Advance pr

MW01492468

"With clarity, wit, and insight, Andrea Bonime-Blanc cuts a searing path through a stale and acrimonious debate over 'AI safety' versus 'AI ethics' and asks a fundamental question: What does it mean to govern and lead, now that the Pandora's Box of uncontained technology is open? There is no one else that could have written this book, and I could not recommend it more highly."

—Alison Taylor, clinical associate professor, NYU Stern School of Business, and author of the award-winning book *Higher Ground: How Business Can Do the Right Thing in a Turbulent World*

"In *Governing Pandora*, Andrea Bonime-Blanc not only provides a comprehendible and clear overview of AI, quantum, and the other 'exponential' technologies changing our world but also offers concrete, helpful advice on how individuals at all levels can mitigate risks, amplify opportunities, and become responsible leaders at times of great disruption."

—Adam Segal, Ira A. Lipman Chair in Emerging Technologies and director of the Digital and Cyberspace Policy Program at the Council on Foreign Relations

"In *Governing Pandora*, Bonime-Blanc offers an invaluable framework for how business leaders should approach a world of exponential technological development, exponential opportunities, and exponential risks. It's a must-read for anyone interested in responsibly building our future."

—Daniel Dobrygowski, head of governance and trust at the World Economic Forum

"As directors, we've been told every new technology is 'game-changing'—but now it actually is. So how do we govern in the age of exponential change? Look no further. Dr. Andrea Bonime-Blanc cuts through the noise in *Governing Pandora*, giving corporate directors the straight talk and tools they need to keep up in a world that's evolving faster than we can refresh our feeds."

— Nora M. Denzel, director of the National Association of Corporate Directors

"*Governing Pandora* is a timely and incredibly thoughtful book that should be a constant companion for industry leaders as they think about the bounty and jeopardy possible with this exponential technology."

—Vikram Sharma, operating partner at S2G Ventures

"In *Governing Pandora*, Andrea cuts a path through the tech news, information, and data tsunami as well as the general confusion and even frustration many feel about the overwhelming pace and thrust of frontier tech. Her primer on five categories of exponential technologies and the practical 'exponential governance mindset' will set the reader on the right course to further learning, open-minded exploration, and responsible tech decision-making."

—Coco Brown, founder and CEO of the Athena Alliance

"All board members should read this book and imagine what the future holds for the companies on whose boards they serve. There is no time to waste to understand and pinpoint and govern the risks and opportunities of the coming technology tsunami."

—Helle Bank Jørgensen, CEO of Competent Boards and author of *The Future Boardroom: How to Transform in Turbulent Times*

"*Governing Pandora* is a remarkable contribution to the discourse on exponential technologies. In this timely and incisive book, Andrea masterfully employs the metaphor of Pandora's Box to illustrate how these technologies have been unleashed onto the global landscape—bringing both transformative opportunities and profound challenges. With eloquence and clarity, she asserts that 'exponential technology requires an exponential governance mindset.' Whether you're a policymaker, business leader, or curious reader, *Governing Pandora* offers invaluable perspectives and practical guidance for navigating the ethical, social, and organizational complexities of our rapidly advancing technological age."

—Olajobi Makinwa, former chief of transparency, anticorruption, and intergovernmental relations in Africa for the United Nations Global Compact

"The era of naive optimism about transformative technology as a force for human progress is squarely behind us. Yes, new technologies continue to offer immense opportunity for supercharged growth. But today they not only unleash creative destruction in the marketplace but also threaten to destabilize core societal and political foundations, degrading trust and undermining our geopolitical order. Companies and governments now have a much greater responsibility to ensure that their technologies are used responsibly. *Governing Pandora* is a critical new contribution that illuminates this new and far more dangerous world of exponential technology change, calling on leaders at all levels and across all sectors to be responsibly courageous in the adoption and governance of new technologies."

—Friso van der Oord, senior vice president of content at the National Association of Corporate Directors

"With clarity and foresight, *Governing Pandora* empowers business leaders to make informed and responsible decisions in a world transformed by Gen-AI and emerging technologies. This indispensable guide is essential for anyone shaping a future that balances risk with opportunity and seeking a trustworthy path into the new technological era."

—Kristina Podnar, global digital policy expert for the Data & Trust Alliance and author of *The Power of Digital Policy*

"As a biotech start-up CEO and scientist, I see firsthand how rapidly advancing technologies are reshaping industries—and how boards, executives, and decision-makers must evolve to keep pace. *Governing Pandora* is more than just a guide; it defines a new field of governance that will be essential for the future of business. With sharp insights and real-world strategies, this book equips leaders to embrace innovation while mitigating risk, ensuring they don't just react to change but stay ahead of it. A must read for anyone serious about governing in the age of technological disruption and geopolitical change."

—Michael T. Marquardt, CEO of Epi-One, Inc.

"Aptly named, *Governing Pandora* is both optimistic and realistic at the same time. Bonime-Blanc draws out the great impacts emerging technologies will have while integrating their attendant risks and responsibilities. Her inclusion of quantum's effects on risk and polyrisk, adaptive governance, and tech trustworthiness are great examples of the depth with which she tackles critical issues. The book is loaded with practical suggestions for countries, companies, and colleagues to consider in order to future-proof our collective paths ahead."

—Tom Patterson, global lead for emerging
technology security at Accenture

"Andrea Bonime-Blanc presents a detailed exploration of the AI-driven risks and opportunities of emerging technologies in this far-reaching book, presenting examples from across industries to describe the 'Age of Pandora.' The book offers an actionable guide for both operational leaders and board directors as they look to manage and govern exponential tech developments."

—Ryan McManus, founder of Techtonic and board director of
Nortech Systems, Empower, and the National Association
of Corporate Directors' New York Chapter

"Governance of AI and other rapidly advancing technologies is a topic that every board member must care about. Dr. Bonime-Blanc's engaging book is full of real-life examples and practical tips for leaders in any industry."

—Maya Bundt, non–executive director and board
member of the CyberPeace Institute and chair of the
Cyber Resilience Chapter of the Swiss Risk Association

"For those leaders who want to navigate with confidence this new world of exponential technology and generative AI, *Governing Pandora* is the guidebook to help you survive and thrive in this rapidly changing time. In an easy-to-read style, Andrea Bonime-Blanc makes sense of this chaotic and thrilling world and shows us that with careful planning and thoughtful governance, we can be productive leaders providing protection and opportunity for all our important stakeholders."

—Mark Kollar, partner at Prosek Partners

"In *Governing Pandora*, Dr. Bonime-Blanc lays out what's really going wrong in tech—and how to fix it. A seasoned watcher of tech trends and an expert

corporate operator, she also shares her sharp insights on AI and its impact on business. This is like being inoculated against tech hype."
—Tarah Wheeler, CEO of Red Queen Dynamics and senior fellow at the Council on Foreign Relations

"An insightful explanation of how accelerating technology governs our future and an impressive guide to how decision-makers can help to keep all of us on a safe path, *Governing Pandora* not only makes an iron-clad case for accelerated governance but also provides practical guidance."
—Marcel Zumbühl, CISO of Swiss Post

"Technology is accelerating. Policy and leadership must catch up—and this book shows how. It equips all decision-makers with the mindset and tools to govern in this era of exponential change."
—Alexander Romanishyn, policymaker, economist, and former deputy economy minister of Ukraine (2020–21)

"*Governing Pandora* is an essential read for anyone interested in the transformation of technology with ethics and integrity, and for those tasked with growing their tech platforms without harming society and their reputations. Andrea provides an essential road map for board members, C-suite leaders, and key stakeholders intent on rolling tech forward without rolling ethics, compliance, or integrity backward. The book is wonderfully written and a true must-read."
—Richard Bistrong, CEO of Front-Line Anti-Bribery LLC

"Andrea's book addresses one of the fastest accelerating challenges facing society, our economies and organizations, and even our personal lives in the twenty-first century. This book is not about crisis management. Exponential change is not a single shift but a continuous change of circumstance. The need for tech-savvy leadership, ESG awareness, and ethical leadership has become clear. This book is a must-read for those charged with overseeing change and everyone who seeks to understand the nature of the exponential change we are only beginning to experience. As Andrea states, in the Age of Pandora, we must be both innovators and stewards."
—Anthony Smith-Meyer, executive director of the Institute for Financial Integrity and Sustainability

GOVERNING PANDORA

GOVERNING PANDORA

LEADING IN THE AGE OF GENERATIVE AI AND EXPONENTIAL TECHNOLOGY

ANDREA BONIME-BLANC

FOREWORD BY DANTE A. DISPARTE

Georgetown University Press / Washington, DC

The publisher is not responsible for third-party websites or their content. URL links were active at time of publication.

Cataloging-in-Publication Data is on file with the Library of Congress
ISBN 978-1-64712-667-4 (hardcover)
ISBN 978-1-64712-668-1 (paperback)
ISBN 978-1-64712-669-8 (ebook)

∞ This paper meets the requirements of ANSI/NISO Z39.48-1992 (Permanence of Paper).

EU GPSR Authorized Representative
LOGOS EUROPE, 9 rue Nicolas Poussin, 17000, LA ROCHELLE, France
Email: Contact@logoseurope.eu

27 26   9 8 7 6 5 4 3 2 First printing
Printed in the United States of America
Cover design by James Keller
Interior design by Paul Hotvedt

If it be now, 'tis not to come; if it be not to come, it will be now;
if it be not now, yet it will come: the readiness is all.
—Shakespeare, *Hamlet*, Act 5, Scene 2

To my very own Hamlet-quoting prince (and husband) in this journey
we call life: I'm grateful it was then, grateful that it's now, and
hopeful that it will be for many tomorrows to come.
And the readiness for it all . . . is all.

Contents

Foreword by Dante A. Disparte   ix
Acknowledgments   xv

Introduction   1

Part I: Preparing for the Age of Pandora—
Understanding the Global Tech Megascape
1. The Global Tech Megascape: The Situational
   Awareness Imperative   11
2. Rise of the Exponential Machines: Tech Turbocharges Tech   34

Part II: Triangulating the Age of Pandora—
An Exponential Tech Whirlwind Tour
3. Generative AI: Everything, Everywhere, All at Once   51
4. Biotechnology: From CRISPR to SynBio   81
5. Exponential Materials: From Silicon to Tiny Skyscrapers   96
6. Frontier Computing: From Cloud and Edge to Quantum
   and the Metaverse   108
7. Autonomy: From Killer Robots to Smart Cities   122

Part III: Surviving and Thriving in the Age of Pandora—
Developing the Exponential Governance Mindset
8. Leadership: Turbocharging 360 Tech Governance   137
9. Ethos: Embedding Responsible Tech Culture   161
10. Impact: Integrating Stakeholders into the Tech Loop   178
11. Resilience: Deploying Polyrisk and Polycrisis Preparedness   199
12. Foresight: Unleashing a Future-Forward Tech Strategy   227

**Part IV: Futureproofing in the Age of Pandora—
Deploying the Exponential Governance Mindset**

13. Futureproofing Ourselves and Our Organizations:
Tips and Typologies   249

14 . Futureproofing the Global Commons: Exponential Frontiers   263

Notes   289
Selected Bibliography and Additional Resources   311
Index   315
About the Author   325

Foreword

The modern age is increasingly defined by code, collective behavior, and technology, rather than by historical social and organizational norms. Gone are the days when predictable human behaviors could be translated into accurate economic, political, and social forecasts. There is a new force in play that does not respect or conform to classical governance and societal norms—and this force, as described by Dr. Andrea Bonime-Blanc's capable pen, is a technology-fueled Pandora.

We have opened Pandora's technology box by unleashing a veritable global arms race of spending, breakthrough product developments such as artificial intelligence (AI), and novel business models powered by edge technologies. From basic cyber dependency propelled by connecting virtually every device to the Internet, to formless cloud networks serving as the veritable invisible backbone of the global economy, the stage is set for a disruption at a world scale. On one hand, there will be winners who learn how to adapt and harness technological change or who are the architects of these changes, such as Silicon Valley's tech titans. On the other hand, the likeliest losers in the greatest technology contest of our times risk being consigned to analog irrelevance, unless they adapt to new ways of doing business and leading their organizations. As the adage goes, manage risk or it will manage you. Dr. Bonime-Blanc offers readers an alternative path to being overwhelmed by events and technology competition—she proposes practical ways in which we can govern Pandora.

In our quest to find new business models and unlock new forms of value or resilience, in no small measure because our existing systems have reached a point of diminishing returns, we have created truly exponential ways of operating. From distributed systems like blockchain and open source developments, which have conspired to reinvent money itself; to biotechnology and bioscience, which can either prolong or shorten life; to the rise of intelligent machines and potentially sentient ones with artificial general intelligence, the responsibility to govern Pandora, or be governed by it, depends very much on moving the central premise of this book from theory to practice: Leaders and corporate boards must move beyond creating the mere semblance of good technology governance and toward a more agile and risk-aware approach that expects disruption and can steer their organizations through turbulent waters.

One thing is clear, despite all the perils and promises of the Age of Pandora, is that people and organizations must not take their hands off the proverbial technological governance wheel, any more than they can take their eyes off the future. A durable question for organizational leaders, technologists, and policymakers alike is just because you can do something with technology does not mean you should. The Internet and software are indeed consuming every facet of life and the global economy, but technology need not take control—least of all if we hope to preserve any semblance of organizational form. Rather than regard technology as a threat, the governance precepts espoused by Dr. Bonime-Blanc call for pragmatic approaches to readying people and organizations to not only survive but to also thrive in this age of profound technological change.

In so doing, Dr. Bonime-Blanc also makes a case for optimism about technology, rather than a deep-seated technophobia. For example, the COVID-19 pandemic revealed many preexisting vulnerabilities among businesses, governance structures, societal norms, and economic models. Agile companies were not just able to survive the COVID-19 pandemic but also to thrive and even gain market advantage based on their pre-pandemic technological capabilities and the organizational flexibility of their people. Something as simple as the enablement of remote work—beyond the sight of watchful managers—would have consigned rigid technophobic companies to losses in productivity and employee loyalty, if they adopted a prepandemic posture where remote work was a perk rather than a feature of a resilient, technology-ready organization. While there is often no substitute for the human connections and spontaneity that are possible when we occupy the same space, many organizations have struggled with returns to work and center city policies—since the

Age of Pandora has blown apart corporate form and the very definition of office work.

Agile organizations, by contrast, would follow many of the precepts of technology governance outlined in *Governing Pandora*—not least of which is being adaptable to both the upside and possible consequences stemming from emerging technologies, rather than confronting technological change with rigidity. Dr. Bonime-Blanc empowers boards and C-suite executives to anticipate change, mount collective defenses, and, most of all, place leaders in potential control of technological effects, rather than in their path, where they could be caught flat-footed. This is the domain in which *Governing Pandora* informs broader organizational strategy and strategic response.

Other areas of optimism include profound changes under way with extremely powerful technologies that are nearly within reach of all humanity. From a full suite of financial services that have historically presumed wealth as a precursor to investing, to enabling novel expansions of human productivity with AI reaching scale with little or no advertising spent, companies that will successfully compete in this environment defined by rapid technological change and developers will harness these new tools, just as they harnessed past generations of technological advances. In short, AI is not likely to take your job or consign your organization to irrelevance, but rather to serve a competitor that effectively harnesses it. Herein lies both the opportunity and the risk with breakthrough technologies becoming ubiquitous—the people and organizations that successfully harness them are likeliest to own the future. Without guardrails, however, as is deftly described in this book, unchecked technological change will indeed sow havoc in organizations, markets, and, indeed, society writ large. This makes *Governing Pandora* in equal measure a management manifesto and a survival guide for the twenty-first century.

One of the critical areas of organizational transformation is the speed with which technology spending and resilience have become decoupled. Herein lies a key priority for the governance layer in an organization: boards can no longer derive reasonable assurance that a novel technology risk is managed merely because a technology leader says so. Instead, the classical corporate governance process must not only anticipate disruption but must also ready the organization to disrupt itself, making it everyone's business to stay in business. In the Age of Pandora, gradualism and the presumption of orderly market transitions will not make for a lasting strategy. All too often, management teams and boards toe the line on their governance accountabilities for emerging technologies. What *Governing Pandora* demonstrates is that managing technology risks and opportunities cannot remain a check-the-box activity for leaders; it must become a part of the fabric of overall corporate governance. This much was true with the advent of cyberrisk management, and it remains an evergreen technology governance priority today.

Stalwart tech titans themselves may look vulnerable to the same technological forces they helped unleash by opening Pandora's Box. For example, in the AI space race, which has nation-state levels of investment and competitive stakes, China's hitherto-unknown start-up DeepSeek was launched in January 2025 and evaporated more than $2 trillion in the market value of tech-stock darlings because it showed the world an alternative, relatively low-cost AI model compared with the heavy capital requirements sought by US firms like OpenAI. Some likened this event to AI's "Sputnik moment," because it served as a national wake-up call that not only will superintelligent computing be accessible to everyone but that it is also not preordained that the latest technology will be developed in the United States or by its values-aligned actors.

Similar strains of disruption, risk, and opportunity will arise as all other cutting-edge technologies come of age. Quantum computing, long thought to be decades away, is increasingly becoming a commercial reality. This will profoundly blow apart the cybersecurity industrial complex that has endeavored (with a checkered scorecard of success and false confidence) to patch up the weak links of the Internet. At the same time, postquantum cyberresilience is no longer a far-flung mythological state but rather a broad market necessity, lest every facet of a functioning economy—from the presumption of privacy to the resiliency of critical systems and infrastructure—remain vulnerable to disruption. In the upgrading of our digital commons on which the modern economy relies, trillions of dollars of new market value will go through creative/destructive cycles. The companies that embrace, drive, and govern this change will not only own the future; they will also help tame it and perhaps even thrive in the Age of Pandora.

Dante A. Disparte, Chief Strategy Officer and Head of Global Policy and Operations at Circle

Acknowledgments

I came across a wonderful quote not long ago that captures the essence of our time at the intersection of humanity, governance, and technology. It is from Edmund O. Wilson, a renowned sociobiologist, who in 2018 stated, "The real problem of humanity is the following: We have paleolithic emotions, medieval institutions, and godlike technology."[1] And he wrote that before the release of ChatGPT in 2022 and the unleashing of generative AI and other exponential technologies!

This quote perfectly encapsulates the focus of my book: understanding the interconnection, intersection, *and disconnect* between human emotions, governance, and the rise of the exponential machines. I hope this book will encourage my readers to think about these interconnections (or disconnections) more deeply and to act upon whatever you encounter in this space more responsibly.

Writing the acknowledgments is both the hardest and easiest part of writing a book. I didn't get here alone. First and foremost, I thank my family, who provided all the patience and moral support—and quite a few insights—along the way! There are so many who played an important role directly and indirectly in my being able to write this book, and the hard part is making sure I leave no one out. The easy part is being thankful and grateful for so many friends, colleagues, and even strangers (no longer) who were willing to provide advice, suggestions, and corrections and who helped me find my voice along the way. To all those who did, thank you!

Gratitude goes to the many reviewers and commentators who provided numerous comments and contributions on early manuscripts: Michael T. Marquardt, Peter Tomczak, Daniel Dobrygowski, Nora M. Denzel, Friso van der Oord, Maya Bundt, Mercina Tillemann Perez, Joyce Li, Meghan Anzelc, Erin Essenmacher, Hernan Huwyler, Maureen Conners, Matthew Sekol, Christopher Hazard, Alexandra Lajoux, Vikram Sharma,

Olajobi Makinwa, Tom Patterson, Margaret Preston, Valmiki Mukherjee, Tarah Wheeler, Marcel Zumbuehl, and Alexander Romanishyn.

There are so many more to thank for their wisdom and influence: Noble Ackerson, Carrie Anderson, Cyd Brandvein, Jacqueline E. Brevard, Herman Brill, Earnie Broughton, Oscar Cartagena, Edna Conway, Kate Duffy, Clara Durodie, Nichola Dyer, Lauren Ferrari, Azish Filabi, Kenneth Frankel, Kevin Fumai, Andrea Gori, Stephanie Goutos, Sergio Guzman, Pat Harned, Richard Haass, Jeff Hoffman, Andrew Jones, Georg Kell, Carolyn Kissane, David Koenig, Ed Levy, Heidi Lorenzen, Vishwas Manral, Kavya Pearlman, Willem Punt, Andreas Rasche, Anna Ransley, Ana Rold, Jay Rosenzweig, Avril Sisk, Shane Szarkowski, Vilhelmiina Vulli, Suilin Yap—thank you! A special thank-you goes to my friend and frequent collaborator over the years, Dante Alighieri Disparte, who took valuable time from his crazy schedule to write a fabulous foreword for this book. He represents that rare combination of being a deep technology expert, a risk manager and governance practitioner, and a stalwart of responsible business.

A final shout-out of deepest gratitude goes to the Georgetown University Press team, most especially to Hilary Claggett, senior acquisitions editor, who had the bright idea of asking me to submit a book proposal after she saw an article I wrote on governing exponential technologies in the fall of 2023. And here we are a couple of years later—thank you, Hilary, for your amazing foresight, guidance, and perseverance! And thank you to Elizabeth Sheridan-Drake, editorial and production coordinator, and her team for the fantastic work organizing and implementing the production and the beautiful design of the book!

The next period humanity will go through requires foresight, guidance, and perseverance (times the 8.2 billion humans on earth at the time of this writing) as we are about to face the intersection of human emotion, governance, and the continued unleashing of godlike technologies. I hope this book will help us get there safely.

I for one vote for an optimistic future in the midst of a concerning present. But it is up to each and every one of us to make it so—through thoughtful action and resilience. Thank you for reading.

Introduction

We are entering the exponential Age of Pandora. The technology box has been opened. Exponential technologies—good, great, bad, and ugly—have been released into the global wild. And they will not and cannot be put back into this box.

This leaves humanity with only one option: develop exponential tech navigation. Develop exponential tech responsibility to stakeholders. Develop exponential tech governance. Develop an exponential attitude to collaboration across borders, across sectors, across disciplines—vertically and horizontally—into an interconnected, multidisciplinary, interoperable, constantly changing, evolving, responsible technology governance ecosystem. Exponential tech requires shared exponential responsibility. Exponential tech requires an exponential governance mindset. And this matters at every level of life—the planetary, the civic, and the biological.

What if policymakers had rapid access to an extreme weather forecasting tool like Nvidia's FourCastNet, which is graphics-processing-unit-accelerated, trained on 10 terabytes of Earth system data, and able to provide seven-day forecasts in a fraction of a second, generating potential effects based on thousands of scenarios. Would policymakers be better prepared to radically modify traditional climate crisis planning for disasters, such as the hurricane-wind-induced urban wildfires devastating large swaths of Los Angeles as I write this book?

What if you live in a democracy that has held national elections and it is proven that coordinated disinformation campaigns using social media, social engineering, and generative AI (GenAI) make it clear that the results were skewed and corrupted, thus requiring a new election? This happened in Romania in 2024. Given that 2024 was the year of the most elections around the world ever—including in the world's most populous democracies (India and the United States)—is it clear that disinformation and social engineering campaigns did not skew or corrupt the election results in those countries, or in your country? How will we ever know for sure? What would you do if reliable medical sources, with the assistance of GenAI and other advanced biotech tools, told you that your chance of a specific deadly cancer was 90 percent and that a gene-editing solution and customized, personalized cancer treatment could minimize or eliminate this chance?

The release of ChatGPT in late 2022 marks the advent of this new Age of Pandora. Though I have been working on the governance of change for a long time, the release of ChatGPT and the OpenAI governance and leadership saga surrounding it got me hyperfocused on what this new era of GenAI means practically to decision-makers, boards of directors, policymakers, students, and the average global citizen.

So I wrote this book. And this book is for all those leaders and others who are struggling to keep up with the tsunami of technology developments, events, information, and crises that we are living through, partly because of the advent of multiple exponential technologies. Indeed, traditional approaches and protocols to governing technology are not designed to govern our emerging Age of Pandora. Digital illiteracy, from the boardroom and the C-suite to national and international halls of political power, is sorely wanting and is a "massive handicap to progress."[1]

This book is for anyone interested in understanding, navigating, and thriving in this rapidly changing, simultaneously dangerous and thrilling time. The book is not only about the governance of GenAI and its ability to tectonically reshape our future; it is about how other cutting-edge technologies—in biotech, materials science, automation, and frontier computing—are developing exponentially, intertwining with GenAI and with one another to radically reshape our collective future.

Having served as an executive, adviser, and board director for numerous for-profit, nonprofit, public-sector, university, and professional associations for over three decades, I have always been fascinated by the intersection of governance and change—especially the change occasioned by technology. I have served in C-suite and senior executive roles at an electric power company, a global media giant, a professional services start-up, and a global tech company. I have served on fascinating tech and cyber start-up boards and advisory boards and have spent much time trying to dissect the intersection of tech and change with governance, leadership, ethics, and sustainability—and provide actionable, practical solutions on how to tackle such change optimally.

My purpose in writing this book is to awaken your excitement and interest in all things at the cutting edge of tech—exponential tech—and to offer you, my reader, a practical and constructive framework to understand your material issues at the intersection of governance and exponential technology so that you can be a responsible, value-added, and productive leader in the age of GenAI and exponential technology—the Age of Pandora—for the full benefit and protection of your most important stakeholders.

Overview

Why use the word "Pandora" in the title and throughout this book? Pandora was the "giver of all things." Pandora was the first mortal woman. She was created in retribution to one god's actions against the greatest god, Zeus (all male). She had many gifts—garments, grace, beauty, jewelry, floral wreaths, and also a few less laudatory characteristics—deceitfulness, shamelessness, and the gift of gab. As soon as she was "revenge" married off to another god, she opened her famous box, and all the ills (and some good things) of the world were let loose. And thus it is the case with the exponential technologies that we, twenty-first-century humans (a collective "Pandora," as it were), are letting loose onto the world. These technologies are full of blessings through incredible inventions and cures, and they are full of sorrows through a slew of new and unexpected dangers.

I would like to introduce my own twist on the Pandora myth: Through the explosion of exponential technology into the world, we are witnessing the release of not only nasty tech things but also hopeful ones. Indeed, this book accentuates the hopeful over the nasty, though we must always be alert to the mix of the two—the upside and downside, the opportunity and risk, the promise and danger—the duality of it all. And that is what we do in this book, and why I call it "Governing" Pandora.

The Pandora's Box aspect of the equation helps us refer to the release into the human wild of technological unknown unknowns—things, effects, and developments that can be bad and ugly but also potentially good and great. And thus decision-makers and leaders need a navigational tool to understand, triangulate, survive, thrive, and futureproof our Age of Pandora. That is what this book is about. But unlike the negative inferences usually made about Pandora's Box, I would like the reader to think of a more nuanced and multifaceted Pandora's Box—one that releases not only nasty and ugly tech but also useful and even superb tech. This book is about understanding the contents of this Pandora's Box that have been released (exponential technologies) and to offer a road map for navigating this new landscape, because we are on a voyage of discovery into parts unknown and as such, we do not know what to expect. Thus preparation, resilience, excellent risk management, and overall good governance—what I call the exponential governance mindset in this book— are not only "nice to haves" but also imperative "must haves."

I have spent my life and career looking at the world through a dual risk and opportunity lens—the fact is that we often face both at any given time, especially when there is great change. As a corporate executive for almost two decades, I have served in roles ranging from general counsel and chief risk officer to head of global ethics and corporate responsibility—from nitty-gritty risk and liability-protecting roles to roles requiring creativity, value protection, and creation. And I have also experienced entrepreneurship, having founded and run a successful international business for over a decade. In all this, I have always had a forward-looking gaze on everything—one that is intent on understanding facts, trends, and triangulating the future, preparing for it, and surviving and thriving in it.

Hence, my great interest in both global risk and opportunity. Though I am not a technologist, in one of my corporate executive roles, I was put in charge of figuring out cybersecurity. And that was in the first decade of the 2000s. I learned a super valuable lesson: Cybersecurity was less about information tech and technology and much more about governance, risk, resilience, and leadership. After that, in my consulting and board roles over the past decade, I have done research reports and practical work in cyber, AI, and a number of other technologies—always through these governance lenses.

Indeed, I have written this book from the perspective of a governance, risk, ethics, and sustainability practitioner and expert, aiming to equip decision-makers of all kinds (local, national, international), at every organizational level (board, C-suite, management, front lines) and in every sector (business, nonprofit, governmental, educational), with a road map of basics to approach, understand, evaluate, develop, and execute responsible, effective, creative, and innovative governance for the current and coming exponential age of generative AI, synthetic biology, nanotechnology, quantum, and beyond—what I call later in this book the "exponential governance mindset."

These capabilities, like technologies at any time in human history, will be deployed by all kinds of humans—the full spectrum, from the most emotionally intelligent to the purely sociopathic. This means that we are at a moment, at an inflection point, the expanse of which we have never seen before, which allows exponential capabilities and asymmetric power to be deployed for both constructive and destructive purposes. Leaders must be sensitive to what can go right and what can go terribly wrong, but they must be so in measured and considered ways. The sky is not falling (yet), but there are slow (and not-so-slow) burning, insidious effects that can accumulate over time if not properly recognized and managed and then happen suddenly and potentially catastrophically. We may (almost certainly will) not be able to control all the downsides, but we most certainly must try. Because this can become an existential matter.

Given the complexity, velocity, volatility, and uncertainty of the book's subject matter, I aim to keep the reader focused on its central point: decision-makers and leaders must seek not only to understand the contours and substance of the exponential technologies exploding all around us but also, and almost more important, they must pay attention to the process of navigating this complex and multifaceted tech journey—a tech

Scylla and Charybdis, as it were—where we are forced to deal simultaneously with life-changing opportunity and extreme danger (and everything in between). In the process of this navigation, it will be essential to have responsible leaders. Indeed, the central question this book seeks to answer is, "What does it mean to be a responsible leader in the age of exponential technology—the Age of Pandora?"

Structure of the Book

This book is divided into four parts; each revolves around what a leader needs to know and do to be or become a responsible decision-maker in the Age of Pandora. Part I, "Preparing for the Age of Pandora: Understanding the Global Tech Megascape," addresses the "why" of our journey by sketching five tech-related global megatrends and providing an overview of the exponential technologies dealt with in the book, providing us with the context and situational awareness needed for our journey. The five megatrends start with the fact that we are being asked to govern the potentially ungovernable—"Governing the Ungovernable: Tech at the Speed of Light." The second megatrend—the "Socioecology of Tech: In Search of Planetary Love"—provides a technological take on our collective planetary responsibility to tackle climate change and its deep interconnectedness with society and biodiversity. For the third megatrend "Geopolitical Techtonics: Tech in the Political Landscape," I analyze the intersections between frontier technologies and politics at three levels: global, national, and organizational. The fourth megatrend, which speaks to economics, is called "Techonomics: Quo Vadis Tech Economics?" and reviews how new tech intersects with three different types of models— identifying an "owner," "stakeholder," and "state" model—as well as a nonstate model—the "borderless tech billionaire model." And, finally, the fifth megatrend addresses a topic near and dear to my heart that is deeply embedded throughout the book: "Tech Trust and Trustworthiness: The Responsible Leadership Imperative."

Part II, "Triangulating the Age of Pandora: An Exponential Tech Whirlwind Tour," explores the "what" of the Age of Pandora by detailing five key exponential technology groups: GenAI, biotechnology and syn-thetic biology, the cutting edge of materials science, frontier computing, and the world of advanced automation and autonomy. The purpose of part II is to encourage leaders to explore the technologies that are most important to them and their work and to engage in continuous education on these topics—anything less will not be good enough for the Age of Pandora.

Part III, "Surviving and Thriving in the Age of Pandora: Developing the Exponential Governance Mindset," addresses the "how" by provid-ing leaders with an exponential governance mindset toolkit with five key elements—revolving around leadership, ethos, impact, resilience, and foresight. The overarching theme of part III—as manifested specifically in each of its five chapters—is to equip leaders and decision-makers with a future-forward mindset that can deal with and continuously adapt to the changes, challenges, and opportunities of the Age of Pandora. In chapter 8, "Leadership," we explore three types of tech actors—the "tech masters of the universe," the "tech enablers and worker bees," and the "tech guardians of the universe." Also in this chapter, the focus is on encouraging the building of 360 technology governance within organiza-tions—whether corporate, governmental, or nonprofit—by creating fully integrated top-down, bottom-up, and middle-out technology governance.

In chapter 9, "Ethos: Embedding Responsible Tech Culture," we un-derscore the deep need to embed responsible tech culture. We do so by first exploring the tech culture wars between accelerationists (or tech op-timists) versus "decelerationists" (tech doomers and whistleblowers) and then by looking at a variety of examples along a spectrum of tech "respon-sibility" including at OpenAI, Microsoft, and Accenture.

In chapter 10, "Impact: Integrating Stakeholders into the Tech Loop," the focus is on stakeholders and how leaders need to incorporate their needs, interests, and expectations into the tech loop. We explore a variety of stakeholder resources, including from Just Capital, and the Athena Alliance, and the connection with the environment, society, and gover-nance and with sustainability. We also review several examples of what it means to integrate stakeholders into the tech loop, including children in the metaverse, data centers in the desert, digital cash for war refugees, and drivers and surveillance.

The fourth element of the exponential governance mindset is explored in chapter 11, "Resilience: Deploying Polyrisk and Polycrisis Preparedness." This chapter is all about organizations truly understanding the global risk context, and being polyrisk- and polycrisis-ready to deal with uncertainty. We explore a wide variety of resources and paint a big-to-smaller universe of global strategic risk, exponential tech risk, and AI risk. We look at examples of the convergence of the virtual and physical worlds, the emergence of digital twins, and the accelerating nature of cyberinsecurity.

Part III's chapter 12, "Foresight: Unleashing a Future-Forward Tech Strategy," outlines key components for an effective tech strategy that incorporates situational awareness (as explored in chapter 1), systems thinking, tech risk intelligence, tech-opportunity readiness, and scenario planning, with examples and tactics deployed vis-à-vis the UN Sustainable Development Goals, the UK Cyber Security Centre, the Magnificent Seven megatech companies, and much more.

Part IV, "Futureproofing in the Age of Pandora: Deploying the Exponential Governance Mindset," addresses the "who" and the "where to." In other words, how can we individually and collectively futureproof ourselves for the Age of Pandora? Chapter 13, "Futureproofing Ourselves and Our Organizations: Tips and Typologies," provides professional tips and ideas for developing a personal exponential governance mindset as well as ideas on how organizations can futureproof themselves. Finally, in chapter 14, "Futureproofing the Global Commons: Exponential Frontiers," we talk about futureproofing the "global commons"—a term that ordinarily refers to the oceans, the air, the Arctic, Antarctica, and Space but which I suggest should be consciously expanded to the Virtual Global Commons as well. By examining four exponential tech frontiers—the biological, the mechanical, the planetary, and the virtual—with specific examples, I hope to leave the reader with an appetite to learn and explore more and to do so with a responsible exponential governance mindset.

Buckle up, we are about to start navigating through the Age of Pandora!

I

PREPARING FOR THE AGE OF PANDORA

Understanding the Global Tech Megascape

1

THE GLOBAL TECH MEGASCAPE

The Situational Awareness Imperative

I have been analyzing multiyear megatrends through my work for many years, and I have published previously on the subject in chapter 1 of my book *Gloom to Boom*, and through annual reports called "The ESGT Megatrends Report."[1] Through these publications, I strived to identify the most important global megatrends affecting our day-to-day life and translate their meaning for each of us as global citizens and professionals.

In today's rapidly changing, sometimes daunting, frequently exhilarating world, gaining situational awareness of the big multiyear megatrends is absolutely central to decision-making success—whether you are a businessperson, policymaker, board member, running a nongovernmental organization, or a government official. We need leaders, deciders, and influencers to be situationally aware. We need our leaders to understand global megatrends.

So this first chapter sets that situational awareness context for what we will discuss later in the book—governing exponential technologies in the Age of Pandora. Here you will find a snapshot and explanation of what I consider to be the five most important global megatrends that intersect with technology (what I am calling the "Global Tech Megascape") to put this Age of Pandora in context and help you to navigate successfully.

Table 1.1 provides an overview of the five megatrends discussed in this chapter. Because this book is deeply focused on the technological aspects of these global megatrends, this chapter focuses mostly on the technological megatrend (Megatrend 1), while paying heed to the other

Table 1.1 The Global Tech Megascape: The Leadership Situational
Awareness Imperative

Megatrend	
1	Governing the ungovernable: *Tech at the speed of light*
2	The socioecology of tech: *In search of planetary love*
3	Geopolitical techtonics: *Tech in the political landscape*
4	Techonomics: *Quo vadis tech economics?*
5	Tech trust and trustworthiness: *The responsible leadership imperative*

Source: Author.

four, but mostly to highlight their interconnectivity to the technological
revolution we are undergoing.

Megatrend 1: Governing the Ungovernable—Tech at the Speed of Light

Since this book is about exponential technology and how leaders and
decision-makers can best manage and oversee its successful, beneficial,
trustworthy, and safe development and deployment, we need to start with
one of the biggest megatrends of our times: tech disruption at the speed
of light, or what I often call "governing the ungovernable." How does today differ from yesterday and the day before? Why is so much exponential
technology being invented, almost at the speed of light, suddenly in the
twenty-first century? Why is there a prospect for so much more disruptive
and exponential tech in the foreseeable future?

What do I mean by the ungovernability of exponential tech? Very simply, the fact that technological change is taking place at lightning speed
in all shapes and forms all over the world, often without appropriate governance, risk management, safety, ethical considerations, or sustainability impact assessments. These shapes and forms range from GenAI to
quantum and from nanotechnology to neurotechnology—from crypto to
robotics, and from materials science to the metaverse. Here is a sampling
of disruptive and exponential technologies, many of which we examine
in this book:

- AI / generative AI
- Autonomous vehicles
- Biotechnology
- Blockchain
- Cloud computing
- Cryptocurrency
- Digital twins
- Energy storage
- Fusion
- Internet of Things
- Materials science
- Metaverse / augmented reality / virtual reality
- Nanotechnology
- Neurotechnology
- Quantum computing
- Robotics
- Spatial computing
- Semiconductor chips
- Synthetic biology
- Three-dimensional printing

Government institutions, regulators, and boards are simply unable to keep up with the breadth, depth, speed, variety, and decentralized nature of tech disruption. And on top of that—"tech is turbocharging tech," meaning that one kind of tech is making other types of tech change and disrupt even faster. Think of how AI and biotechnology are combining to find, create, and deploy faster cures. Or how geospatial engineering and AI are combing to revolutionize meteorological forecasting. Or how biotech and nanotech are collaborating in creating biological implants. Or how AI, robotics, and facial recognition tech are combining to deploy drones, and police and military robots, for law enforcement, surveillance, warfare, and terrorism.

The innovators, technologists, and inventors are way ahead of the rest of us—including, alarmingly, those who are supposed to manage the social commons, like legislators and regulators. Indeed, in many cases, private-sector technologists have a lot more money and influence than do governments and regulators to attract the right investments, employee talent, creativity, and even popular support (consider Elon Musk's use of his X social media platform).

This is happening everywhere—from places of great concentrated power, money, and influence, like Silicon Valley, Abu Dhabi, and China, to almost anywhere in the world where there is enough access to technology, data, digital devices, compute capacity, and related tools like the cloud. And this access can be deeply asymmetric, including that by dangerous actors such as rogue nation states, criminal and terrorist organizations, and the proverbial guy in his mother's basement with lots of tech and nothing better to do.

We have already seen in the past one or two decades what benign and malign cyberactors have accomplished with increasingly disruptive and creative cyber technologies on numerous fronts—the legal, the illegal, the criminal, and the geopolitical. What some of the emerging exponential technologies might achieve will put some of the cyber developments we have experienced so far to shame in both impact and speed.

Tech Changes Everything

Have you ever stopped to think why change—specifically, tech-enabled change—has been happening so rapidly and so broadly in recent years? Have you thought about how this change may be affecting other aspects of life in ways knowable and unknowable, noticeable and unnoticeable?

For those of us who were alive and conscious in the latter part of the twentieth century, certain things—certain human behaviors—seem to be quite different today from what they used to be. I do not think it is nostalgia that we might feel that way. The reason we are seeing so much simultaneously dramatic and rapid change—especially in social culture and human behaviors—is obvious: it has everything to do with the rapidity and acceleration of disruptive technological change over the past thirty years, which has accelerated even more in the past few years. It is as if tech has turbocharged tech.

As a human species, we have never seen so much dramatic, disruptive change in such a compressed period of time. This tech explosion is in turn changing and molding human behaviors and our cognitive functions in fast, unknown, unpredictable, and uncontrollable ways. Just think about how social media (which did not exist until the first decade of this century) has affected behaviors and cognition, especially in children—humans at their earliest and most absorptive point in brain and behavioral development. Think TikTok-first "digital natives."

These waves of tech-induced change started with the rise and spread of the Internet in the 1990s. A lot of the world was suddenly able to access and process information and data in a hyperefficient and rapid manner (certainly compared with pre-Internet days). In the 1980s, I researched and wrote my PhD dissertation on Spain's transition to democracy using a typewriter, accessing original documents and people in analog ways. Digital work was not an option then.

After the Internet became a thing, the tech revolution continued into the early twenty-first century with the invention and democratization of social media and our ability to access it (and feed it) via our smartphones. The value of Facebook in its original incarnation was that it was a way to connect with friends and family around the world. Suddenly, we could conduct group and individual conversations and networking, and could share photos, videos, and stories in real time. For those privileged to have access to Internet, computers, and digital devices, the world became our digital oyster.

Of course, the digital oyster that the Internet plus social media represented also presented significant and alarming downsides, including the rapid and explosive spread of child pornography; the rise of the deep and dark webs; the use of "outlaw" webs for drugs, arms, and human trafficking; hate-filled chat rooms; terrorist planning; spying; and other forms of negative human behaviors, including violence—physical, digital, and psychological.

All this Internet and social media activity in turn was accelerated by amazing advances in and the miniaturization of silicon chips, semiconductors, and computing power, which in turn led to the adoption of increasingly smaller and more portable computers and handheld devices (the iPhone in 2007 and the iPad in 2010). For a terrific history of chip development and its meaning for the development of technology generally, check out *Chip War: The Fight for the World's Most Critical Technology* by Chris Miller.[2]

Now, in the mid-2020s, we are experiencing an unprecedented expansion of data analytics, information processing, computing capacity, algorithms, large language models, and generative AI (GenAI). Let us just wait to see what the further miniaturization of chip capacity and then quantum computing (and other technologies) do to all this in the next decade and beyond.

From Analog to Digital Natives

For those who were young adults or adults in the late twentieth century, and who are analog natives rather than digital natives (let alone TikTok-first digital natives), walking around on the street (or even biking or driving) while looking at screens was not a thing. Indeed, if someone walked down the street talking to themselves in the late twentieth century, the default assumption was that that person was a little strange or deranged. Nowadays, we automatically think of someone walking down the street (or biking or driving) while talking into the air as engaging in a conversation with another person through their ear/headphones—whether they are or not. Indeed, they may not be talking at all but instead reading, watching videos, TikToks, an X thread, and so on. We have seen the videos of Tesla drivers on autopilot apparently sleeping or watching movies (and in some cases dying in a crash). More recently, when Apple released its $3,500 Vision Headset, a video circulated on social media of a Tesla driver wearing the Apple Vision headset, driving down the highway while gesticulating and engaging in spatial computing. I do not think humans were designed—at least for now—to multitask this heavily, let alone multitask through various screens, spaces, and activities—simultaneously, without consequences. But I may be wrong.

Indeed, we have all defaulted to split-screen personalities—one that is physical, and one that is mental or virtual—both in private and in public. Even the most capable and disciplined among us will be distracted by multiple sensory overloads. We should not be surprised that we are witnessing a variety of less than functional, dysfunctional, and heretofore unseen disruptive or dangerous human behaviors alongside all the benefits we undoubtedly get from these innovations.

The Human (Tech) Condition

This inexorable rise of new, disruptive, and, in some cases, exponential technology has had a wide variety of effects on the human condition. As someone with artists and musicians in my own family and circle of friends, I have had a front row seat to how new tech business models have affected individual musicians, writers, actors, and other creative folk—largely adversely, while expanding the financial benefits to businesspeople and technologists deploying new music, visual, and other "creative" technology business models—venture capitalists, private equity inventors, and tech inventors (e.g., the owners and shareholders of, and investors in, Spotify, Apple Music/iTunes, YouTube, and TikTok). The Hollywood screenwriters (the Writers Guild of America) and actor members of SAG AFTRA, through the Hollywood strikes of 2023, were professionally existentially concerned that GenAI (especially) might be used to brainstorm creative ideas, write scripts, replace writers, and even actors. An AP headline in September 2023 stated that "In Hollywood Screenwriters' Battle Against AI, Humans Win (for Now)."[3]

Though they may have won the battle—"for now"— the war is ongoing. Actors' greatest concern is that movie and TV studios will either mess with their likeness and/or entirely replace them with AI-generated images, video, and/or voice. The actors' unions won their strike two months after the writers did—in November 2023—as depicted in this *Wired* headline: "Hollywood Actors Strike Ends with a Deal That Will Impact AI and Streaming for Decades."[4] Again, this is perhaps a battle won, but the war on human actors and human writers—and other creatives—is only just beginning.

The effects of new technology have also happened at individual and social-neurological, cognitive, and behavioral levels, with basic human behaviors changing with the usage and pervasiveness of these new technologies. This is starkly illustrated in the research and work of leading behavioral scholars like Jonathan Haidt (especially on the effects of social media on teenagers),[5] or the work that Tristan Harris and Aza Raskin have done through Jeff Orlowski's film *The Social Dilemma* and their work at the Centre for Humane Technology.[6]

In *The Social Dilemma*, the creators were among the first to systematically explore the harm and risks of social media by underscoring through numerous expert citations and interviews—including with technologists themselves—the serious downsides of unfettered social media, including the addictive quality of such media, and, what is more troubling, addiction by design, mental health consequences, and the spread of misinformation and disinformation, among several serious themes.[7]

Harris and Raskin go on to underscore the potential downsides of GenAI in their 2023 talk "The AI Dilemma," which points to many of the more extreme and existential AI dangers that some are concerned about.[8] For example, the Future of Life Institute (led by the AI/tech luminary Max Tegmark) issued the "Open Letter to Pause Giant AI Experiments" in March 2023 (the "FLI Letter"), signed by many leaders in the tech community and beyond (including Elon Musk).[9] The letter advocated pausing GenAI experiments for six months. While the FLI Letter had a public impact on the conversation at the time (just a few months after OpenAI released ChatGPT), it by no means paused the development of GenAI experiments. If anything, GenAI pioneers everywhere (including Anthropic, Meta, Google, and others) doubled down on their work, releasing new closed and open source models throughout the next year and later.

But the FLI Letter did serve an important purpose: it alerted the world to the outsize significance of what had happened with the release of ChatGPT a few months earlier, something of which the larger public may not have been fully aware in terms of its exponential significance and impact. Indeed, the FLI Letter opened up the dialogue about AI and GenAI to a conversation between experts and others about how existential and even dangerous GenAI could become, especially if GenAI reached artificial general intelligence status, taking over from humans to run the world one day.

Far from pausing experimentation, the FLI Letter has led to an explosion of experimentation both in controlled and uncontrolled ways—through the release of large language models like Llama by Meta, something we explore in great detail in several chapters of this book.[10]

A Fifth (or Exponential) Industrial Revolution?

Tech change is happening at such lightning speed these days that one might ask: have we already entered the Fifth Industrial Revolution, or something we might call the Exponential Industrial Revolution or the Postindustrial Revolution or maybe the First Virtual or Digital Revolution? If so, how does this differ from the Fourth Industrial Revolution? We just barely started the Fourth Industrial Revolution, according to some scholars and think tanks; and if we are to believe that GenAI and some of the other disruptive exponential technologies we examine in this book are indeed as revolutionary and game changing as they appear, perhaps we have turned another corner in the evolution of humanity and planet Earth.

Table 1.2 provides an overview of industrial revolutions to date, and figure 1.1 provides a schematic of several groupings of exponential technology that have been sprouting over the past one to two decades that may provide grist for the mill that we have indeed turned the corner to the new Exponential Industrial Revolution.[11] The rest of this book looks at the details of this broad statement, but I suggest that perhaps we are there

Table 1.2 Four (or Five?) Modern Industrial Revolutions

Revolution	Year	Characteristics
1	1784	Steam, water, mechanical production equipment
2	1870	Division of labor, electricity, mass production
3	1969	Computer, electronics, and the Internet
4	1990s	Barriers between humans and machines dissolve
5?	Mid-2020s?	Exponential Industrial Revolution
		Rise of Exponential Technologies

Source: Author.

Figure 1.1 Exponential Technologies and Their Convergence

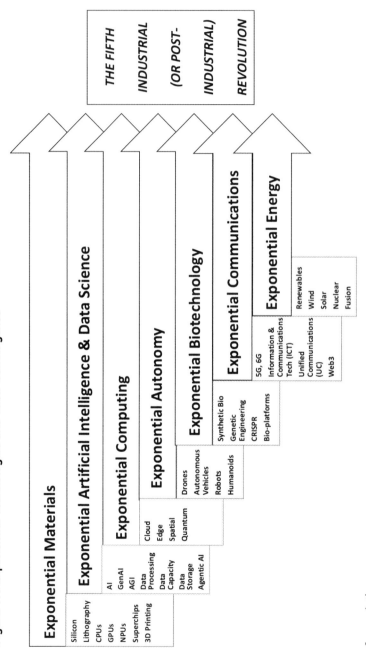

Source: Author.

already, mostly because of the unleashing of GenAI and its interconnectivity with and acceleration of many other technologies.

Megatrend 2: The Socioecology of Tech—In Search of Planetary Love

As the world becomes increasingly subject to the predictable and unpredictable effects of climate change, global warming, melting polar caps, and more, the interconnection between life on Earth—what I like to call the socioecological triangle—and technology is critically important, maybe even existentially so. I, like many others who are experts and scientists in this space, believe we are at a turning point to show the planet some love . . . or else. New and exponential technologies can be outsized contributors to addressing some of our greatest climate challenges and with showing that planetary love.

An Interdependent Socioecological Triangle

What is the socioecological triangle, then? This megatrend focuses on the intersection of technological change and the components of the socioecological triangle—climate, biodiversity, and humans. One depends on the other, and is affected by and affects the other. Foreseen and unforeseen or foreseeable and unforeseeable effects and consequences ensue when important developments take place in one realm with material effects on or correlation with another realm. The next subsections outline several examples of these interconnected relationships in the context of pandemics, deforestation, and heat.

Pandemics

Zoonotic viruses spreading from one species to another because of deforestation (biodiversity decline) and population growth and encroachment on biodiverse forests are becoming more common. Some scientists believe that COVID-19 represents one such case, becoming the first major global pandemic in a century, leading to the death of millions and creating long-term health consequences for many millions more.[12] The socioeconomic, political, and other consequences of the COVID-19 pandemic are still being felt, analyzed, and studied, but we know already that it has had a variety of social effects: work from home, social distancing, the use of immersive technologies, changing medical services delivery, and much more.

Deforestation

The uncontrolled, illegal, and corrupt logging of key forests along the equator (the Amazon River in Brazil for agricultural purposes, and the Congo River's forests for mining) push critical climate issues to the brink, and potentially beyond the brink, which could lead to greater and faster coastal flooding, eliminating islands in the Pacific and affecting cities and coastal zones around the world.[13]

Heat

The years 2023 and 2024 were the hottest ones on record. The inability of the world to come together more seriously and materially to maintain the 1.5 degrees above the baseline from the Industrial Revolution will lead to continuing climate devastation; indeed, in 2024 the Earth traversed the 1.5 degree red line.[14] The oil and gas industry and its supporters and entourages around the world continue to control governments, international organizations, and policy (witness COP28 and COP29, where the chairmen of these two global conferences were from oil-rich countries).[15] And it does not help that increased and often extensive drought-induced wildfires (like those in eastern Canada in the summer of 2023 and in Los Angeles in January 2025—their "wet" season) have exacerbated the carbon emissions we have been so impotent to tackle successfully over the past few years. All manner of climate consequences will follow without further effective global, regional, and local collaboration.

Socioecology and Technology

What does technology, especially exponential technology, have to do with the rise of complex socioecological risk, and what can responsible leaders do about it? There is a robust and concerted effort under way led by the United Nations with respect to its Sustainable Development Goals and the search for digital and technological solutions to these seventeen goals, bringing business, governments, and civil society together to find solutions, including climate-tech, social tech, health tech, fintech, and the general application of digital solutions to our most serious climate, biodiversity, and social challenges.

In the innovation space, there is a veritable explosion of activity and invention in this area worth mentioning, including new forms of energy storage and energy sources, such as thermal and mechanical systems, and batteries, including lithium-ion, flow, lead acid, sodium, and others designed to meet specific power and duration requirements, not to mention new modular nuclear plants under development. All these technologies can be paired with software that controls the charge and discharge of energy.[16]

And then there is the long-distance dream of nuclear fusion, which occurs when two atoms slam together to form a heavier atom, as when two hydrogen atoms fuse to form one helium atom. This is the same process that powers the Sun and creates huge amounts of energy—several times greater than fission (the process used for nuclear power). It also does not produce highly radioactive fission products. Scientists are currently studying fusion reactions; but because they are incredibly difficult to sustain, there is a long road to making them commercially and publicly viable.[17]

The Rise of Social-Impact Tech: The World Food Program, Google, UNHCR, and Circle

Finally, amazing strides are being made in what could be called social-impact tech, a great example of which has been taking place in an innovation incubator system within the World Food Program's Innovation Accelerator Program (IAP). Through the IAP, the connection between the dire effects of climate change (and other conditions, e.g., war and civil conflict) on the well-being of large swaths of the human population is fought every day using advanced technological tools. Under the rubric of #DisruptHunger, the IAP had twenty different start-up accelerators in 2024, focusing on innovative finance, frontier technologies, AI, and blockchain. These programs are looking to identify and scale disruptive solutions to global hunger. And business is involved, too—Google has funded the World Food Program USA through the IAP to leverage technology to improve emergency response, supply chain efficiency, and support for small-scale farmers in vulnerable communities. This grant will fund an acceleration program for developing and scaling up ten ventures, integrating advanced technologies like AI and blockchain. The IAP also focuses on projects in the food distribution space as well as digital pay solutions.[18]

Even the digital currency or crypto world has entered this space with Circle, the issuer of the digital currency USDC, providing digital cash to support war refugees fleeing Ukraine in the Ukraine-Russia war, by supporting the UN Refugee Agency with an innovative and integrated solution to deliver digital cash assistance to displaced persons and other war-affected Ukrainians.[19]

Megatrend 3: Geopolitical Techtonics—Tech in the Political Landscape

How does technological change intersect with geopolitical tectonic change? In this section, we connect two critically important megatrends: the rapid rise of exponential tech and the deep tectonic geopolitical and political shifts that are taking place at the global, national, organizational, and virtual levels. Key themes include superpower GenAI and other exponential tech competition and cooperation, the rise of exponential tech regulatory programs, the fight against misinformation and disinformation, and the tech threat to democracy.

Geopolitical Techtonics on the Global Stage

At the global level, we are witnessing several geopolitical techtonic developments. Chief among them is the deployment of high-tech weaponry and capabilities in the war in Ukraine and in the various war or conflict zones in the Middle East (Israel/Gaza and vicinity and the Red Sea). The war in Ukraine is the first full-scale war deploying a wide gamut of new tech in warfare—from autonomous and semiautonomous weapons (like all manner of drones) to cyberwarfare, surveillance tech, and open source intelligence.

Globally as well, there is the ongoing superpower competition between the United States and China on all things exponential technology, especially GenAI and chips. The fight is about who will gain an upper hand on GenAI and related technologies, including who will control the design, creation, distribution, and application of superchips—such as the graphics-processing units that Nvidia makes. With one catch: TMSC, the Taiwan-based chip manufacturer, currently controls 60 percent of the world's chip manufacturing and 90 percent of world production of the highest-end superchips (namely, those made by Nvidia) while in the crosshairs of China for a possible takeover, invasion, or other disruption.[20] As Taiwan's new premier stated at the beginning of his term in early 2024: "Taiwan has already mastered advanced semiconductor manufacturing, and we stand at the center of the AI revolution. . . . We are a key player in supply chains for global democracies. . . . With every step forward that Taiwan takes, the world takes a step forward with us." [21]

From a global geopolitical business standpoint, and beyond the complex nuances of United States / China / Taiwan tensions, several other global geopolitical techtonic developments are also taking place, including the emergence of other tech power centers in the Middle East (Israel, the United Arab Emirates, and Saudi Arabia) and in Asia (Singapore, Japan, and South Korea). Europe continues to be an important innovation center but is hampered, as some argue, by its more rigorous regulatory approach to exponential tech—best exemplified in its EU AI Act of 2024 (discussed in detail later in this book), which takes a risk-based approach to prioritizing human and social rights over unfettered innovation.

In Africa, we see several tech initiatives, including the Africa Observatory on Responsible AI, which has developed a number of regional reports, some in conjunction with the United Nations, looking at two key opportunities for harnessing AI to benefit humanity—first, to leverage AI to "advance development priorities in the region"; and second, to use "AI to address inequalities in critical sectors, such as education, health care, agriculture, finance and access to basic services."[22]

Global tech battles are also happening virtually through social media platforms like TikTok, X (formerly Twitter), Facebook, YouTube, and Telegram. These battles are more about the control of toxic content, which flourishes on some/most of these platforms, and the pushback from the platform providers against any form of control. The Telegram story is still unfolding as I finish writing this book, but it may be the tip of the spear of democratic governments beginning to hold platform owners accountable for criminal and human rights violations, including the distribution of child pornography, criminal arms and drug transactions, misinformation and disinformation with effects not only on human rights but also on the electoral process, and even the stability of democracy. In response to these many tech-enabled threats, several initiatives—some public, some private—have emerged over the past few years to combat tech-enabled toxicity, among them are NewsGuard, which reviews the reliability of news online; Recorded Future, a threat intelligence company; and Clemson University's Media Forensics Hub.[23]

However, as a cautionary note, at the time I am finishing this book, Mark Zuckerberg, CEO of Meta (parent of Facebook) has unilaterally announced the dropping of all existing content guardrails in favor of an X-like "community comments" section, which experts are cautioning will lead to new floodgates of toxicity on Facebook and related sites.

Geopolitical Techtonics on the National Stage

In a discussion of geopolitical techtonics, it would be a serious omission to not mention the internal national effects of tech's actual and virtual polarization and warfare. There is the deployment of surveillance technologies on citizens and populations—with different approaches from authoritarian, democratic, and illiberal states. We see the interference with freedoms and elections by foreign and domestic actors—their use of disinformation and misinformation, deep fakes, and other GenAI-driven visuals to influence political discourse and the use of social media for good and for not so good. In 2024—when the most people in the world (4 billion) lived in countries where national political elections were held (some more democratic, some less), the importance of clean, transparent, and precise voting and results—without polarization, toxicity, interference, and cyberattacks—was critical. The consensus of experts is that misinformation and disinformation blossomed like never before, including significantly in the United States.[24]

Geopolitical Techtonics at the Organizational Level

Finally, it bears mentioning that all these geopolitical techtonics have a direct and indirect effect on each of us as people living wherever we live and our entities—whether corporations, nongovernmental organizations, agencies, universities, and the like. There has never been a greater need for boards and management to run their companies with resilience programs—risk, crisis, and business continuity programs and constant futureproofing, including understanding geopolitical risk and opportunity.

Indeed, the World Economic Forum's "Global Risks Report" for 2025 identifies for the first time a geopolitical global strategic risk—"state-based armed conflict"—as the number one current global risk, by far, followed by "extreme weather" and another geopolitical risk as the third—"geoeconomic confrontation." Both these geopolitical risks remain in the top ten for the next two years, with the first one at third.

Geopolitical issues can materially affect tech planning and strategy, including cybersecurity GenAI-driven cyberinsecurity; the dangers of defective AI and GenAI infecting products and services; the issue of data provenance; and the deployment of new, often-untested and potentially contaminated technologies. In other words, there has never been a time when entities need a diversity of experts to triangulate their tech profile more and connect it back to governance. The "NACD 2024 Technology Leadership in the Boardroom Blue Ribbon Commission Report" does a great job connecting the dots back to the duties and responsibilities of corporate directors in this space.[25] This is a theme that we address repeatedly throughout this book: what leaders like board members need to consider in their oversight of technology-influenced geopolitical governance.

Megatrend 4: "Techonomics"—Quo Vadis Tech Economics?

"Quo vadis" is a Latin term that roughly translates to "where are you go-ing?" So, in this section, we focus on a megatrend about where technoeco-nomic (or "techonomic") leaders and decision-makers must navigate for the foreseeable future, in the context of how the economic environment is informed by and informs the new technology environment.

Three Nation-State Approaches to Techonomics Worldwide

From an economic systems standpoint, we have seen the movement from Milton Friedman's concept of pure "shareholder capitalism" of the 1970s and 1980s to a broader concept of "stakeholder capitalism" in recent de-cades—one that, while still making profitability the core objective of the corporation, also takes into account the most important other stakehold-ers beyond shareholders and owners—like employees, customers, gov-ernment, regulators, and suppliers. And then, of course, there are the more state-directed economies, sometimes called "state capitalism" but often not really capitalist at all, best exemplified by the current Chinese state capitalism or postcapitalism economic model. We also see this state capitalism model prevalent to different degrees in a wide spectrum of na-tions, ranging from illiberal democracies to authoritarian and totalitarian states.

If we look at how these economic systems approach technology and innovation, we can uncover some further nuances. At this time, there are essentially three approaches to or models of tech economics or techonom-ics, summarized in table 1.3.

There is the "Owner Techonomic Model," prevalent in somewhat-tech-unregulated free market economies (like the United States); there is the "Stakeholder Techonomic Model," where the interests of stakeholders (in addition to owners) are subject to greater regulatory protection (as in the EU); and there is the "State Techonomic Model," where the state has most control of the economics of technology, best exemplified by China.

Table 1.3 Three Approaches to "Techonomics" Worldwide

Owner Techonomic Model (United States, United Kingdom, and most free market economies with lesser individual rights regulations)	Stakeholder Techonomic Model (EU countries, Japan, South Korea, Australia, and other free market economies with individual regulatory protections)	State Techonomic Model (China, United Arab Emirates, Saudi Arabia, and most illiberal democracies and authoritarian states)
• Favors shareholders and owners • Other stakeholders are on their own • Accelerates innovation • Ignores many human rights protections	• Favors stakeholders • Owners and shareholders are held more accountable • May dampen innovation • Augments human rights protections	• Favors the state • Controls other stakeholders (sometimes including owners) • State-directed innovation • Stakeholders may be "protected" but controlled

Source: Author.

This latter model is also extant in a variety of countries, with the common threads being that the state is in greater charge of the economy, there is less or no free market capitalism, and the interests of stakeholders are subjugated to state direction and discretion, including tech surveillance and social scoring techniques.

Each of these systems has its pros and cons, though the State Techonomic Model would appear to be the harshest in terms of stakeholder rights, well-being, and effects, along with the possible absence of robust innovation due to state controls. Under the Owner Techonomic Model, as best exemplified by the US approach, while innovation and economic growth have been unleashed by the economic system, the interests, rights, and well-being of many citizens are not properly protected. For example, the United States still does not have a federal privacy law after decades of attempts to create one. So this model, while favoring the overall economy and the business class—especially the billionaire tech and "broligarch" class—it has left the average user on his or her own trying to protect against the toxicity, social media addiction, misinformation and disinformation, and general polarization allowed to run rampant on US-based social media platforms. In the Stakeholder Techonomic Model, prevalent in the EU countries, the trade-off appears to be more one where stakeholders and their human rights are broadly protected—especially those of more vulnerable groups—but innovation may be somewhat dampened by heavier regulatory burdens.

Techonomics; Environmental, Social, and Governance Issues; and Sustainability

Another deep connection exists between new technologies and the overall global economy and that is the interconnection between tech and sustainability or tech and environmental, social, and governance (ESG) issues. I have long written about this subject, as have others, and much of this book contains examples, concepts, and practical suggestions on the interconnection of sustainability and technology. Suffice it to say here that in the United States and a couple of other countries, these topics have become part of a toxic and polarized political debate in recent years. But these topics continue to be deeply important to business in general and especially to tech companies because these matters affect business planning, strategy, risk management, and other important components like supply chains and customers.

This interconnection of sustainability or ESG and technology will continue to be powerful, especially because of mounting environmental (energy and water) concerns for the big tech companies and in terms of innovation. Though the Trump Administration has issued executive orders and policies to counter Biden Administration climate laws, aspects of the US Inflation Reduction Act of 2022 (investing in climate measures at $369 billion over the coming decade) and the US CHIPS and Science Act of 2022 ($53 billion) remain in place for now. Both together and separately, these are some of the biggest US government investments ever made in climate and technology. Whether businesses speak loudly or "greenhush" about their ESG and sustainability advances, they know that for their strategy, risk management, and governance to work favorably, productively and profitably, they will need to continue integrating ESG and sustainability into their foresight.[26]

A Fourth Techonomics Approach: The Borderless Tech Billionaire Bros

There is yet another, still-developing approach in the world of techonomics—something that is brewing and still unclear. It involves the rise of a superwealthy, superpowerful clique of mostly Silicon Valley–based—what some are calling "broligarch"—class of mostly white men who are innovators, investors, financiers, and independent men of tech. Elon Musk, Sam Altman, Peter Thiel, Marc Andreessen, and Ben Horowitz belong in this group. Mark Zuckerberg, Jeff Bezos, and a few others should be included as well. Their power and influence got a turboboost with the Musk-financed political victory of Donald Trump to a second presidency with another tech supported "bro," J. D. Vance, as his vice president. The common theme is that this class of powerful men act beyond borders, often with impunity—they are an almost-untouchable privileged class of hypersuccessful people, revered by some, hated by others, who are at the cutting and bleeding edge of technology. They have billions to spend, and sometimes pursue wild ideas (remember Sam Altman looking for $7 trillion to build a new chip conglomerate?). They share dreams of power and more money, have built super luxurious, fully stocked, remote bunkers in case artificial general intelligence gone wrong happens, are also supporting "independent cities," and do pretty much whatever they want, as long as they can get away with it.[27] Which brings us to the last megatrend, which is all about responsibility, trust, and trustworthiness in this Age of Pandora, a subject that runs throughout this book.

Megatrend 5: Tech Trust and Trustworthiness—The Responsible Leadership Imperative

One of the notable coincidences or perhaps interconnected developments of our times is the rapid rise of exponential tech and the continuing and alarming decline in trustworthy leaders—whether in government, media, business, or nonprofits. If you only look at the twenty-plus years of the Edelman Trust Barometer measuring leadership trust in the aforementioned four institutional categories, you will find a steady and so far, unrelenting decline in trust by global stakeholders in over twenty-five countries surveyed each year.[28]

This leadership trust decline (or even vacuum in some cases) has serious implications for the development of exponential tech guardrails and responsibility. Indeed, leadership trustworthiness and irresponsible or ungovernable tech can become a vicious cycle. The GenAI-infused deployment of deep fakes, disinformation, and cyberinsecurity in the corporate and political worlds, plus the rise of pervasive surveillance and its effects on stakeholder trust, are key themes explored in this book.

What do we mean by responsible, effective, and ethical? Why are those the most important qualities of future tech leadership? In chapter 8—"Leadership: Turbocharging 360 Tech-Governance"—and chapter 9—"Ethos: Embedding Responsible Tech Culture"—I discuss many of the nuances of what it means to have good to great leadership and a responsible tech culture in this Age of Pandora. I also share in those chapters a variety of resources from the likes of Just Capital, the Harris/ Axios poll, the World Economic Forum's Digital Trust framework, and others to provide guidance on creating that responsible ethical future we all need. Suffice it to say here that "tech trust and trustworthiness and the responsible leadership imperative" is the single most important embedded theme that runs through this entire book. In part IV, I provide practical suggestions and frameworks for all of us as individuals, members of organizations, and global citizens to deploy in furtherance of a safer, more equitable, more beneficial tech future. Developing and deploying the situational awareness of knowing what the global tech megascape looks like at any given time is critical to having and maintaining trustworthy and responsible tech leadership.

2

RISE OF THE EXPONENTIAL MACHINES

Tech Turbocharges Tech

The central question that this book addresses is: How does an effective and ethical leader manage the onslaught of new tech in a deeply complex and interconnected world to maximum stakeholder benefit? The world is changing rapidly and broadly. Exponential technologies—exponential machines—are rising and spreading everywhere. Leaders and decision-makers need to be prepared to govern and manage these technologies urgently but thoughtfully. While not all leaders and managers will have to deal with all exponential technologies, each of us will undoubtedly have to deal with a variety of these technologies directly or indirectly (especially GenAI). For this, we must develop an exponential technology management and governance mindset—something we explore in great depth in part III of this book. This exponential governance mindset means being curious, open to change, humble, prepared for what is next and willing to learn and stand corrected, early and often. Chapter 13 goes into depth about the qualities and characteristics needed in our leaders in this Age of Pandora.

In my 2020 book *Gloom to Boom*, I began to explore the concept of future tech and reviewed materials from Imperial College that looked at the 100 "future most disruptive technologies." I was completely fascinated with the upper-right-hand quadrant of its explorations—the most distant and highest-impact technologies. Table 2.1 recreates this upper-right-

Table 2.1 The Future's Most Disruptive Technologies

Higher	Ei Space elevators	Vr Fully immersive virtual reality	Co Artificial consciousness	Qt *"We can't talk about this one"*
	Is Invisibility shields	Ph Factory photosynthesis	Th Transhuman technologies	Te Telepathy
Socio-economic disruption	Qs Quantum safe cryptography	Cp Cognitive prosthetics	Ud Data uploading to the brain	Rd Reactionless drive
Lower	Me Internet of DNA	Tc Thought control machine interfaces	Dr Dream reading and recording	Wh Whole Earth virtualization
		Sooner	*Time*	*Later*

Sources: Assembled by the author from the Imperial College of London's "Table of 100 Disruptive Technologies"; see Jake Kanter, "Academics Created a Periodic Table of Mind-Blowing Tech and It's a Handy Guide to How the World Will Change Forever," *Business Insider*, August 4, 2018, https://amp-businessinsider-com.cdn.ampproject.org/c/s/amp.businessinsider .com/imperial-college-london-table-of-disruptive-tech-will-blow-your-mind-2018-7.

hand quadrant and portrays future imagined technologies that appear pretty insane—but perhaps not impossible—like a space elevator, artificial consciousness, telepathy, transhuman technologies, dream reading, and recording thought control.[1]

Are these future technologies "exponential" technologies? Maybe some of them are; but not necessarily all. "Exponential technology" does not solely refer to future technologies but also to current or future tech that has certain key characteristics, mainly that the tech is happening with amazing velocity, uncertainty, and potential volatility—often with deep asymmetry in its use and deployment and, almost always, interconnectivity with other tech.

This chapter lays out basic parameters and gives an overview of what exponential technologies are. In part II, we will explore large categories of exponential tech, from GenAI and biotechnology to advanced materials, computing, and autonomy. By no means is the coverage here intended to be comprehensive or even in depth—that would be nearly impossible. But by selecting these large categories of exponential technologies currently under development, we hope to shine a light on matters leaders and decision-makers must pay attention to and prepare for now. The purpose is to stimulate the reader's interest in going deeper, where it makes sense for you to do so. The goal is to help you develop the exponential governance mindset we talk about throughout the book.

Exponential Tech Changes Everything . . . Exponentially

In 1993, Vernor Vinge, in a paper delivered to NASA, made this prescient observation: "The acceleration of technological progress has been the central feature of this century; . . . we are on the edge of change comparable to the rise of human life on Earth. The precise cause of this change is the imminent creation by technology of entities with greater than human intelligence. There are several means by which science may achieve this breakthrough (and this is another reason for having confidence that the event will occur): (1) the development of computers that are 'awake' and superhumanly intelligent (to date, most controversy in the area of AI relates to whether we can create human equivalence in a machine. But if the answer is 'yes, we can,' then there is little doubt that beings more intelligent can be constructed shortly thereafter); (2) large computer networks (and their associated users) may 'wake up' as a superhumanly intelligent entity; (3) computer/human interfaces may become so intimate that users may reasonably be considered superhumanly intelligent; and (4) biological science may find ways to improve upon the natural human intellect. The first three possibilities depend in large part on improvements in computer hardware. Progress in computer hardware has followed an amazingly steady curve in the last few decades. Based largely on this trend, I believe that the creation of greater than human intelligence will occur during the next thirty years."[2]

So, are we there yet? Not quite, but we are much closer than we were in 1993. Indeed, while we have not yet reached a level of superhuman intelligence (one that goes above and beyond what we know humans can do today, even with the assistance of AI and GenAI), all four of the developments Vinge mentions are in full swing—especially with the advent of GenAI, increasingly tiny and exponentially more powerful superchips, the miniaturization of digital devices, and biotechnological innovations. The debate continues to rage on whether and when we might reach the next exponential moment in AI—achieving artificial general intelligence, into which we will delve deeper in chapter 3. For the purposes of our journey in this book, exponential technology is a technology that by virtue of its own properties can grow rapidly, sometimes unexpectedly so, drawing on (and/or accelerated by) other technologies (including other exponential technologies) for such growth, which in some cases may double in power and/or size and/or reduce dramatically in cost in a short period of time and much more rapidly than expected.

ChatGPT/Perplexity: Asking for a Friend—What Is Exponential Technology?

In my explorations of exponential technology, I queried two GenAI exponential technologies—ChatGPT4/ChatGPT4o, from OpenAI; and Perplexity AI, from Perplexity—for their definitions of exponential technology. Here are each of their responses when I prompted "What is exponential technology?"

From GPT4o:[3]

Exponential technology refers to technologies that evolve at an accelerating rate, often doubling in capacity or efficiency while simultaneously decreasing in cost usually following a pattern similar to Moore's law in computing. These technologies often have the potential to disrupt existing industries, create new markets, and lead to rapid societal change. The defining characteristic of exponential technologies is their rapid rate of advancement, which often outpaces our ability to anticipate their full impact on society and the economy.

Next, I posed the same query to Perplexity AI—first in January 2024, and then in late August 2024. The answers are a little different each time:

Exponential technology refers to innovations that double in capability or performance over a short period of time, often while halving in cost. These technologies have the potential to disrupt various industries and significantly impact our daily lives.[4]

Exponential technology refers to technologies that experience rapid growth in power or performance while simultaneously decreasing in cost. This concept is often associated with Moore's law, which observes that the number of transistors on a microchip doubles approximately every two years, leading to a doubling of computer processing power over the same period."[5]

I also asked both ChatGPT and Perplexity to list the most important exponential technologies for me in both early 2024 and late summer 2024. A comparison of the two large language model (LLM) responses over a six-month period shows mostly overlap but a few differences, as table 2.2 demonstrates. ChatGPT includes Quantum Tech (which Perplexity does not) and augments its initial categorization of types of exponential technologies to include robotics and three-dimensional printing (while deleting "renewable energy technologies" for no apparent reason). Perplexity has the interesting category "exponential innovation" in its earlier list (deleted from the later one), which refers to the "combination of core technologies," an insightful take that corresponds to what I call the "interconnectivity" of exponential technologies (discussed later in this chapter) and to the idea of tech turbocharging tech. Perplexity, unlike ChatGPT, also includes in its list of exponential tech the Internet of Things, virtual/augmented reality and wearables, autonomous vehicles, and synthetic biology.

The purpose of querying these two different LLM services at two different times was twofold. First, I thought it would be very important to use the tools of exponential tech to understand aspects of exponential tech. But second, and more important, the purpose is to show that there can be differences, disagreements, mistakes, and other things happening within the GenAI "black box," which no one knows about when we query GenAI. And because this tech is changing so fast and is not always reli-

Table 2.2 Comparing ChatGPT4/ChatGPT4o and Perplexity Responses to My Query: "What Is Exponential Technology? Provide Examples"

ChatGPT4 Responses, March 2024	Perplexity AI Responses, March 2024
• Artificial intelligence and machine learning • Quantum computing • Biotechnology • Nanotechnology • Blockchain and distributed ledger technologies • Renewable Energy Technologies	• AI • 3D printing • Internet of Things • Virtual reality, augmented reality, and wearables • Exponential innovation (defined as "the combination of core digital technologies like computing power, data storage, and bandwidth fueling exponential innovation across various industries.")
ChatGPT4o Responses, August 2024	Perplexity AI Responses, August 2024
• Artificial intelligence and machine learning • Quantum computing • Biotechnology • Nanotechnology • Blockchain and distributed ledger technologies • 3D Printing (additive manufacturing) • Robotics	• AI • 3D printing • Internet of Things • Robotics • Autonomous vehicles • Blockchain • Synthetic biology

Source: Author, with the assistance of ChatGPT4 /ChatGPT4o and Perplexity AI.

able or transparent, we require a human in or on the loop (something we explore in detail in chapter 10) at all times to provide the judgment, context, a moral compass, and experience that these models do not (for now) have. If I had to settle on one being more useful than the other, I would say that Perplexity did a slightly more sophisticated job than ChatGPT4o in selecting and explaining exponential technology categories.

The Exponential Technologies We Explore in This Book, and Why

Checking with a more traditional source of true and tried tech research—"Gartner's Emerging Tech Impact Radar 2024"—we can learn a lot as well.

Table 2.3 Gartner's Emerging Tech Impact Radar for 2024

Current, "high" or "very high" impact, 2024–25:
- GenAI
- Knowledge graphs

1–3 years, "high" or "very high" impact, 2025–27:
- GenAI-enabled virtual assistants
- Digital Twins
- Multimodal AIs
- Responsible AI
- Leo-satellite mega constellations
- AI chips
- Blockchain
- Human-centered AI
- Intelligent applications

3–6 years, "high" or "very high" impact, 2027–30:
- Smart spaces
- Tokenization
- Hyperscale edge computing
- Vision transformers for vision computing
- Self-supervised learning
- Neuromorphic computing
- Private 5G
- Decentralized identity
- Privacy enhancing technologies

6–8 years, "high" or "very high" impact, 2030–32:
- Quantum processors
- Spatial computing
- Web3

Source: Author, based on Gartner research.

Table 2.3 offers a breakdown of what Gartner considers the highest-impact (in its lingo, "very high" or "high") emerging and cutting-edge technologies in the coming few years broken down by time horizon.[6] Gartner also classified as medium- or lower-impact several additional technologies or implementations, including autonomous vehicles, synthetic data, AI avatars, and behavioral analytics.

Based on the foregoing and additional extensive research, I derived two criteria for my selection process of exponential technologies we must consider. First, these technologies and technological applications are already extant or under deep development (or both) and are being (or are about to be) mainstreamed into global business through widespread adoption. Second, these technologies serve as living, breathing examples of the challenges and opportunities that leaders—in business, government, and civil society—are already facing and will continue to face in the near term. Both criteria underscore the need for a governance, risk, ethics, and impact mindset reset for decision-makers in the future. Based on these considerations, I have chosen to explore five exponential technology categories in this book: AI and GenAI, biotechnology and synthetic biology, advanced materials, frontier computing, and autonomy, each of which is explored in part II, in chapters 3 through 7.

Our Lenses on Exponential Technology

These are the five foundational exponential technologies that my peers and others without tech backgrounds will need to understand to deploy the exponential governance mindset we discuss in the second half of this book. My approach is not that of an engineer, biologist, or data scientist; it is that of a social scientist—someone who looks at the frameworks, approaches, and systems that are important for society, the economy, governance, and futureproofing the planet from a policy standpoint. My experience is that leaders and board members within the communities at the nexus of science, industry, and policy will also find this approach useful.

From a governance standpoint, decision-makers—at both the board and executive levels—must understand the content, characteristics, and contours of new technologies their entities are creating, developing, acquiring, integrating, and/or implementing. They need to be equipped—with different degrees of detail and hands-on control—with the information necessary to understand how exponential technologies are or are not integrated into their business and business model and why and why not.

From a risk (and opportunity) management standpoint, the disciplined and holistic vetting of the impact and likelihood of potential downsides (and upsides) of an exponential technology must be an integral part of both enterprise risk management and strategy. Indeed, a concept I have long operationalized is one that states that knowing your risks provides a blueprint for knowing your opportunities. That is why it is so critically important for organizations (regardless of sector) to have effective risk management and risk governance that help identify opportunities for the creation of better or new processes, products, and services.

The evaluation of the ethical implications of the developing tech must be a north star of exponential technology invention, integration, process, and outcome. Ethics experts need to work hand in glove with technologists and engineers and be part of the full life cycle of exponential technology inception, design, integration, implementation, troubleshooting, and sunsetting. While a code of ethics is always a good start, it is wholly unsatisfactory if it remains a piece of paper or a webpage instead of a fully operationalized, endemic and intertwined set of organizational practices.

Finally, appreciating the impact of exponential technologies is crucial for the environment, society, the global commons, and key stakeholders. We must take into account stakeholders' most important expectations of our organizations to undertake considered action and protect and enhance reputations. This means understanding the key stakeholders an organization has at the individual, community, national, and international levels, and the implications (if any) for biodiversity, climate, and the planet. The full panoply of issues to consider include health, safety, security, well-being, survivability, preservation, resilience, and more, as we will discuss in detail in parts III and IV.

The Five Attributes of Exponential Technology

There are five key attributes of exponential technologies that appear again and again when we look at the various types of technologies that can be characterized as exponential. These are velocity, volatility, uncertainty, asymmetry, and interconnectivity as seen in Figure 2.1. Not all exponential technologies have all these attributes at all times, but these attributes help

Figure 2.1 Five Exponential Technology Attributes
Source: Author.

us to understand the unique nature—challenges and opportunities—of exponential technology. Let us briefly examine each attribute.

Velocity

The velocity of a technology's development is much greater—exponentially so—than what might be expected, at least for a time. This also means that both velocity of degradation and velocity of improvement can be greater. What this means to leaders and decision-makers is that they are operating at a severe disadvantage if they do not assume this mindset. It also means that they may gain advantages, including competitive advantages, if a business, for example, consciously adopts a velocity assumption. For instance, the velocity of development of GenAI models has been nothing short of head snapping for a swath of established and emerging companies—from OpenAI, Anthropic, and Meta to Perplexity

AI and Xai—publishing exponentially new and improved GenAI models every few months. Also, this requires corporate consumers to be hyper-vigilant about what they are using, how reliable it is, and whether it has been materially superseded by competitors, rapidly making what they are using today less than desirable or even obsolete.

Volatility

Closely related to velocity, volatility means that we do not really know where an exponential tech is going from the standpoint of safety, security, ethics, and impact—that is, overall governance. Our ability to control, limit, or close down technologies at any stage of their development or deployment is not a given.[7] The implications for leaders and decision-makers is that they need to be more prepared than usual to identify, understand, and mitigate future risk and new, emerging risk. This means, in turn, that in an organizational setting, enterprise risk management, information tech audit, and information security teams and their leaders need to keep pace with, or even be ahead of, the potentially unpredictable effects of the use of these technologies, especially negative or harmful ones.

Uncertainty

The possibility of unknown, unpredictable, unintended (as well as intended) consequences—positive, negative, and/or neutral—is greater. We are truly peering into the unknown and potentially unknowable. What this means for decision-makers is that they must prepare for uncertainty by developing resilience and preparedness practices and frameworks, like crisis management; business continuity; personal, data, and asset protection plans; and related practices like red teaming and scenario planning.

Asymmetry

Many of the exponential technologies that we explore are and will be deployable asymmetrically—that is, a small, under-the-radar entity or even individual person who can, if successful, have exponentially greater or asymmetric effects. What this means in practice for leaders and decision-makers is that, for example, they need to be ready for the erstwhile guy in his mother's basement mounting a cybersecurity attack on a national defense department's computer system. An asymmetric case like this occurred in the now-famous and very expensive MGM Grand and Casino Resorts cyberhack of 2023, with a seventeen-year-old arrested in the United Kingdom in connection with this attack.[8]

Interconnectivity

Although not uncommon for previously known and established technologies, it is almost a given that most exponential technologies are interconnected—dependent, enabled, and boosted—by other exponential or more established technologies. Leaders must become fully aware of these interconnectivities. On the negative side of this equation is the bad actor capable of deploying interconnected GenAI, SynBio, and a semiautonomous drone to deliver a terrorist attack to an urban environment. On the positive side of the equation, think of geospatial tech and GenAI intertwining to deliver critically important catastrophic weather information in advance of it hitting a location allowing for life-saving measures to be taken.

Exponential technologies do not exist in silos or alone on an island. Each scientific and engineering development is informed and influenced by both the past and the present and by advances, successes, and failures in multiple other disciplines, as well as by trends and megatrends in the environment, society, economy, governance, and geopolitics. It is therefore incumbent on us to think of every technology we talk about in this book and in our work and world as a multidimensional phenomenon that is constantly morphing, metamorphizing, influencing and being influenced—and all of this much faster than ever before.

The Exponential Tech Paradox: Innovators Are Not Always Stewards

A pervasive theme of this book is that because we are going through faster cycles of inventing, launching, and adopting new technologies, there is barely any time or opportunity to examine the parameters, characteristics, possible risks, and potential stakeholder effects of this tech. Therefore, we are relying almost exclusively on the creators and funders of tech to spot, account for, and mitigate potentially harmful consequences.

The problem is that tech creators and funders (innovators) are often members of a very small, select, homogeneous, privileged group of mostly (white) men in tech companies and private equity firms, located mostly in Silicon Valley, who are largely focused on rapid—"move fast and break things"—accomplishments. While some do (or profess to) pay sufficient heed to the critically necessary stewardship part of the equation, many do not.

Even tech giants like Google—which have the deepest of pockets and supposedly the guardrails set up internally to integrate risk, ethics, governance, and impact considerations into the development of their new tech—have from time to time been unable to apply basic digital trust parameters. Witness Google Gemini's semidisastrous unveiling of the LLM text-to-visual capability in early 2024, where Nazi figures appeared as members of a variety of races (none of them white) and President Lincoln appeared as a Black gentleman. To its credit, the company quickly acknowledged the issue and worked on fixing the problem, apologizing for "inaccuracies in some historical image generation depictions" pausing "Gemini's ability to generate images featuring people."[9]

The problem is that the technologists and funders often have no idea of (or do not want to know) what the foreseeable, unforeseeable, intentional, or unintentional consequences and effects of their new tech will be—partly because they are hyperfocused on innovation, growth, and returns. There is nothing wrong with this. But something is wrong with a model that says that you can forge forward with exponential technologies that you do not fully understand yet, without inputs from other critical functions—governance, risk, ethics, and impact, among them. In addition to some of the large established players that have more accountable digital trust models (Microsoft, Google), others have put their money where their mouth is on tech ethics—Mozilla and Salesforce come to mind. In both these companies' cases, their leadership has made it a priority to develop responsible technology, with strong governance in place and a proactive culture of tech ethics. But nothing is forever, and firms that did well yesterday and today on these fronts may not do so tomorrow, when there is a change of leadership, for example.

A recurring theme seems to be that the companies developing these exponential technologies often do not include the right or precise tests, guardrails, and quality controls in the process of creation because they are viewed as impediments to progress and fall into the maligned "cost center" category of the business. Another theme is that these leaders are in a big hurry to get products to market, to be first to introduce new products or improvements (witness the fast and furious release of new and more powerful LLMs) in the competitive landscape before their products and/or services are properly vetted and ready for prime time.

Most of this happens within these organizations and far from the eyes of watchful stakeholders—like regulators and ethicists—who, given an early chance to peer into the tech, might help create safer or more ethical choices. But they are excluded from these early stages for "good reasons"—namely, speed to market, competition, short-term cost—generally viewed as ballasts for progress.

In other words, investors and the capitalists have full control over exponential tech products and services until they are ready to be released into the commercial wild, at which time other stakeholders have their first shot at analyzing the governance, risk, ethics, and impact contours of the tech, without the benefit of understanding what went into its development. These experts—the guardians and stewards of tech—are, by definition, disadvantaged and underresourced. And thus, when it comes to exponential technologies, humanity does not have proper safeguards in place. We discuss this phenomenon in detail in chapters 8 and 9.

There are different economic models, of course, depending on geography, jurisdiction, type of government, and so on. What I have described above is more pertinent to the free market capitalist model prevalent in the United States and a few other jurisdictions. There are more regulated models—the European Union comes to mind, especially because it has enacted the EU AI Act, which provides a risk-based model that some critics complain is too heavy on regulations and too light on incentives for innovation (discussed later in this book). And then there is the more autocratic, statist model—which can be capitalistic or state controlled—where China comes to mind as the prime example. In China, this model is one in which the state has almost absolute control of communications, technology, a walled-off Internet, social media, and the economy, and it carefully controls what each person has access to and what that person does online and virtually through social scoring and other means.

Not to be lost in this description of the exponential tech paradox is of course the massively positive opportunities that these new technologies provide to the world. Think of the vaccines we got in less than eleven months to combat COVID-19. With GenAI, so much has been revolutionized in just a few short years in efficiency, productivity, research, and more. We can only imagine what will happen when Quantum computing becomes a reality. This is the conundrum we face: We want the amazing qualities and benefits of these technologies, and we want them now, but we also want them without damaging or life-threatening downsides. We want the instant gratification of tech solutions, but we do not want them to bite us back or worse. What we ultimately want is that the innovators be human-centric stewards too. And that is the trick.

This reality requires a concomitant response from those of us who have relevant expertise. We must have a conscious awareness, a continuing education, a sense of preparation, a readiness for deployment, and willingness to repair things that are happening and will happen. This means first being a conscientious, alert, communal, and helpful human. It means prepping for, triangulating, surviving in, thriving in, and future-proofing the Age of Pandora.

Part II

TRIANGULATING THE AGE OF PANDORA

An Exponential Tech Whirlwind Tour

3

GENERATIVE AI

Everything, Everywhere, All at Once

Let us start by level setting on all things AI by defining artificial intelligence (AI), generative AI (GenAI), and the ultimate in AI, which we have not yet reached: artificial general intelligence (AGI). According to AWS, AI "is the field of computer science dedicated to solving cognitive problems commonly associated with human intelligence, such as learning, creation, and image recognition. Modern organizations collect large volumes of data from diverse sources like smart sensors, human-generated content, monitoring tools, and system logs. The goal with AI is to create self-learning systems that derive meaning from data. Then, AI can apply that knowledge to solve new problems in human-like ways."[1] Or as I would put it more simply: AI is humanity's attempt at reaching human intelligence through artificial means—that is, computationally.

Google offers this definition of GenAI: it "refers to the use of AI to create new content, like text, images, music, audio, and videos. Generative AI is powered by foundation models (large AI models) that can multitask and perform out-of-the-box tasks, including summarization, Q&A, classification, and more. Plus, with minimal training required, foundation models can be adapted for targeted use cases with very little example data."[2] Or, as I would simplify it: GenAI is an expanded version of AI that builds on it and offers multimodality, exponentially improving the chance of reaching human intelligence artificially or computationally.

According to Gartner, AGI would be a "form of AI that possesses the ability to understand, learn and apply knowledge across a wide range of tasks and domains. It can be applied to a much broader set of use cases and incorporates cognitive flexibility, adaptability, and general problem-solving skills."[3] Or, as Mark Zuckerberg put it when asked what AGI was, "I don't have a one-sentence pithy definition. . . . You can quibble about it, general intelligence is akin to human level intelligence, or is it like human-plus, or is it some far-future super intelligence."[4] And my take on AGI? It is humanity's attempt to unleash a form of artificially created or computationally arrayed intelligence beyond GenAI into a domain of supra-human superintelligence.

As these definitions from AWS, Google, Gartner, and Zuckerberg, respectively, (and my own admitted oversimplifications) underscore, GenAI is a form of AI that goes beyond the versions of AI we have seen over the past several decades (especially if we harken back to the modern inception of AI around World War II and the Turing Machine), while AGI—an even more exponential form of AI than GenAI—is something we have not reached yet and over which there is much debate and even disagreement as to if and when we will reach it.[5]

For those who have followed the various twists and turns in the development of what is considered to be AI today, the Turing Machine, developed by Alan Turing during World War II, is considered the birth point of modern AI (see sidebar 3.1). It is so because through his work, Turing demonstrated that anything that is computable by a human using an algorithm is also computable by a machine. The Turing Test, as it came to be known, became the criterion by which to judge whether a machine could exhibit intelligence equivalent to or perhaps even better than human.

A key Turing Test question for our times is whether through the fast, even exponential, advances we are witnessing in GenAI, we have reached the point of passing the Turing Test. In other words, are our most advanced GenAI iterations imitating the human mind yet, or do we still have a way to go? In my humble opinion, we are not there yet, simply based on the fact that while GenAI is indeed conquering feats of overwhelming intelligence gathering, interpretation, and construction—often in a way that is far superior to what can be done by a single or even multiple human brains—the emotional intelligence, judgement, and depth of per-

---

Sidebar 3.1

The Turing Machine and Why It Is So Fundamental for Developing AI

The Turing machine was created by Alan Turing in 1936 and laid down a conceptual framework for understanding computation even before computers were created. Turing envisioned machines capable of advancing beyond their original programming, essentially conceptualizing AI before the term was coined. Turing is known for having conducted the Turing Test in 1950 which revolved around an idea of an "imitation game" to test whether a machine could mimic a human's thinking. This became a fundamental part of the conceptualization and development of AI. Turing worked on something called the "Automatic Computing Engine," which was designed to mimic the human brain in a way that predates the concepts of neural networks and machine learning. He attempted to deploy this on chess playing. Turing's work in this space provided the essential early mathematical framework for understanding computation that later became a vital part of developing AI algorithms and systems.

Source: Coursera, "The History of AI: A Timeline of Artificial Intelligence," www.coursera.org /articles/history-of-ai.

---

ception humans bring to the table has not and may not be translatable into a machine—at least not yet. Time will certainly tell, and nothing is off the table in terms of the possibilities.

A fundamental question of our times is why have AI, and especially GenAI, burst so prominently, some may say exponentially, onto the scene suddenly in the early 2020s? It was not truly until the dawn of the twenty-first century when we saw the convergence of several key factors that explain the birthing of GenAI two decades into this century. The ever-significant expansion of data collection and analytics; the constant miniaturization of increasingly powerful semiconductor chips, central-processing units (CPUs), and general-processing units (GPUs); and the resulting explosion in "compute" power—have all culminated (for now) in the incarnation of GenAI over the past few years.

Experts identify 2017 and the introduction by Google of "transformers" as the turning point, when AI changed dramatically from what it had been before that time—pretty much increasingly powerful information and data processing and algorithms—to what it is in its GenAI manifestation in the 2020s: an interactive, multimodal, constantly learning vehicle that becomes smarter and more powerful the more compute power it achieves and the more it learns from humans and other data sources. It was on August 31, 2017, that Google AI researchers announced the concept of the transformer.[6] "Transformers are a type of neural network architecture that transforms or changes an input sequence into an output sequence. They do this by learning context and tracking relationships between sequence components. For example, consider this input sequence: 'What is the color of the sky?' The transformer model uses an internal mathematical representation that identifies the relevancy and relationship between the words color, sky, and blue. It uses that knowledge to generate the output: 'The sky is blue.'" Organizations use transformer models for all types of sequence conversions, from speech recognition to machine translation and protein sequence analysis. Table 3.1 provides a side-by-side comparison of the differences between AI and GenAI.

It is in some of these differences that we can find the reason why GenAI has caught on in such a transformational, indeed exponential, manner both in its upsides—the creativity and applications, and in some of its downsides, for example, its transparency challenges. Let us now explore key issues and themes for GenAI.

Key Issues and Topics for GenAI

It is hard for any of us not to be overwhelmed by the multiple fire hydrants (not just hoses) of GenAI and AI information generally and the multiplicity of parallel technological developments since the release of ChatGPT in November 2022. We need to learn as much as possible but also understand how to skinny this tsunami of information down to what is useful and important for each of us personally and professionally.

Here are a few topics of interest that, by the time you read this, will have probably been superseded and/or overwhelmed by newer and shinier GenAI- and AI-related topics. Nevertheless, it is important to under-

Table 3.1 Major Differences between AI and GenAI

Type of Difference	Traditional AI	GenAI
Overview	Includes a range of methods, from rules-based systems to deep learning, capable of solving complex tasks typically requiring defined objectives and data sets	Extends AI capabilities to create new content and adapt dynamically, breaking boundaries of specific-task constraints.
Learning	Task-specific performance: focused on solving narrowly defined problems (e.g., play chess, diagnose diseases)	Expansive performance: learning and adapting across multiple fronts at once
Applications	Task-specific systems: Using fixed logic or trained models (e.g., spam filters, Alexa)	Broader systems: Rules can change with new inputs (adaptive learning).
Data creation	New data that are created are based on user behavior and preferences generate insights and predictions.	New data, new content creation (e.g., music, visuals, text, code) go beyond traditional AI to include new music, poetry, etc.
Manifestations/Uses	Narrower application: While AI can have a wide range of uses, including complex predictive modeling and decision-making systems, AI has a narrower application than GenAI.	Broader application, chatbots conversing, new media creation, multimodal discourse, and more
User Interaction	Limited interaction with or learning from user, more static, minimally adaptive interaction based on predefined or trained models, presentive and less dynamic than GenAI	Enhanced interaction with and broad and far ranging multimodal learning from user
Transparency	Ranges from fully transparent to opaque as to rules and interpretation	Less transparent, more "black box"; difficult to interpret, almost entirely opaque

Source: Author.

stand these topics. They are, in no particular order, the criticality of having high-quality data to feed into GenAI (including synthetic data); the importance of reinforcement learning from human feedback; the debate between open source and closed source models; inferencing; hallucinating; and the GenAI "black box" problem.

Data: Garbage In / Garbage Out and the Setting
of New Data Standards

Alexandr Wang, CEO and founder of Scale AI, said in an interview with Bloomberg TV in May 2024 that the GenAI revolution is based on three pillars: data, compute (computing power or capacity), and algorithms. Compute is led by Nvidia, algorithms by OpenAI, and data are the focus of Scale AI, which seeks to solve the data challenges to enable a leap from GPT4 to GPT10 by ensuring that we have the means of production to do all that.[7]

Some of the data challenges include the provenance and quality of data fed into an algorithm—if you feed in garbage, you will get garbage. Also, if you feed in biased, unfair, discriminatory data, it will produce skewed results. If you feed in data collected in violation of privacy and other human rights, you have yet another set of challenges. And if you feed in intellectual property (copyrighted information) obtained without permission, you may face a series of legal and litigation challenges. There are regulatory requirements that need to be observed in certain jurisdictions; if you do not, you may be subject to regulatory fines or lawsuits. Integrating and scaling the data is key. And then there are ethical issues having to do with the use and application of data outputs, including misinformation, disinformation, and intellectual property theft.

And then there is the new frontier of synthetic data creation which some hope will transpire broadly as more traditional data sources dry up. In other words, large language models (LLMs) have already hoovered up much of the data on the Internet, for example, even though data are always changing as well. By creating synthetic data that mimic real-world data through algorithms and simulations, the hope is that ample and sufficient data will be available to feed the constantly growing GenAI data

Sidebar 3.2
What Are Synthetic Data? Risks and Opportunities

"Synthetic data" are information that are artificially manufactured rather than generated by real-world events. They are created algorithmically and used as a stand-in for test data sets of production or operational data to validate mathematical models and train machine learning (ML) and deep learning models.

Risks:

1. Lack of realism and accuracy
2. Bias and unfairness propagation without great quality control
3. Difficulty in verifying and validating data quality
4. If only source of data for AI model, limited usefulness
5. Possible model degradation
6. Cybersecurity risks especially if there are hard to detect hallucinations
7. Ethical concerns if deployed in sensitive fields like health care
8. Degradation of data quality over time

Opportunities:

1. Enhanced privacy and security (and compliance with relevant regulations)
2. Unlimited data generation
3. Cost-effectiveness
4. Improved/turbocharged AI and ML development
5. Risk free testing, experimentation
6. Greater control over data quality and format
7. Reduced bias, more fairness
8. Collaborative and accessible

Sources: Cameron Hashemi-Pour et al., "What Is Synthetic Data? Examples, Use Cases and Benefits," TechTarget, www.techtarget.com/searchcio/definition/synthetic-data; author.

intensive beast (see sidebar 3.2). However, some of the key challenges for synthetic data revolve around human oversight of synthetic data creation, human orchestration of deep neural networks, privacy differentials between real data and synthetic data, measurable accuracy, data evaluation and validation, and, finally, the role of alignment teams.[8]

On the good news side of the ledger, business, governmental, and societal efforts are under way to develop high-integrity data—whether real or synthetic—in the continuing development of GenAI. Among the most prominent is the Data & Trust Alliance, a nonprofit consortium of twenty-nine leading businesses and institutions that deploy data and AI in business. Its mission is to "develop practices that enhance trust in data, in AI models, and in the people and processes through which they are deployed." So far, the alliance has developed Data Provenance Standards— the first cross-industry metadata standards "to bring transparency to the origin of data sets used for both traditional data and AI applications" and it is working on additional standard setting in this space.[9]

Reinforcement Learning from Human Feedback

GenAI has indeed turbocharged AI, in part because of "reinforcement learning from human feedback," a type of machine learning (ML) that uses human feedback to improve ML models to create more efficient ways of self-learning and to develop reward systems that are aligned with human needs and objectives. Reinforcement learning trains software to make better and more accurate decisions.

Though reinforcement learning from human feedback was used before GenAI became pervasive, together with GenAI it has become a major contributor to the unique features of GenAI as we no longer depend on only data to "teach" LLMs but can now rely on immediate human feedback as well to correct, enhance, augment, or reinforce the data. There are major differences between traditional AI and GenAI, mainly pointing at the turbocharged nature of GenAI—with more capacity, speed, and frequently precision than its precursor. Such differences can be seen around several factors—from learning and applications to use cases, interactivity, and transparency.

The Debate on Open Sources versus Closed Sources

Another important differentiation of the forms of GenAI that are being released into the wild is the difference between those created with open source code versus those programmed with closed source code:

- *Open source software* is source code that is publicly available, accessible, modifiable, and distributable by anyone to anyone, anywhere. Because it is free and open to all, it lends itself to collaboration, community, and crowd-sourced improvement.
- *Closed source software* is source code that is proprietary, confidential, and accessible only to those who have created it or make it available to others through payment or licensing arrangements. Because of its closed and payment-led character, it is more restricted and less collaborative, and is subject to slower modification or improvement.

Table 3.2 provides a shorthand summary of the characteristics, pros, and cons of open source versus closed source and examples for both. This information helps to illuminate a raging debate that is taking place in the GenAI space between the likes of Yan Le Cun, chief data scientist for Meta, who is a passionate advocate for open source (though experts differ on whether Meta's AI is indeed open source), and others like the leaders of OpenAI, who fear the adverse, potentially high-risk effects of handing the "keys to the GenAI source code kingdom" to anyone anywhere around the world. Underlying both concepts at least in the for-profit world, is the tension between those like Zuckerberg at Meta who believe they have the greatest prospects for new revenue through open source strategies and those like Sam Altman from OpenAI who believe a closed source model is more lucrative (while also extolling its better "safety" qualities).

Those who favor the open-source model argue that it provides for greater transparency of data inputs, coding, and algorithm construction, which in turn can translate into better security and regulatory compliance (e.g., with the European Union's AI Act). They also emphasize the communal aspects of the open source model, in that almost anyone can contribute and collaborate on improvements not to mention customization, innovation, and accessibility. Those on the other side of the equation—that is, who favor the more closed, proprietary model—argue that their experts (and not just anyone) are able to consistently quality control

Table 3.2 A Comparison between Open Source and Closed Source Software

Point of Comparison	Open Source Software	Closed Source Software
Principal Characteristics and Differentiators	Source code is freely accessible to public Volunteer-driven Community support Free education Encourages innovation No confidentiality or proprietary restrictions Crowd-sourcing produces better code development Security concern: Greater danger of bad actor usage	Source code is not freely available to the public Company or organization-controlled Company/seller support Education for a price Suppresses widespread innovation Proprietary and confidential source code Profit-driven—purchased or licensed Flaws may not always be caught Security depends on company
Examples	Linux Mozilla Firefox WordPress Llama (though debated)	Microsoft Windows Adobe Photoshop Apple iOS OpenAI
Advantages/ benefits	Collaboration and community Transparency Flexibility Cost efficiency	Stability Support For-profit model
Disadvantages/ detriments	Less support and documentation More complexity and fragmentation Monetization challenges	High cost of entry Burden of customization Lack of transparency Security dependency on vendor

Sources: Leanne Mitton, "Open Source vs. Closed Source Software," Splunk, April 4, 2024; Kinsta.com; author.

and update the software and provide a robust infrastructure with greater embedded security that also allows for scalability and reliability.

These pro and con arguments will continue to rage, and hybrid solutions will also become more common; but at the heart of these arguments, in my opinion, is the issue of security and security vulnerability and, for now, the open source model is definitely more susceptible at least in theory, to direct nefarious interference by third parties as well as the cyberinsecurity of data, algorithms, and solutions (table 3.2).

Turbocharged Inferencing: Another Frontier

Another expanded frontier for GenAI is what is called "inferencing."[10] Inferencing is a process that a machine learning model uses to develop conclusions from new data. Inferencing can happen even when the desired results of such an exercise are unknown. According to Joyce Li: "Inference is a core part of every Gen AI application now. When you send ChatGPT a question, ChatGPT runs the query against its model and this process is called model inference. This is why we typically see two types of AI model costs at the AI model companies: training costs and inference costs. While inference itself is not new, making it efficient, cost-effective, and scalable enough for widespread deployment is indeed a crucial frontier in AI development."[11] Self-driving cars provide a good example of inferencing, where such a car's AI learns about symbols and signs in one context or location and is able to extrapolate (inference) into a new context or location.

Almost any real-world application of AI relies on AI inference. Some of the most commonly used examples include LLMs, predictive analytics, email security recognizing spam / malicious emails, scientific and medical research that depends on interpreting data, and finance models trained on past market performance that can make (nonguaranteed) inferences about future market performance. As compute becomes more powerful and extensive with the building of supercomputers, inferencing and the predictive capability that comes with it will become even more pervasive.

The GenAI "Black Box" Problem

Another challenge all companies producing GenAI models are facing is what is being called the "black box" problem. In essence, it means that there is very little transparency in what goes on inside the box of the GenAI model in understanding and deciphering how AI makes decisions, choices, and outputs. This is especially challenging in complex ML models with deep neural networks. AI scientists understand what is going into these models and what is coming out, but they do not really understand what is going on inside the "machine."

Hence, the issue of hallucinations, incomplete or incorrect data, out-right fakery, and invention, have become some of the key concerns in the developments of the many now publicly available GenAI products and services. This becomes a huge challenge in areas of security and safety, especially where accountability is key, such as in health care, cybersecurity, financial products, and education. The ethics of all this has also become critically important to understand. There is some movement to address and solve this problem through explainable AI—processes and methods that allow AI scientists to understand what happens inside the "black box"—the use of open source models, and eventually effective regulatory models.[12]

A Word on Artificial General Intelligence

AGI is not something most experts expect to happen rapidly (though there are real disagreements on the timeline for that, too). In a helpful piece from McKinsey, the consulting firm identifies several major obstacles to the achievement of AGI rapidly. First comes the issue of visual perception—most vividly represented by the failure to get autonomous vehicles to mimic the depth, breadth, and type of human visual capabilities. Similarly, audio perception is seen as another human quality that robots are not quite able to fully integrate, at least not yet.[13] Natural language processing and fine motor skills are two deeply human skills that robots are not quite capable of conquering either. And it goes on from there—most of these skills and qualities being intrinsically human, like problem solving, navigating, and creating, though it is important to note that GenAI tools are getting increasingly sophisticated and capable of solving complex and difficult problems.

In the area of the arts, McKinsey's explainer seems overly sanguine when it claims that "ChatGPT may be able to write a sonnet, but it is not yet ready to rival human-level creativity." Tell that to the innumerable musicians, writers, actors, and filmmakers who are currently pondering their livelihoods. And last but certainly not least, the McKinsey piece identifies social and emotional engagement as a critical obstacle to AGI. Indeed "humans themselves struggle to correctly identify emotions; AI that is capable of empathy is still a distant prospect." To which I would add: Unless a future tech-world is capable of injecting human personality into an AI, this particular trait will be difficult to attain in a chatbot. [14] However, it is important to make the caveat that studies show that in some cases, GenAI can be as empathetic or more than some humans. This was the case "in a cross-sectional study of 195 randomly drawn patient questions from a social media forum, where a team of licensed health care professionals compared physician's and chatbot's responses to patient's questions asked publicly on a public social media forum. The chatbot responses were preferred over physician responses and rated significantly higher for both quality and empathy."[15] So, those of us who are human, should not get too smug about being more empathetic than arrays of GenAI chatbots. I would add another critically important nuance to this list of challenges to achieving AGI—and it is giving GenAI judgment and ethics or what some might call a moral compass. The thing that most differentiates humans from robots, AI or AI-enabled robots is that we humans do have something akin to a moral compass, an emotional radar system, and a decision-making core that help us discern matters based on our own experiences, our character, and what we learn along the way.

Of course, not all humans have a moral compass or ethical core, as we know all too well—being subject to traits like narcissism, hubris, sociopathy, and more. Thus, humans can also make awful and damaging decisions without the help of AI or robots. The real danger lies in the scenarios where the compromised humans have access to and use the exponential power of technology to achieve their nefarious ends. Even in this age of fakery, disinformation, misinformation, nasty disagreement, and worse, we still have the ability to debate, judge, and decide what is largely more beneficial versus detrimental to those affected. Thus, I challenge the creators of GenAI to create anything akin to this human judgment in all its imperfections—in the data, the algorithms, and the compute power they are deploying.

The Exponentiality of GenAI: Its Five Attributes

So, what makes GenAI "exponential"? Returning to the characteristics of exponential tech we first described in chapter 2, let us look at why GenAI is an exponential technology that in turn requires all of us—especially decision-makers—to assume an exponential governance mindset not only for GenAI itself but also for many other technologies and exponential technologies like automation and robotics, biopharma discoveries and treatments, new materials deployed in consumer products, and the like, most of which contain GenAI. Why is this the case? It is because GenAI is the most "interconnected" of all the exponential technologies out there today.

Velocity

The sheer velocity, ferocity, and volume of data and compute capacity that have come online over the past decade through the increasing miniaturization of chips, especially over the past handful of years (witness the Nvidia-led superchip revolution, which is discussed in chapter 5), partially explains why we have seen such a rapid growth of GenAI. Not only did OpenAI make its ChatGPT available to the public in November 2022, but an explosion of other providers—offering both closed source and open source versions of their own GenAI LLMs—came to the fore shortly thereafter. See table 3.3 for a list of popular open source and closed source GenAI models. An explanatory note regarding Meta's popular Llama model is in order: it is not listed in table 3.3 because it is not really open, but Meta claims it is. Many experts in the field—including the standards setter, the Open Source Initiative—specify that the Llama model is not open and indeed accuse Meta and others that claim to be open but are not of "openwashing."[16]

All this velocity and compute power are being supercharged by the likes of Nvidia's constant transformation of its AI-powering GPUs. To quote Nvidia CEO Jensen Huang at his 2024 company commercial conference: "We're in the beginning of this AI computing ramp, . . . and we're in the beginning of the accelerated computing ramp. It's going to last a few years."[17]

Indeed, Geoffrey Hinton, a 2024 Nobel laureate, known as the "godfather of AI," a pioneer of AI and LLM, and a former academic who joined Google and DeepMind not long ago, resigned from Google (after collecting multimillions). He only then started speaking out about the unpre-

Table 3.3 Sampling of Open Source and Closed Source GenAI Models

Open Source (Publicly Available, Modifiable, and Distributable by Anyone)	Closed Source (Proprietary, Subscription, or by Invitation Only)
• BLOOM (Hugging Face) (multilingual language) • MPT-30B (used by NVIDIA H100 GPUs) (language) • DALL-E Mini (Craiyon) (text to art generator) • Stable Diffusion (art generator) • Text2Video (text to video creator)	• GPT-4o (Open AI) • ChatGPT-4 (Open AI) • ChatGPT (Open AI) • Copilot (Microsoft) • Alpha Code (Google DeepMind) • DALL-E (Open AI) • Gemini (Google) • Firefly (Adobe) • Claude 2 (Anthropic) • Make-a-Video (Meta) • Perplexity.ai

Source: Author.

dictability and dangers of our reaching AGI and being unable to control it as humans, and revised his prediction of when we will reach AGI from thirty to fifty years to five to twenty years. But he added: "I now predict 5–20 years but without much confidence. We live in very uncertain times, it's possible that I am totally wrong about digital intelligence overtaking us. Nobody really knows which is why we should worry now."[18]

However, others—all experts—would argue that we are far, far away from achieving AGI—perhaps even centuries. We explored above some of the reasons revolving around some potentially unsurmountable obstacles, at least for the medium to long terms. AWS enumerates three key challenges to the development of AGI. The first is the inability for AI currently to make the connections or interconnections necessary between domains, something humans are more used to doing, even if imperfectly. Second and third are two human-centric qualities that future "sentient" AGI will be hard-pressed to muster; one is *sensory perception,* or what Fei Fei Li calls "spatial intelligence,"[19] which requires physical environment interaction—which would involve creating robots that can perceive their environment in the same way humans do—a tall order. The other is similarly challenging: *emotional intelligence*—something that even some humans do not have. And without emotional intelligence there is no creativity.[20]

Volatility

Because GenAI is moving so fast and so unpredictably, we must brace ourselves for potential volatility. What kind of volatility? The kind that can lead to false answers, hallucinations, corrupted data producing discriminatory results, fake information, incorrect solutions, and much more. Thus, the GenAI data sets must be subject to deep and broad quality assurance, provenance standards, constant vigilance, and testing. There must be humans—competent ones, of course—in the loop. This potential volatility is a two-way street: On one hand, we need lots of quality controls and assurance from both machines and humans to ensure that whatever data that is being fed into the GenAI models have been vetted for provenance, integrity, and reliability. On the other hand, we need responsible use of the GenAI—user misuse of GenAI tools can also account for much of its potential volatility.

There are several efforts under way to lead to such provenance integrity. As mentioned above, the Data & Trust Alliance is a prominent nonprofit, nonlobbying entity of numerous industries in the private sector collectively representing almost $2 trillion in revenues dedicated to sharing best practices across industries and disciplines to accelerate learning and to develop new practices and tools to advance the responsible use of data, algorithms, and AI. Its motto: "Every data enterprise must be a responsible steward of data, algorithms and AI." Among its members: American Express, Humana, IBM, Meta, Nike, UPS, and Walmart.[21]

At the same time, humans deploying these AI tools and techniques must be responsible as well. There are several examples of lawyers who have consulted ChatGPT for their casework without fully vetting whether ChatGPT regurgitated true or false information—that is, fake case law. For example, there was the case of the New York lawyer who in his court room brief cited cases that turned out to be entirely fake and made up by ChatGPT. This incident occurred during a personal injury lawsuit filed by Roberto Mata against Avianca Airlines. Steven A. Schwartz, of the law firm Levidow, Levidow & Oberman, representing Mata, used ChatGPT to supplement his legal research only to cite nonexistent, hallucinated cases and end up being reprimanded and fined by the court. This illustrates the need for quality control on both ends of the GenAI spectrum—data inputs with responsible humans in the loop, and data outputs with responsible humans in the loop.[22]

Uncertainty

This discussion segues nicely into a consideration of the uncertainty and unpredictability of GenAI. While the tech titans—inventors, enablers, and investors—know more than the average user about the unpredictability of the tech they are developing, in the case of GenAI it could have enormous implications because the tech titans do not know everything that can happen and are generally in a rush to build bigger, better, faster GenAI that will get them first to some form of AGI.

Indeed, this scenario may be playing itself out most visibly and concerningly at OpenAI, where the goal of achieving AGI has been directly and indirectly touted as its be all and end all, with many both internally and externally raising deep concerns about achieving such goals without endangering safety and security. For example, there has been much speculation about the slow departure from OpenAI of its chief scientist and cofounder, Ilya Sutskever. He sided with the original nonprofit board of OpenAI (of which he was a member) in the November 2023 dismissal of CEO Sam Altman; but when Altman was reinstated five days later, Sutskever changed his mind and apparently never returned to the office. In May 2024, Sutskever's official departure from OpenAI was announced. There has been speculation in the marketplace that Sutskever "saw" something that might have been AGI in the OpenAI work he was supervising, that it scared him, and that he did not trust Altman to place the proper security and safety guardrails around it.

One more disturbing thing became clear: After leaders of its superalignment team resigned, OpenAI disbanded it. The superalignment team was created in July 2023 to ensure that superintelligent systems under development were developed with humans and risk in mind. Its principal work centered on mitigating rogue AI scenarios, ensuring AI systems follow instructions accurately, maintaining human oversight, building a human-level automated alignment researcher, and addressing some of the key risks associated with deploying advanced AI systems such as misuse, economic disruption, disinformation, bias, discrimination, addiction, and overreliance.[23]

Sam Altman's move to disband the superalignment team was met with great surprise, skepticism, and criticism in the AI community, especially the half that worries about profit motivations being the sole focus for the accelerated development of increasingly more powerful GenAI or, as one of the group's leaders, Jan Leike, who later resigned, put it on Twitter/X: "OpenAI must become a safety-first AGI company." He said that building GenAI was "an inherently dangerous endeavor" and that Open-AI was more concerned with releasing "shiny products" than safety.[24]

Asymmetry

GenAI tools are enabling the democratization, decentralization, and empowerment of access to extraordinary compute power. The upside is that almost everyone with access to Internet connectivity and computer devices (which is not everyone but increasingly a majority of humanity), will have access to GenAI tools like ChatGPT, Llama, and others. That will help us increase productivity, learn new things, invent, and turbocharge other activities in the health care, education, financial, entertainment, and other sectors.

The downside is that almost anyone can now gain access through these tools to information (a recipe, e.g., for a toxic biological weapon) to do nefarious and nasty things and worse. GenAI has already done a lot to enhance the ability of small, decentralized groups and hard-to-find individuals who want to undertake a cyberattack, build bombs, disrupt air traffic controls, and engage in personal surveillance. The use of GenAI in cyberattacks and in cyber defense is steadily increasing. For example, the North Korean–supported Kimsuky Group has been reported to use Gen-AI to burrow into US think tanks to gather information to create more convincing phishing emails and other forms of cyberattacks.[25]

As individual and organizational cyberattacks in the form of more sophisticated, GenAI-enhanced social engineering, deepfakes, and malware take place, firms like Microsoft, IBM, and SentinelOne are developing GenAI-enhanced cyberdefenses, including AI-driven email security programs, threat detection programs across platforms, and programs that synthesize threat intelligence and are capable of being subjected to queries and conversations by users.[26]

The asymmetry of GenAI is also on blazing display in its ability to allow the smallest of units (all the way down to one individual) to create, develop, and deploy weapons of war or terrorism. The war in Ukraine is the first full-scale war in which the asymmetric power of technology is on full display, with Ukrainian engineers, technologists, and others building countless homemade frequently lethal drones. Likewise, in cyberspace, the Ukraine war has seen the development of homegrown, often asymmetric, capabilities utilizing drones, cyberattacks, crowd-sourced and commercial tech, AI and autonomous systems, and even space technology (e.g., the use of Starlink satellites).[27] Thus, the asymmetry factor makes GenAI in its current and future incarnations a double-edged sword—one that is a lot sharper than any coming before it.

Interconnectivity

A final characteristic of exponential technology is that it does not operate in isolation, in silos, alone. Indeed, GenAI is only possible because of the convergence of multiple trends and factors—like amazing progress in the miniaturization of silicon chips, the development of lithography and optical lenses, the exponential growth of GPU capacity, and so much more, which in turn has allowed for a maximization of compute power.

GenAI is also unique among most technologies in that it touches almost everything, as we discuss in the next section of this chapter, where we explore the global nature of GenAI, the abundance of GenAI-driven opportunities in every sector, GenAI as a multidisciplinary and cross-functional phenomenon, how GenAI turbocharges other technologies, and how GenAI has a multifaceted "polyrisk" profile.

The Many Faces of GenAI: Everything, Everywhere, All at Once

In this section, we briefly review the multifaceted nature of GenAI with the purpose of underscoring its pervasiveness. It is as if a tsunami penetrated every part of an island where we—humanity and the world—are the island. Ever since the launch of ChatGPT in late 2022, we have been regaled monthly if not weekly with new versions of multimodal GenAI that get better, faster, and more amazing every time—converting text to graphics, text to audio, voice to video, text to video, text to code, and every other permutation thereof.

GenAI Is Global

There is not a geographical corner of the planet that AI and GenAI have not reached—with the assistance of other technologies, such as communications, the Internet, the Internet of Things, social media, and the like—almost everyone everywhere has access to or is somehow touched by GenAI all at once.

Geographically speaking, GenAI of course is deeply rooted in Silicon Valley and the United States. But beyond US frontiers, we have a variety of manifestations of GenAI in multiple and multifaceted ways—from start-ups, incubators, and investors everywhere to all manner of business, civil society, and governmental activity, and sometimes collaboration in and from every corner of the world.

According to several studies and surveys, the United States has the largest share of GenAI companies, accounting for about 53.2 percent of the global total. The United Kingdom follows the United States, with 7.2 percent of generative AI companies worldwide. Israel and Singapore are leading in global interest in generative image AI, particularly with tools like Midjourney. The Philippines, Singapore, and Canada show high search interest in generative AI tools, with the Philippines having the highest search volume. India, Indonesia, and Japan are emerging as significant players in the AI landscape. In the case of China, some of their largest established technology companies, like Tencent and Baidu, are at the forefront of developing GenAI.[28] If we take the lens of which countries are doing the most in leading GenAI research, we find that China is at the forefront of adopting GenAI, with a high percentage of organizations using the technology. China announced the game-changing, apparently cheaply produced but superpowerful GenAI produced by a small start-up, DeepSeek, in early 2025 and has also filed a significant number of patents related to generative AI, indicating strong research-and-development ef-forts in this area.[29] But when we are talking about regulations and legal developments regarding AI and GenAI, the European Union is at the forefront, with its enactment in 2024 of the EU AI Act, the world's first comprehensive risk-based AI and GenAI regulatory framework. How-ever, there have been developments in many other countries and regions as well.[30] As of the date of this writing, there are laws in place or under development as shown in table 3.4.[31]

Table 3.4 Jurisdictions Around the World with AI or GenAI Regulations/ Frameworks Approved or under Development, as of August 2024

International Organization	Status
Group of Seven	AI regulation mandate member state compliance with international human rights law
United Nations	New draft resolution on AI encourages member states to implement national regulations
Organization for Economic Cooperation and Development	AI recommendations encourage member states to adopt trustworthy AI
Council of Europe	Developing new Convention on AI to safeguard human rights, democracy, rule of law in the digital space covering governance, accountability, and risk

Region/Country	Status
Australia	Voluntary AI Ethics Principles
Brazil	Under development
Canada	At federal level expected; not yet provincial
China	Interim AI Measures approved, targeting specific, administrative regulation of GenAI services
Czech Republic	Enacting EU AI Act nationally
European Union	EU AI Act approved 2024
France	Participates in EU AI Act plus looking at sector specific laws
Germany	Evaluates AI specific legislation needs
India	National frameworks inform approach to AI regulation
Israel	Promotes responsible AI innovation through specific policies
Italy	Evaluates AI-specific legislation needs
Japan	Adopts soft law approach to AI governance, but hard law advancing in legislature

continued

Table 3.4 *continued*

Region/Country	Status
Kenya	National AI Strategy & Code of Practice expected to set foundation of AI law
Nigeria	Draft National AI Policy under way to pave way to comprehensive national AI strategy
Norway	Position paper informs approach to AI, sector specific legislative amendments
Saudi Arabia	Relying on guidelines for now
Singapore	AI frameworks guide ethical and governance principles, sector specific regulations
South Africa	In process of obtaining inputs for a draft National AI plan
South Korea	AI Act to be consolidated body of AI law once approved by National Assembly
Spain	Creates Europe's first AI supervisory agency, active with EU AI Act
Switzerland	National AI Strategy aims to finalize AI regulatory proposal in 2025
Taiwan	Draft laws and guidelines under consideration
Turkey	Multiple guidelines use of AI in various sectors
United Arab Emirates	Several decrees and guidelines some related to data protection laws
United Kingdom	Flexible framework with sector-specific laws
United States	Relies on presidential executive orders federally; some state legal developments

Sources: Compiled by the author from a White & Case memorandum.

There are very significant additional nongovernmental or international private / public / civil society initiatives worldwide—represented by the African Observatory on Responsible AI, by work coming from the Association of Southeast Asian Nations, and by UNESCO's MENA Observatory on Responsible AI, just to name a very few—where civil society, business, and sometimes government are involved in national, regional, and international dialogues, projects, and initiatives on AI. There are hugely significant university and think tank efforts under way as well; and, of course, the United Nations itself has a major global AI initiative, the UN AI Advisory Group.[32]

GenAI Opportunity Is in Every Sector

Another way in which GenAI is interconnected with so many aspects of life on Earth lies in its deployment in every sector, industry, business, type of organization, and agency. See figure 3.1 for just a few of the sectors GenAI touches.

At the time of this writing, GenAI use cases were being developed all over the world, especially in the larger start-up and technology hubs. While the preceding year, 2022–23, was the year of GenAI discovery, with most of us learning for the first time of its marvels, 2025 and beyond

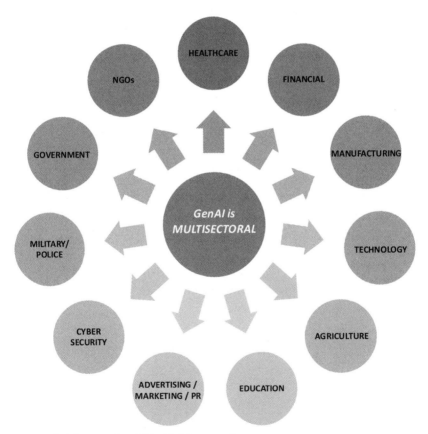

Figure 3.1 Generative AI Is Multisectoral
Source: Author.

will be focused on testing whether these discoveries will survive the test of time. We will need to understand whether many of the extraordinary investments and claims being made about the capabilities of GenAI will translate into real, actionable, groundbreaking, and profitable products and services. From now on, the focus will be on developing measurable and observable GenAI productivity, creativity, and other boosts to human, social, economic, political, and business activity. For example, will the top global technology companies' extraordinary investments in Nvidia GPUs and other GenAI-related expenses—like energy and cooling facilities (amounting to about $200 billion between now and 2026) translate into profitable products and services embedding GenAI that Microsoft Copilot or Google DeepMind or Meta's Facebook, Instagram, and WhatsApp—are developing?

This ferocious inundation of AI and GenAI capabilities has created a wide variety of opportunities that are still sorting themselves out (see figure 3.2). But chief among them are efficiency and productivity gains, performance improvements, automation of repetitive tasks, creativity and innovation, acceleration of technical automation, and so much more.

GenAI and its myriad deployments are exploding everywhere and infusing every sector, every walk of life, and all forms of social and business activity. The real question—yet to be definitively answered in the short term—is whether excitement and investment are leading to concomitant gains. One can break down the many uses of GenAI by sector. Let us start with some of the more hard-core industrial cases involving more traditional industries and then move into sectors that rely more heavily on services and creativity.

For example, in manufacturing, GenAI has been already very successfully deployed in several respects. We have seen GenAI involved in predictive maintenance, as in the case of SparkCognition's Darwin AI platform that analyzes data from machinery sensors to forecast potential failures and to optimize maintenance schedules. We have also seen product design optimization take place, as in the case of Autodesk Generative Design, which uses AI to explore variation in a design fast and efficiently to provide alternatives that optimize materials usage, strength, and cost.[33]

Figure 3.2 Generative AI Productivity and Value Creation
Source: Author.

In the entertainment and creative sectors—music, art, and film—we are seeing deployments of GenAI such as in DALL.E and Midjourney helping create visual content like images, patterns, and textures. Creative types are using GenAI for idea creation and brainstorming through tools like ChatGPT and Anthropic. In a twist of fate that may hurt a broad swath of creative people in music, GenAI tools are being used to create music, composing harmonies, melodies, and to analyze existing music. We have gone from AI telling us what piece we are listening to to GenAI composing for us.[34]

In the marketing and ad sector, among others, content is being created by GenAI geared at specific audiences; for example. GenAI is being deployed to generate new product designs and prototypes. GenAI has become a must have in terms of customer service becoming ever more sophisticated, seamless, and productivity enhancing. In one article alone, 100 of the top GenAI applications are listed, with a multitude of ever-changing examples illustrated.[35]

Another fruitful sector for GenAI deployment is the health care and pharmaceuticals sector, where drug discovery and patient interaction platforms have become essential tools without which a business or facility may very well become competitively disadvantaged or worse—go out of business. Take the example of Insilico Medicine's use of GenAI to predict the effects of drugs on specific genetic profiles, something that is being done broadly in the health care community to accelerate the development of personalized treatments. And who has not interacted already with some of the GenAI-infused patient platforms, which are beginning to dominate the health care information management ecosystem?[36]

In the software space, we have GenAI assisting developers in creating, optimizing, and finalizing code to such an extent that some are beginning to question whether human coders will still be needed in the relatively not-too-distant future. Indeed, in an article, the Coursera staff identified twenty examples of GenAI applications across industries, as summarized in table 3.5.[37]

GenAI Turbocharges Other Technologies

Unlike most other exponential technologies, GenAI is integral and thereby deeply interconnected with almost every other technology and exponential technology. GenAI turbocharges synthetic biology and genetic engineering. GenAI is involved in augmenting the capabilities of robots and autonomous vehicles. Without GenAI, spatial computing would not be possible. GenAI infuses every other exponential technology in one way or another. The next chapters in part II show in many different ways how interconnected GenAI is to all these other technologies and exponential technologies. See figure 3.3 for a sampling of this phenomenon.

Table 3.5 GenAI Applications Across Industries

Industry	Applications
Health care and pharmaceuticals	Enhancing medical images
	Discovering new drugs
	Simplifying tasks with patient notes and information
	Personalizing treatment
	Detecting cancers
Advertising and marketing	Generating marketing text and images
	Generating personalized recommendations
	Creating product descriptions
	Enhancing search engine optimization
Manufacturing	Accelerating the design process
	Providing smart maintenance solutions for equipment
	Improving supply chain management
Software development	Generating code
	Translating programming languages
	Automating testing
Financial services	Creating investment strategies
	Communicating and educating clients and investors
	Quickly drafting documentation and monitoring regulation
	Detecting fraud
Media and entertainment	Creating audio and visual content
	Composing music
	Generating highlights for sports and events
	Managing tags to better manage content
Education	Personalized learning for developing expertise, individualized learning styles. and special education requirements
Defense industry	Data processing and intelligence, including in communications infrastructure
	Equipment development and maintenance
	Optimization of large-scale deployments, including terrain and weather, such as troop and equipment organization

Source: Author.

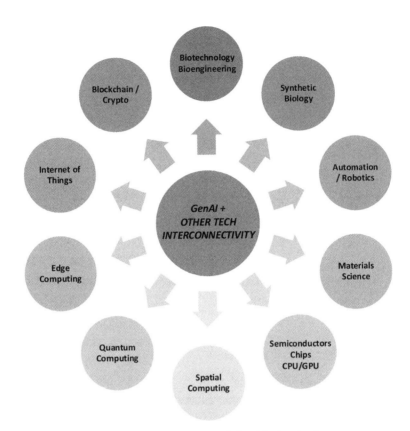

Figure 3.3 Generative AI Turbocharges Other Technologies
Source: Author.

GenAI Is Multidisciplinary and Cross-Functional

As I hope has become abundantly clear by now, GenAI requires all hands on deck—a multidisciplinary team, with cross-functional collaboration, to ensure the high-quality development of GenAI itself or the treatment of products and services containing GenAI. Figure 3.4 provides an overview of some of the key functions and disciplines that need to be educated and up to date, as well as contributing to the management and oversight of tech (including GenAI) in your organization.

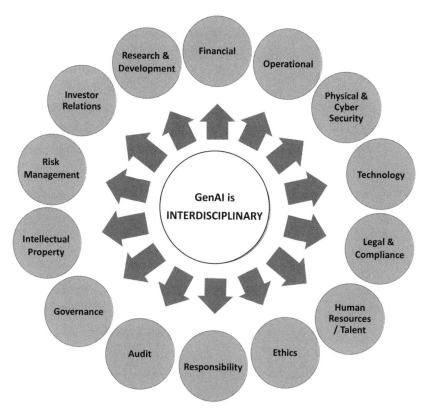

Figure 3.4 Generative AI Is Multifunctional and Multidisciplinary
Source: Author.

GenAI Polyrisk Is Everywhere

When one discusses risk, the logical next question is how to mitigate it. And thus, we have a world of burgeoning new and transformed risks that GenAI and other exponential technologies bring up, which we are all struggling to identify, understand, and mitigate, and yet we also expect regulators at local, national, and international levels to know what to do about all this novelty and new danger.

As table 3.4 earlier in this chapter makes clear, there are many efforts internationally at developing both soft and hard guidelines and regulations to manage AI, and especially AI risk. In addition to the one's men-

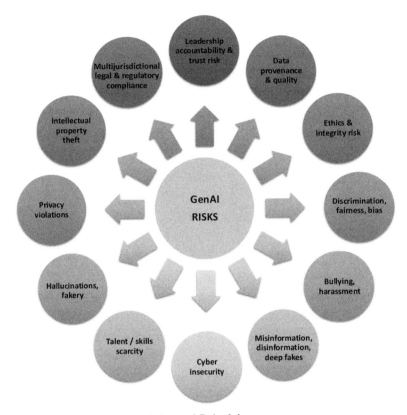

Figure 3.5 Generative AI Risks and Polyrisks
Source: Author.

tioned in that table, there is a recent effort to undertake a comprehensive look at AI risk under an initiative called the AI Risk Repository.[38] This is an ongoing, constantly refreshed, comprehensive database of risks from AI systems that is based at the Massachusetts Institute of Technology. We discuss its very helpful framework as well as the overall concept of achieving resilience as part of the exponential tech mindset—which includes understanding and addressing our polyrisk and polycrisis times—in chapter 11. For now, suffice it to serve as another illustration of the many faces of GenAI risk, as shown in figure 3.5.

4

BIOTECHNOLOGY

From CRISPR to SynBio

This chapter explores the contours of biotechnology and exponential biotechnology and explains why exponential biotechnology is everybody's business—not only that of the people involved directly in its creation, development, policymaking, or deployment. Exponential biotechnology has strategic and tactical implications for all of us—as individuals, as global citizens, as stakeholders, and, sometimes, as decision-makers.

Biotechnology

Before we can understand what constitutes "exponential" biotechnology, let us understand what "biotechnology" is. Here are several definitions of "biotechnology" that provide a sense of what it is in essence—the combination of biology and engineering. According to the industry association BIO, "At its simplest, biotechnology is technology based on biology—biotechnology harnesses cellular and biomolecular processes to develop technologies and products that help improve our lives and the health of our planet."[1]

The marriage of biology and engineering yields real, tangible outcomes. *National Geographic* defines biotechnology as "the use of living systems and organisms to create new technologies. On the simpler end of the spectrum, baking bread with yeast is an example of this interdisciplinary science. On the more complex side, genetic engineering, biochemistry, and molecular biology are pushing boundaries in an effort to treat illnesses, develop new biofuels, and grow plants more efficiently to feed more people."[2]

According to some sources, the actual term "biotechnology" was first coined by a Hungarian engineer, Karl Ereky, in 1919.[3] Others consider the fictional character of Frankenstein's monster to be one of the most important literary figures literally embodying the marriage of biology and engineering. Indeed, according to Ashish Swarup Verma and colleagues, "Biotechnology from fiction, myth, and reality can be simply understood by reading the novel and watching the movie *Frankenstein*. In this science fiction, Frankenstein has created a human life which became a monster, this monster became the reason for the destruction of Frankenstein, the creator of human life."[4]

In this chapter, we glide from biotechnology's peril to its promise, with an eye on what constitutes the cutting edge—the exponential nature—of biotechnology today. Let us start with historical examples of bioterror to set the tone for the more promising end of the spectrum.

Bioterror: The Deadly Downsides of Weaponized Biotechnology

The specter of biotechnology gone wrong that the Frankenstein story evokes brings us to a consideration of biotechnology beyond its strict definition—the threat we have come to know as "bioterrorism." Biological weapons can be derived from a variety of sources—from viruses and bacteria to fungi and other toxins. They have been used as weapons since time immemorial. For example, in the year 1155, Emperor Barbarossa poisoned water wells with human bodies in Tortona, Italy. In 1346, Mongols catapulted the bodies of plague victims over the city walls of Caffa, Crimea. A century and a half later, the Spanish mixed wine with the blood of lepers and then sold the wine to their French enemies in Napoli. Vivid, biodestructive examples like these continued throughout history, including dealmaking, not to use such bioweapons, as in 1675, when the Germans and French first made a deal not to use poisoned bullets.[5]

What makes biological weapons so threatening is the need to identify the biological agent used in the first place (which is a hugely difficult undertaking) and the urgency of finding solutions, antidotes, and other mitigating measures. Perhaps the most notorious case in the United States happened right after the terrorist attacks on September 11, 2001, when anthrax spores were mailed through the US Postal Service to numerous recipients, five of whom died (because of inhalation) and eleven of whom survived (theirs were subcutaneous, not inhaled cases).[6] In 1995, in what came to be known as the Tokyo Subway Sarin Attack, a cult called the Aum Shinrikyo first tried to deploy biological weapons, such as anthrax and botulinum toxins, in the subway system but failed before resorting to Sarin gas more "successfully," causing twelve deaths and over five thousand injured.[7]

Bioterrorism agents today come in many shapes and forms, and what makes this space even more alarming is that the advent of synthetic biology (SynBio) has brought a whole new level and capacity for the deployment of biology above and beyond anything we have discovered in nature before. Indeed, the interconnection of biotechnology with GenAI has only turbocharged humans' ability to find new and potentially dangerous biological agents. Add that to new semiautonomous and autonomous delivery systems like drones and we are in for unpleasant and potentially devastating incidents. Table 4.1 shows some of the biologic agents we know of and the diseases they cause:[8]

Under the global strategic technology risk category "Adverse Outcomes of Frontier Technologies," the World Economic Forum's "Global Risks Report for 2025" identified "Losing Control of Biotech" as a short-term (two years) and long-term (ten years) risk. Its main points are summarized in sidebar 4.1.[9]

Biopromise: The Amazing Upsides of Biotechnology

Though the weaponization of biotechnology can be catastrophic, advances in biotechnology, especially in health care and medicine, have brought us to the threshold of discovering customized cures to some dreaded, heretofore incurable, diseases, including a wide variety of rare cancers. The fact that more people can increasingly now get specialized, literally customized, cancer treatments based on their own genetic makeup is something

Table 4.1 Bioterrorism Biologic Agents and the Diseases They Cause

Biologic Agent	Diseased Caused
Bacillus anthracis	Anthrax
Clostridium botulinum toxin	Botulism
Yersinia pestis	Plague
Variola major	Smallpox
Francisella tularensis	Tularemia
Filoviruses (e.g., Ebola, Marburg) and arenaviruses (e.g., Lassa, Machupo)	Viral hemorrhagic fevers
Brucella species	Brucellosis
Epsilon toxin of Clostridium perfringens	Food poisoning
Salmonella species, Escherichia coli O157:H7, Shigella	Food poisoning
Burkholderia mallei	Glanders
Burkholderia pseudomallei	Melioidosis
Chlamydia psittaci	Psittacosis
Coxiella burnetii	Q fever
Ricinus communis (castor beans)	Ricin toxin poisoning

Source: Bio.org, "What Is Biotechnology?" www.bio.org/what-biotechnology.

Sidebar 4.1
World Economic Forum, "Global Risks Report 2025": Adverse Outcomes of Frontier Technologies—Biotechnology Risk Key Takeaways

- It is becoming easier for threat actors to make use of advances in biotech to modify or create new biological agents, which if released could lead to pandemics or be used in targeted biological attacks.
- While biotech is offering groundbreaking solutions for health issues, these can come with new risks, from possible clinical complications to unknown long-term effects.
- Unless comprehensive global ethical boundaries are set for biotech developments, ethical concerns are likely to be disregarded by some, leading to new sources of division and conflict within societies.

Source: World Economic Forum, "Global Risks Report 2025," January 2025.

that we could only dream about just a few years ago. While the cost of some of these groundbreaking discoveries continues to be high, the rise of competition from specialized start-ups and solutions will likely drive those prices down over time.

DNA, RNA, and mRNA

Let us look at some basic concepts, like DNA, RNA, and mRNA. According to Nature.com, "What do a human, a rose, and a bacterium have in common? Each of these things—along with every other organism on Earth—contains the molecular instructions for life, called deoxyribonucleic acid, or DNA. Encoded within this DNA are the directions for traits as diverse as the color of a person's eyes, the scent of a rose, and the way in which bacteria infect a lung cell."[10]

RNA, ribonucleic acid, is "present in all living cells that have structural similarities to DNA," according to the National Human Genome Research Institute. "Unlike DNA, however, RNA is most often single-stranded; . . . some RNAs are involved in regulating gene expression. Certain viruses use RNA as their genomic material."[11]

The discovery of mRNA-based COVID-19 vaccines during the worst pandemic in a century saved millions of lives, partially by cutting short the period in which the disease could replicate, mutate, and develop into more resistant viral forms. What scientists globally were able to achieve in record time (less than a year, in contrast to the many years and even decades needed in the past to develop effective vaccines against dreaded diseases) was nothing short of miraculous. They did this through mRNA, which is defined as follows: "Messenger RNA (abbreviated mRNA) is a type of single-stranded RNA involved in protein synthesis. mRNA is made from a DNA template during the process of transcription. The role of mRNA is to carry protein information from the DNA in a cell's nucleus to the cell's cytoplasm (watery interior), where the protein-making machinery reads the mRNA sequence and translates each three-base codon into its corresponding amino acid in a growing protein chain."[12]

Though mRNA techniques were being developed for many years, two

leading vaccine providers—Moderna and Pfizer/BioNTech—were able to
rapidly deploy mRNA vaccines. Here is how they work, as explained by
the Centers for Disease Control and Prevention: "To trigger an immune
response, many vaccines put a weakened or inactivated germ into our
bodies. Not mRNA vaccines. Instead, mRNA vaccines use mRNA created
in a laboratory to teach our cells how to make a protein—or even just a
piece of a protein—that triggers an immune response inside our bodies.
This immune response, which produces antibodies, is what helps protect
us from getting sick from that germ in the future."[13] Many of the advances
that have been taking place, especially in bioengineering and genetic engineering, can be traced back to DNA sequencing and to CRISPR.

CRISPR

What is CRISPR? The National Human Genome Research Institute
defines CRISPR (short for "clustered regularly interspaced short palin-
dromic repeats") as "a technology that research scientists use to selec-
tively modify the DNA of living organisms. CRISPR was adapted for use
in the laboratory from naturally occurring genome editing systems found
in bacteria."[14] It is a powerful technology that allows scientists to correct
disease-inducing genetic defects in all manner of organisms and forms
of life—from plants to animals, including humans. Some of the key diseases that scientists are seeking to address through CRISPR technology
include muscular dystrophy, sickle cell anemia, cystic fibrosis, and a wide
variety of cancers.

Of course, with every amazing technology there are potential trou-
bles, ethical and beyond. Some of the key concerns with CRISPR have
to do with unethical and perhaps even criminal or security concerns, including the causation of unintended consequences that affect humans,
embryos, and plants. For example, something called "genetic mosaicism"
can occur during the editing of embryonic cells, which can lead to some
cells incorporating the edits and others not. Worse yet is the possibility
of intentional changes made to one specific human being which then
becomes part of their future generations. The editing of human sperm,
eggs, or embryos (what is called "germline editing")[15] or, as the coau-

thors of a *Scientific American* piece, "The Dark Side of CRISPR," put it, "its potential ability to 'fix' people at the genetic level is a threat to those who are judged by society to be biologically inferior."[16] Put that together with efforts by the Masters of the Universe—that is, billionaires and millionaires intent on living forever who are investing in all manner of new biotech and wanting to extend their lives by decades or longer—and a cornucopia of new societal, health equity, inequality, security, safety, and health issues rise to the surface. Cases in point: Peter Thiel, Jeff Bezos, Sergey Brinn, Larry Page, Larry Ellison, and Elon Musk are focused on extending their lives dramatically by investing in a variety of antiaging, revitalization, and GenAI tools and techniques that will extend their already highly privileged lives. Whether the discoveries and advances that they help fund can extend to the general population remains to be seen.[17]

Exponential Biotechnology

Since this book is about sensitizing us to the realities of exponential technology, let us now turn to what we mean by *exponential biotechnology*. As we discussed in chapter 2, several attributes make a technology exponential, and while not every exponential technology has all five attributes, we argue that most exponential technologies exhibit a majority if not all of these attributes to greater or lesser extents:

- *Velocity* of development, change, or improvements in the technology
- *Volatility* of results—will the tech be safe, containable, guardrailable, or the opposite?
- *Uncertainty* of direction; unintentional or unintended consequences of the technology
- *Asymmetry* of usage—will the technology be restricted to creators and developers, or will any user be able to find and deploy the technology from anywhere?
- *Interconnectivity* with other tech—the tech in question is deeply interconnected, sometimes codependent, and frequently turbocharged

by one or more other technologies (some of which may also be exponential like GenAI).

When we look at exponential biotechnology, we are looking at biotechnology that is moving faster, is potentially more volatile and unsafe, uncertain, and unpredictable in its direction and impact, uncontainable in its effects if released into the wild wrongfully or negligently, possibly asymmetric in its deployment, and often dependent on other technologies (including—for example, exponential technologies like GenAI, superchips, and autonomy).

I queried Perplexity AI about "exponential biotechnology," and it responded as follows: "Exponential biotechnology refers to the rapid and accelerating advancements in the field of biotechnology, characterized by the doubling of capabilities or processing speed, while costs are halved over time. Exponential biotechnology encompasses a wide range of applications, including but not limited to, genetic engineering, synthetic biology, biopharmaceuticals, and agricultural biotechnology."[18]

As Mustafa Suleyman, the cofounder of DeepMind and Inception AI (and, more recently, senior AI executive at Microsoft) stated as part of his thesis in his book *The Coming Wave*: "Containment is the overarching ability to control, limit, and, if need be, close down technologies at any stage of their development or deployment. It means, in some circumstances, the ability to stop a technology from proliferating in the first place, checking the ripple—of unintended consequences (both good and bad)."[19] Thus, a critical element of exponential biotechnology—just as it is with exponential AI like GenAI—is to have one or more humans in or on the loop with potential human-controlled kill-switches somewhere in that loop, something we discuss in detail in chapter 10.

Categories and Examples of Exponential Biotechnology

Let us look at several categories and examples of exponential biotechnology and what their applications are in the real world. Agricultural biotech is a form of biotech that has been around for a while and continues to be turbocharged with the advent of GenAI. Through techniques developed over time (remember genetically modified corn?), genetically modified crops are being used to increase yields, to improve resistance to pests and diseases, and to enhance nutritional values. Closely related are environmental and industrial biotechnology.

Another exponential biotechnology field that has been around for a little while but, like agriculture, is getting a turboboost from other technologies like GenAI (e.g., providing enhanced climate data) and autonomy (in the form of agricultural seeding drones) is the field of biofuels production, where renewable energy is being produced from organic biomass. A promising exponential biotech field called "bioremediation" uses living organisms, such as fungi and microbes, to remove or neutralize contamination in polluted areas. This helps business entities and government agencies deploy methodologies against hazardous waste management.

There are exponential biotechnology developments in the pharmaceutical and medical fields. For many years, starting with advances in genomic sequencing, and science, and the creation of CRISPR technology, we have seen an explosion of genetic research, product development, and deployment. As we have seen, CRISPR is a revolutionary gene-editing technology that allows for precise, surgical changes to genomic DNA—together with other forms of genetic engineering that allow for the genetic reconfiguration of the genetic composition of genes—including their transfers within and across species. This sophistication and potential scale of biotech change would make Frankenstein shudder.

Additionally, there are "bioplatforms" that enable the deployment of multiple products or applications using a similar underlying core tech. For example, one of the most prominent venture capital technology firms invested in such platforms, Andreessen Horowitz, states: "We used to grow our vaccines; now we can print them. That's a big deal."[20] Andreessen Horowitz is referencing how biotechnology is also interconnected with advanced materials—that is, three-dimensional (3D) printing—another exponential tech. 3D bioprinting is an emerging tech that uses 3D printing methodology to create tissue-like structures for regenerative medicine and other medical research. Andreessen Horowitz goes on to say that

Table 4.2 Overview of Categories of Exponential Biotechnologies

Exponential Biotechnology	Application
Agricultural biotechnology—application of biotechnology to agriculture	Developing genetically modified crops to increase yields To improve resistance to pests and diseases To enhance nutritional value
Bioremediation is the use of living organisms, like microbes and fungi, to remove or neutralize contaminants from a polluted area	An environmentally friendly, cost-effective way to detoxify hazardous waste
Biofuels production uses biotechnology to produce renewable energy from organic biomass	Production of advanced, more efficient biofuels
Biopharmaceuticals; using biotechnology to produce medical drugs	Vaccines Hormones Gene therapies
Environmental biotechnology: the application of biotechnology to solve environmental challenges	Developing microbial systems for waste management and pollution control
Genetic engineering: the direct manipulation of an organism's genes using biotechnologies that change the genetic make-up of cells, including transferring genes within and across species boundaries to produce improved or novel organisms.	Medicine Genetic manipulation
Industrial biotechnology, also known as "white biotechnology," involves using enzymes and microorganisms to produce bio-based products	Application in chemical, food, beverage, detergent, and paper and pulp sectors
Synthetic biology, or SynBio, involves redesigning organisms for specific purposes by engineering them to have new abilities	Medicine Manufacturing Environmental management
Tissue engineering and regenerative medicine use biotechnology to create artificial organs and tissues for use in medical procedures and treatments	Regeneration of damaged tissues and organs

Source: Perplexity AI, "Query: Types of Exponential Biotechnology?" April 8, 2024.

"what's an even bigger deal is that these programs are just the first in a long list coming that will benefit from the same underlying platforms." The firm explains bioplatforms as "new industrialized platforms built on powerful new breakthrough technologies such as biological engineering and artificial intelligence amplify two key superpowers: interrogation and intervention. They allow us to interrogate the dark corners of biology at unprecedented scale and detail, like rapidly decoding full genomes down to the single-cell resolution. Or they allow us to intervene against disease in new ways, by enabling us to engineer complex biological systems (like cell and genes) with specific functions."[21] And, of course, we just reviewed the crowning achievement of recent years in the biotechnology space: the development of mRNA technology, which allowed for the development of vaccines against COVID-19 in record time during the severe global health crisis that saved many millions of people from death and debilitating disease. Table 4.2 provides a summary of these and additional categories of exponential biotechnologies and their applications.[22]

Synthetic Biology: An Especially Exponential Biotechnology

One form of exponential biotech that best represents the cutting-edge nature of exponential biotech is synthetic biology, SynBio. As with every dual-use (or potentially dual-abuse) technology, there are key upsides and definite downsides to SynBio. Let us start with definitions.

According to the Royal Academy of Engineering, "Synthetic biology strives to make the engineering of biology easier and more predictable."[23] Mustafa Suleyman defines synthetic biology as "the ability to design and engineer new organisms or redesign existing biological systems."[24]

According to the US Government Accountability Office, "Synthetic biology is a multidisciplinary field of biotechnology that involves engineering the genetic material of organisms—such as viruses, bacteria, yeast, plants, or animals—to have new characteristics. It has the potential to create useful changes in crops, improved drugs, stronger materials, and more efficient industrial processes. Scientists are also exploring the use of synthetic biology to address environmental challenges by engineering organisms to use carbon dioxide, produce biofuels for vehicles, and transform methane into biodegradable plastics."[25]

SynBio Use Cases

SynBio has a broad variety of use cases and applications. What follows is the tip of the iceberg of use cases that are already under way in three sectors; but these could be replicated in many other sectors. Let us start with defense and industrial production, continue with medicine and health, and conclude with the food sector.

Defense and Industrial Production

Small molecules on demand for the US Department of Defense: The Massachusetts Institute of Technology and Harvard University have showcased their ability to produce via SynBio 6 out of 10 molecules of interest to the Defense Department in less than 3 months, demonstrating how certain shortages might be addressed via SynBio.[26]

Engineered silkworms for spider silk production: Bioengineers have created silkworms that produce spider silk instead of their natural silkworm silk for the purpose of creating materials that are superior in their strength, flexibility, and resilience.[27]

Medicine and Health

CAR-T cell therapy: An example of SynBio in medicine involves the development of individual-specific, personalized CAR-T cell therapy, which is a form of cancer treatment involving the engineering of a patient's T cells to attack cancer cells.[28]

Engineered human immune cells and "living therapeutics": SynBio has been deployed in the creation of what are called "living therapeutics," which represent engineered human or microbial cells. An example of this involves engineered human immune cells that recognize and kill cancer cells.[29]

Microbial production for pharmaceuticals: Pharmaceutical products require microbes for the efficient production of medical agents. This requires integrating "heterologous pathways into designer cells" that will help produce pharma products at a yield that can be better than those that are extracted from plants or fungi.[30]

Food

Plant-based meat alternatives: One of the first companies to deploy SynBio for food innovation was Impossible Foods, when it created its plant-based burgers, which were produced from soy leghemoglobin, a key ingredient in providing meat flavor. This is an example of SynBio providing more sustainable food production with lower environmental effects.[31]

The Future of SynBio

In a prescient 2007 report by the ETC Group, "Extreme Genetic Engineering," the authors provided this definition for SynBio: "the design and construction of new biological parts, devices and systems that do not exist in the natural world and also the redesign of existing biological systems to perform specific tasks. Advances in nanoscale technologies—manipulation of matter at the level of atoms and molecules—are contributing to advances in synthetic biology."[32]

Synthetic biology is also seen as "a field that aims to make biology easier to engineer." Indeed, the easier engineering deployed through SynBio in turn augments the dual-use threat that is so often an intrinsic and, in many cases, unavoidable part of innovation. "Dual use" is best understood as the "potential for the same scientific research to be 'used' for peaceful purposes or 'misused' for warfare or terrorism."

There is a deep concern that the emergence of SynBio allows for a "do it yourself" community of nonexperts or experts outside the mainstream (and outside protected and quality-controlled labs) who can deploy SynBio misuse because of the coming together of several useful technologies and capabilities—GenAI, online access to genomic DNA sequences of pathogenic organisms, the lowering of pricing for certain services, and the like, which in turn provide potentially asymmetric advantages to rogue actors.[33] The dual-use containment conundrum that SynBio presents seriously underscores the dire need for appropriate governance frameworks, effective risk management, ethical guardrails, and impact and sustainability standards.

In an appropriately named 2024 article, "Whack-A-Mole Governance

Challenges for AI-Enabled Synthetic Biology," the author states that "although bio risk is subject to an established governance regime, and scientists generally adhere to biosafety protocols, even experimental, legitimate use by scientists could lead to unexpected developments."[34] He goes on to suggest various approaches to the forward governance of this complex space, suggesting four different approaches—command and control, stewardship, bottom up, and laissez-faire governance. As their names denote, each can be useful but none has the final answer to a rapidly changing, hypercomplex set of issues. Indeed, the author suggests that perhaps the best solution is to deploy such a multipronged governance approach.

And not to get dystopian on SynBio or anything, but Stanford's Existential Risk Initiative produced a future scenario video seeking to underline some of the deep and even existential risks involved with SynBio projecting to 2075, and the picture is not comforting; indeed, it is deeply disturbing. Among the greatest warnings and concerns expressed in this futuristic assessment are the dangers of cascading risks, where SynBio breakthroughs have unintended and unpredictable systemic consequences leading to multiple catastrophic biological events in rapid succession, partly because the interaction between SynBio and other technologies and ecosystems is impossible to fully predict, partly because we are not prepared to deal with these deep uncertainties. Take a look at this alarming but useful forecast and see what you think: the Stanford Existential Risk Initiative's video, *Synthetic Biology Unleashed in the Wild: Global Systemic Risk Scenario 2075.*[35]

Strategic and Leadership Considerations
of Exponential Biotechnology

Returning to a central question of this book, we should ask this about exponential biotechnology: How does an effective and ethical leader manage the exponential nature of some of the biotechnology developments taking place—including SynBio—to maximum stakeholder benefit and protection? The answer must include having a comprehensive understanding of how exponential biotechnology interfaces with your organizational or project footprint, what the risks and what the opportunities for value creation are, and the safeguards from a health and safety standpoint that are being arrayed and observed, including the International Organization for Standardization's standards, auditing protocols, and the like. The only way to do this is to fully understand the expectations of and effects on your most important stakeholders. Ethical and successful leaders in the exponential biotechnology spheres—whether public, private, research, or community based—need to develop a full, agile, and continuing understanding of how best to mitigate the risks and augment the opportunities of such exponential biotech activities and developments.

Why is SynBio—or, for that matter, other forms of exponential biotechnology—important to the average citizen, leader, or decision-maker? It is essential for each of us to understand the contours of these exponential technologies, because they may affect our well-being and also the very nature of life on Earth. The shape and form in which these techs are developed, guardrailed (or not), and applied, will have foreseeable and unforeseeable consequences for the delicate balance of nature. We address many of these questions later in the book, specifically in the exponential governance mindset framework explored in part III and in the future-proofing chapters of part IV.

5

EXPONENTIAL MATERIALS

From Silicon to Tiny Skyscrapers

In this chapter, we delve into exponential materials—a very broad and diverse set of technologies. Similarly to the other chapters in part II, we provide definitions, categories, and examples and conclude with a few observations on the strategic and leadership implications of these exponential technologies. A reminder: in this book, we do not claim to be comprehensive in our treatment of exponential technologies—that would be nigh impossible, given the velocity and breadth of the change taking place. Instead, we touch on some of the exponential technologies that are most visible, with the purpose of illustrating some of our key themes—velocity, volatility, uncertainty, asymmetry, and interconnectivity—to help each of us build an exponential tech management and governance mindset. Thus, there are many technologies that we do not refer to here, not because they are not important but because that is not the purpose of this book. The focus here is on sensitizing the mind to the exponential technology governance mindset, not on being an encyclopedia of exponential tech.

Knowing about these cutting-edge, disruptive, exponential technologies is the business not only of the companies developing them and the researchers studying them but also of policymakers and of each of us as individuals and citizens—from education policy (kindergarten to postgraduate), from business to civil society, and from the most local to the most global, planetary, and even extraplanetary, levels. Because exponential technologies—the ones we examine in this book and the ones we do not—have strategic and tactical implications for all of us—as individuals, as global citizens, as stakeholders, and, sometimes, as decision-makers.

Exponential Materials

Jensen Huang, the cofounder of one of the most successful tech companies of all time, Nvidia, once said, "In the 1920s, water went into a generator, and DC power came out. Now electrons go into a generator, and intelligence comes out."[1]

And so the "generator" is a critical element in the success of the electricity equation as well as the "intelligence" equation that Huang references. What is this "generator," and what goes into it? How does the "generator" Huang is talking about in the present generate "intelligence"? There is a vast area called materials science and engineering that focuses on the wide array of materials that are being used in every type of technology, including chips, superchips, central-processing units (CPUs), and graphics-processing units (GPUs). To understand computing (and the revolution in computing) properly, we also need to understand basic ingredients in the computing revolution—advances in materials science and engineering.

Moore's Law

Chris Miller—the author of the riveting, award-winning book *Chip Wars* —has stated that from the first commercially available chip created in the mid-1960s, the size of a chip has increased 20-billion-fold (as of the writing of this book), from 4 transistors on a chip to 80 billion transistors on a chip in the latest Nvidia Hopper H100 GPU.[2] Indeed, at the time of this writing, Nvidia's own superchips are being superseded by new generations of superchips it is creating and has announced, including latest versions of its Blackwell Ultra GPU for 2025, Vera CPU, and Rubin GPU forecast for 2026. Interestingly, and as part of the exponential growth of these technologies, Nvidia has emphasized that its GPUs are not just

GPUs but entire platforms and ecosystems upon which it is developing software solutions and much more, including improving environmental impacts—reducing energy and water usage.[3]

Moore's law and materials science are intimately intertwined. It was Gordon E. Moore, cofounder of Intel, who introduced a concept (later called "Moore's law") in a paper in 1965 titled "Cramming More Components onto Integrated Circuits."[4] Moore is important both for his technological innovation and for projecting what innovation should look like. This is a summary of the meaning and implications of Moore's law: "Moore's law is the observation that the number of transistors on an integrated circuit will double every two years with minimal rise in cost. Intel co-founder Gordon Moore predicted a doubling of transistors every year for the next 10 years in his original paper published in 1965. Ten years later, in 1975, Moore revised this to doubling every two years. This extrapolation based on an emerging trend has been a guiding principle for the semiconductor industry for close to 60 years."[5]

So, what does Moore's law have to do with materials science? The exponential growth in computing power that has occurred over the past sixty years, and especially in the past decade, has everything to do with materials science and its ability to develop and use advanced materials to minimize the size of transistors on chips and to expand the compute power of the chips themselves while simultaneously reducing their cost exponentially. For an updated consideration of what Moore's law means today, see sidebar 5.1.[6]

Materials Science and Engineering

Let us start with a definition of "materials science." Materials science is a very broad and deep interdisciplinary area—"the field of Materials Science, which encompasses the science, engineering and technology of materials, is an interdisciplinary area involving the structure and properties of matter with application to the design, development and manufacture of real products."[7] The interdisciplinary part of this subject matter derives from this definition—it requires an intersection of physics, chemistry, metallurgy, and several other areas of expertise in science and engineering.

Sidebar 5.1

Steve Jurvetson's Reinterpretation of Moore's Law in 2025

Moore's law is both a prediction and an abstraction. It is commonly reported as a doubling of transistor density every 18 months. But this is not something the co-founder of Intel, Gordon Moore, has ever said. It is a nice blending of his two predictions; in 1965, he predicted an annual doubling of transistor counts in the most cost-effective chip, . . . but he revised it in 1975 to every 24 months. With a little hand waving, most reports attribute 18 months to Moore's Law, but there is quite a bit of variability. The popular perception of Moore's Law is that computer chips are compounding in their complexity at near constant per unit cost. This is one of the many abstractions of Moore's law, and it relates to the compounding of transistor density in two dimensions. Others relate to speed (the signals have less distance to travel) and computational power (speed x density). Unless you work for a chip company and focus on fab-yield optimization, you do not care about transistor counts. Integrated circuit customers do not buy transistors. Consumers of technology purchase computational speed and data storage density. When recast in these terms, Moore's law is no longer a transistor-centric metric, and this abstraction allows for longer-term analysis. What Moore observed in the belly of the early IC industry was a derivative metric, a refracted signal, from a longer-term trend, a trend that begs various philosophical questions and predicts mind-bending futures.

Source: Steve Jurvetson, "Ever-Moore," X post, January 10, 2025, https://x.com/Future Jurvetson/status/1877870052642578464.

So why is materials science so important? By understanding the origins of the properties of materials, these can be used or designed for a wide variety of applications, from microchips and biopharmaceutical solutions to structural steel and building materials. This is why materials science is critical for almost any industry or process, from large-scale engineering projects and aerospace exploration and electronics to information processing, telecommunications, and energy-sector activities. Materials science therefore covers the gamut of natural materials like wood and metals to human-made materials like plastic. There are 300,000 different materials that have been identified, with combinations

Table 5.1 Materials and Their Applications

Material	Application
Metals	Engines, buildings, airplanes. trains
Ceramics	Glass, fiber-optics, furnace
Semiconductors	Computer chips in mobile devices
Polymers	Plastics, Gore-Tex, Plexiglas
Composites	Steel, carbon-fiber bicycle
Biomaterials	Materials part of a living being, i.e., skin
New materials	Aerogels, carbon nanotubes, graphene

Source: Author.

and permutations that can create an almost infinite number of materials possibilities. Table 5.1 shows several categories of materials and the sector or activity in which they are most applied.[8]

As table 5.1 makes clear, materials science also requires materials engineering. So what is "materials science and engineering"? Michigan Tech provides this guidance: "Materials science and engineering seeks to understand the fundamental physical origins of material behavior in order to optimize properties of existing materials through structure modification and processing, design and invent new and better materials, and understand why some materials unexpectedly fail."[9] Which brings us to the question: What is exponential materials science?

Exponential Materials Science

In November 2023, Google DeepMind made this astonishing and ground-breaking announcement: "AI tool GNoME finds 2.2 million new crystals, including 380,000 stable materials that could power future technologies."[10] This is the bleeding edge of exponential materials science—a combination of GenAI and materials science. Indeed, in their scientific paper "Scaling Deep Learning for Materials Discovery," the Google Deep-Mind team published contemporaneously the results of its work combining GenAI and materials science discovery, underscoring this focus: "Novel functional materials enable fundamental breakthroughs across technological applications from clean energy to information processing. From microchips to batteries and photovoltaics, discovery of inorganic crystals has been bottlenecked by expensive trial-and-error approaches. Concurrently, deep-learning models for language, vision and biology have showcased emergent predictive capabilities with increasing data and computation."[11]

Of course, there are always skeptics and folks in the know who may have a different take on such a subject. A *Financial Times* opinion piece by Anjana Ahuja cast doubt on the idea that these many materials are in effect possible or practical. But the point of it is there: With breakthroughs in one scientific area—GenAI—we might find breakthroughs in another, the discovery of new materials being but one of these.[12] Indeed, Ahuja mentions in her opinion that other researchers based in Berkeley had revealed that they had created forty-one novel compounds in their own laboratory using Google DeepMind's database in under three weeks. As Ahuja states: "Only the dullest mind could fail to imagine a giddy future: lines of robotic arms fabricating shiny new AI-designed materials to solve grand challenges like clean energy."[13]

This is indeed an exponential brave new world of materials science. Let us now turn to a few examples of how these exponential materials are being applied to products and services, including, most amazingly, superchips.

Advanced Materials

Several advanced materials have been developed to power computing. Well known among them are lithium-ion batteries, which have exhibited exponential change in both pricing and capacity over the past couple of decades. They have powered smartphones, autonomous cars, and other devices. Tesla Gigafactories is a significant producer of these batteries. Closely related are advances in energy storage, including innovation in solid-state batteries and supercapacitors, which in turn truly supercharge home energy solutions, electric vehicles, and grid systems generally.

Another advanced material is graphene (derived from graphite), which is a one-atom-thick layer of carbon that is 200 times stronger than steel and has superior electrical- and heat-conducting properties. It is being used from flexible device screens and solar panels to protective fabrics and drug delivery systems. Among the leading organizations champion-ing these materials are Samsung, Ford, and the University of Sussex.[14]

Increasingly, we are seeing materials previously discarded becom-ing recyclable, with plastics, polymers, and resins being converted into additional uses, enabling sustainability in automotive, health care, and consumer goods manufacturing. We are seeing fascinating advances in textiles and wearables with temperature and health-monitoring clothing and fabrics, with a wide variety of applications for sweat-wicking sporting goods, daily clothing, and therapeutic purposes. There is a wide array of start-up companies in this space worldwide, as reported in a story by StartUs Insights,[15] and leading companies in this space include Adidas, Nike, and even Google, which has entered the smart textiles market with jacquard technology, which allows textiles to become interactive and be responsive to touch.[16]

There are "metamaterials," which are superengineered products not found in nature, such as the "negative refractive index," which enables super-lenses in photography, science, and medicine. And there are "nano-materials," with structures at the nanoscale that offer unique optical, elec-tronic, and mechanical properties that can be applied to everything from semiconductors to medicine. Nanotechnology refers to the design, pro-duction, and structuring of devices and systems by manipulating atoms and molecules at nanoscale, meaning at 100 nanometers (a millionth of a millimeter or smaller).[17]

And then there is the multifaceted phenomenon known as three-dimensional (3D) printing. Materials for additive manufacturing are be-ing developed especially for 3D printing, allowing for complex structures and customization. 3D printing is an additive materials process used by layering stacks and fusing these stacks of materials to manufacture new parts—anything from a small machine part to something as large as a whole prefab house. The beauty of 3D printing is that it is fast, not ter-ribly expensive, and incredibly varied in its techniques and applications, including for engineering, biotechnology, food, and just about anything that requires "building" a product or structure. Table 5.2 summarizes several of these inventive techniques and the companies behind them.[18]

Table 5.2 Technologies and Companies at the Cutting Edge of Three-Dimensional (3D) Printing Materials Science

Technology	Companies
Fused Deposition Modeling (FDM) uses a spool of thermoplastic filament that is melted and extruded through a heated nozzle to build parts layer by layer.	Ultimaker, MakerBot, Prusa Research
Stereolithography (SLA) uses a laser to cure liquid resin into hardened plastic, creating highly detailed and smooth parts.	Formlabs, 3D Systems
Selective Laser Sintering (SLS) uses a laser to sinter powdered material, typically nylon, into solid structures.	EOS, 3D Systems
Digital Light Processing (DLP) uses a digital light projector to cure photopolymer resin, similar to SLA but generally faster.	EnvisionTEC, Anycubic
Multi Jet Fusion (MJF) uses a printhead to selectively apply fusing and detailing agents on a bed of nylon powder, which are then fused by heating elements.	HP
PolyJet jets layers of liquid photopolymer onto a build tray and cures them with UV light, allowing for multimaterial and full-color prints.	Stratasys
Sheet Lamination involves bonding sheets of material together and cutting them to shape, used for creating prototypes and models.	Fabrisonic, Mcor Technologies
Direct Metal Laser Sintering (DMLS) uses a laser to sinter metal powder into solid metal parts, allowing for complex geometries.	EOS, GE Additive
Electron Beam Melting (EBM) uses an electron beam to melt metal powder in a vacuum, suitable for high-performance metal parts.	Arcam (a GE Additive company)
Binder Jetting uses a liquid binding agent to bond powder particles, which are later sintered to form solid parts.	ExOne, Desktop Metal

Source: Author.

Superchips: "Tiny Skyscrapers"

And then there is the amazing, exponential case of the increasing miniaturization of superchips. The latest microchips have been called "tiny skyscrapers," and it is easy to see why in ASML's explanation of their creation: "Modern chips can have up to 100 layers, which all need to align on top of each other with nanometer precision (called 'overlay'). The size of the features printed on the chip varies depending on the layer, which means that different types of lithography systems are used for different layers. Our latest-generation EUV (extreme ultraviolet) machines are used for the most critical layers with the smallest features, and our DUV (deep ultraviolet) machines for the less critical layers with larger features."[19] As the road map of silicon chip making from ASML in table 5.3 shows, the manufacture of a superchip is a hypersophisticated, complex, and at the same time delicate process, which, if not strictly controlled 100 percent of the time, can lead to product defects.[20]

The Nvidia Phenomenon and Beyond

All this leads us to Nvidia, the most revolutionary of all chip developers. At the time of this writing, Nvidia was one of the three biggest companies in the world, next to Microsoft and Apple—all big tech companies (part of the Magnificent Seven) having achieved a more than $4 trillion valuation. But in comparison with the other Magnificent Seven (or whatever number and nomenclature we are up to at the time you are reading this), Nvidia is unique in so many ways because of its leader/founder—Jensen Huang—and the manner in which it has become one of the most dominant tech players in the world.

Simply put, because Nvidia has been hyperfocused on creating and developing best-in-class graphics-processing units for video games since its founding in 1993, it was in a pole position to pivot and take full advantage of the AI and GenAI revolution. It does not stop there. Huang has become the rockstar of the tech world because he worked hard and mostly quietly for decades on creating, diversifying, and amplifying Nvidia's chip design. Its announced new superchips, hardware, and software solutions are now rolling out almost every year through the end of this decade. Among some of its recently announced products are: [21]

- The Rubin (forecast for 2026)
- Blackwell GPU Architecture, with AI models with trillions of parameters, to be released 2024–25[22]
- Quantum-X800 and Spectrum X800 Communications Technologies
- Project GRooT Foundation Model Humanoid Robots

Table 5.3 How a Silicon Chip Is Made, According to ASML

Step	Explanation
Deposition	The first step in creating a microchip is typically to deposit thin films of materials onto the silicon wafer. These materials can be conductors, isolators, or semiconductors.
Lithography	Lithography, or photolithography, is the critical step in the computer-chip-making process. It involves coating the wafer with photosensitive material and exposing it with light inside an ASML lithography machine.
Photoresist coating	To print a layer of a chip, the wafer is first coated with a light-sensitive layer called a "photoresist," or "resist" for short. It then enters the lithography machine.
Exposure	Inside the lithography machine, light is projected onto the wafer through the reticle containing the blueprint of the pattern to be printed. The system's optics shrink and focus the pattern onto the resist. Where light hits the resist, it causes chemical changes, recreating the pattern from the reticle in the resist.
Computational lithography	The reticle containing the pattern to be printed in the wafer sometimes needs to be optimized by intentionally deforming the pattern to compensate for physical and chemical effects that occur during lithography. ASML machines do this by combining algorithmic models with data from our machines and from test wafers.
Baking and developing	After leaving the lithography machine, the wafer is baked and developed to make those changes permanent, and some of the photoresist is washed away to create a pattern of open spaces in the resist.
Etching	Materials such as gases are used to etch away material from the open spaces created during the developing phase leaving a 3D version of the pattern.
Metrology and Inspection	Throughout the chip production process, the wafer is measured and inspected for errors. These measurements are fed back to the system and are used to optimize and stabilize the equipment.
Ion implantation	The wafer may also be bombarded with positive or negative ions to tune the semiconductor properties of parts of the pattern, before the remaining photoresist is removed.
"Repeat as needed"	This whole process, from deposition to resist removal, is repeated until the wafer is covered in patterns, completing one layer of the wafer's chips. To make an entire chip, this process can be repeated up to 100 times, laying patterns on top of patterns to create an integrated circuit.
Processed wafer	In the final step in production, the wafer is diced into individual chips, which are encapsulated in protective packages. The chip is now ready for your TV, tablet, or other digital device!

Source: ASML, "How Microchips Are Made," www.asml.com/en/technology/all-about-microchips /how-microchips-are-made.

- Generative AI Microservices
- Digital Twin Earth 2 Cloud Platform

According to Nvidia's website, the impact and application of its products and services by industry includes:[23]

- In the automotive sector, NVIDIA DRIVE powers all the top thirty autonomous vehicle data centers.
- Regarding AI factories, more than 40,000 companies use Nvidia's AI technology to power their AI factories.
- With respect to digital twins, Nvidia Omniverse has more than 300,000 individual users and 700 companies in the pipeline.
- In gaming, more than 200 million gamers and creators use Nvidia's GeForce GPUs.
- In health care, more than 1.8 million developers have downloaded the MONAI framework for AI in medical imaging.
- In robotics, more than 1.2 million developers use the Nvidia Jetson platform for AI at the edge.

As this survey of materials science and engineering and the examples from the cutting edge of materials science and engineering demonstrate, we are only at the beginning of the exponential materials science revolution. In addition to GenAI and the materials enabling GenAI (e.g.,

Table 5.4 Definition of a Neural-Processing Unit

A neural-processing unit (NPU) is a specialized unit explicitly designed for executing machine learning algorithms. Unlike traditional central-processing units and graphics-processing units (GPUs), NPUs are optimized to handle complex mathematical computations that are integral to artificial neural networks. They excel in processing vast amounts of data in parallel, making them ideal for tasks like image recognition, natural-language processing, and other AI-related functions. For example, if you have an NPU within a GPU, the NPU could be responsible for a specific task like object detection or image acceleration.

Source: Georgie Peru, "What Is an NPU? Here's Why Everyone's Suddenly Talking About Them," *Digital Trends*, December 27, 2023, www.digitaltrends.com/computing/what-is-npu/.

superchips and CPUs, GPUs, and the latest rage, neural-processing units, NPUs[24]), another critical ingredient in enabling the exponential industrial revolution is the explosion in the capacity and diversity of computing capabilities. (Chapter 6 explores the exponential edge of computing.) See table 5.4 for a description of NPUs.

Strategic and Leadership Considerations of Exponential Materials

How does an effective and ethical leader manage the exponential nature of some of the exponential materials and advancements taking place—to maximum stakeholder benefit and protection? The answer includes understanding how the multifaceted aspects of exponential materials interface with your organizational or project footprint, and what are the risks and opportunities for value creation. And, once again, the only way to do this right is to understand who your key stakeholders are who will be interfacing with the materials science you are providing them with. Ethical and successful leaders in the exponential materials spheres need to immerse themselves in the risks and challenges their new products present before unleashing them on the consumer or other member of the public, and that includes in the case of these materials the environmental and social effects of the materials and their production—the energy, waste, and water implications and beyond.

Many of these structural and tactical issues and questions—similar to those we pose for the other exponential technologies explored in this book—are addressed via the exponential governance mindset framework explored in part III and in the futureproofing chapters of part IV.

6

FRONTIER COMPUTING

From Cloud and Edge to Quantum and the Metaverse

In this chapter we explore several types of exponential computing and some of the top-level opportunity, risk, ethics, and safety considerations associated with each of these technologies.

Computers, Computing, and "Compute"

Much of what Nvidia and others in the chip-making space (like Intel and AMD) are doing in the realm of advancing superchips is furthering what we are calling exponential computing. While computing is a very broad subject, let us start with basic definitions. We will then quickly move on to explaining the cutting edge of computing—from spatial and edge computing to quantum computing—traversing concepts and spaces like the metaverse, the cloud, augmented reality, virtual reality, and nano computing.[1]

Those who saw Theodore Melfi's wonderful 2016 movie *Hidden Figures* may remember that "computers" in the 1950s and 1960s were mainly human—mostly African American women—mathematicians who worked at NASA processing and computing huge amounts of data and information to assist with the mathematical calculations (i.e., computing) needed for the launch into orbit of John Glenn, the famous American astronaut and later senator.

Now that we know what a human computer is, what is a nonhuman "computer"? A nonhuman computer is usually an electronic device that is programmable and that stores, retrieves, and processes data and information to varying degrees of sophistication and capacity. So then, what is "computing"? Computing is a way of calculating or determining outcomes mostly via mathematics and through a physical computer—whether a tiny handheld device or a massive supercomputer.

So, then, what is this latest term being bandied about by the tech-cognoscenti—"compute"? According to the BBC correspondent Richard Fisher, "compute" is "not a verb, but a noun. Compute refers to the computational resources—such as processing power—required to train AI. It can be quantified, so it is a proxy to measure how quickly AI is advancing (as well as how costly and intensive it is too). Since 2012, the amount of compute has doubled every 3.4 months, which means that, when OpenAI's GPT-3 was trained in 2020, it required 600,000 times more computing power than one of the most cutting-edge machine learning systems from 2012. Opinions differ on how long this rapid rate of change can continue, and whether innovations in computing hardware can keep up: will it become a bottleneck?"[2] So, there you have it: the rise of AI and GenAI and the rapid-fire advances in "compute" power are putting all kinds of strains on existing equipment and on natural and human-made/managed resources like water and electricity.

Exponential Computing: From Cloud and Edge to Neuromorphic and Spatial

The "computational capacity of computers has increased exponentially, doubling every 1.5 years, from 1975 to 2009."[3] Likewise, the cost and efficiency of computing is dropping precipitously over time as well—another telltale sign of exponential technology.[4] This ability is pushing innovators and inventors in the computing field to find, develop, and deploy increasingly futuristic and exponential forms of computing power. Among them are the forms outlined in the next subsections—from cloud and edge to neuromorphic, quantum, and spatial. Let us briefly review what each of these exponential computer technologies entails.

Cloud Computing

Cloud computing allows for the expansion of capabilities on our own laptops and computers via the use of cloud services over the Internet for both storage capabilities and compute capabilities. This allows the average user—person or business—to scale their capabilities exponentially for a reasonable fee without the concomitant hardware and storage expenses and necessary periodic upgrades. In theory and depending on the cloud provider, cloud computing also comes with security and privacy services built into the offering.

Distributed Computing

There is another computing services platform called "distributed computing," which arrays multiple computer systems to work on a unique project or challenge that requires the processing of large data sets and that otherwise requires large and complex computer tasks. By having such an array of distributed computers, the computational tasks are run more efficiently than if they were run by one computer.

There are certain distributed computing projects that have been run in this manner—examples include SETI@home and Folding@home. The former is focused on a scientific experiment using Internet-connected computers in the "Search for Extraterrestrial Intelligence" (SETI) and run out of the University of California, Los Angeles.[5] The latter is a citizen scientific experiment using distributed computing to help the fight against global human health threats like COVID-19, Alzheimer's, and cancer. This case of distributed computing requires downloading specific software created by the project lead and participating in running simulations of proteins to exploit biological insights to inform drug discoveries, among other things.[6]

Edge Computing

Edge computing is almost the opposite of distributed computing, in that it pulls computing power and data storage much closer to the location where it is needed—at the "edge" of a network—which in turn provides for faster responsiveness as well as more bandwidth. Use cases include its deployment in autonomous vehicles, the explosion of the Internet of Things, and smart cities.[7] An example might involve a security camera in a remote warehouse that uses AI to identify suspicious activity and that only sends relevant data about such specific activity to the main data center for processing. This saves the system from always having a camera on and transmitting and processing at all times.[8]

High-Performance Computing

High-performance computing (HPC) involves the use of supercomputers and computer clusters to solve advanced computational problems at high speeds. It supports research and innovation in a wide variety of scientific endeavors by providing simulations and other analyses. Examples of HPC use cases include simulation and modeling for autonomous driving, weather forecasting, seismic data analysis, precision medicine, and fraud detection.[9]

Nanotechnology Computing

IBM defines "nanotechnology computing" as using "specialized technology—including computer hardware and algorithms that take advantage of nanotechnology mechanics—to solve complex problems that classical computers or supercomputers can't solve or can't solve quickly enough."[10] It is multidisciplinary, in that it involves computer science, physics, and mathematics that use nanotechnology mechanics to solve complex problems faster than would be the case on classical computers. It includes a focus on both hardware research and application development. It is particularly useful to provide speed boosts to machine learning. Its applicability is likewise wide and diverse, ranging from financial portfolio optimization projects to chemical systems simulations.[11]

Neuromorphic Computing

"Computers that think like humans may be the next big thing in AI," according to the BuiltIn tech reporter Ellen Glover.[12] This statement in essence describes the meaning of "neuromorphic computing," which is "an emerging process that aims to mimic the structure and operation of the human brain, using artificial neurons and synapses to process information."[13] It still has very few real-world applications or use cases, as it is a cutting-edge area of research and development; but its main advantage, if it comes to pass, is that it will be much more efficient than standard computers in both processing capacity as well as energy efficiency.

Organoid and Biocomputing

A still-experimental but entirely outside-the-box approach to computing that the pioneering Swiss company FinalSpark is developing is called "biocomputing." It aims to replace the dominant silicon-based hardware used in computing—which depends heavily on the use of natural resources like energy and water for storage and processing—with biological matter.

This approach uses synthetic biology, "such as miniature clusters of lab-grown cells called organoids, to create computer architecture." FinalSpark rolled out its "Neuroplatform" in 2024—a computer platform powered by human brain organoids available over the Internet for a rental fee of $500 per month.[14]

Spatial Computing: AR, VR, and the Metaverse

We have all heard of the "metaverse," perhaps ad nauseum, without necessarily having experienced it; and if we have, the experience has not always been everything it was promised to be. But the hype was real for several years, to the point that in 2022, Mark Zuckerberg, thinking it was the next big tech thing, in a bid to claim the domain name for himself and Facebook, changed the name of Facebook's parent company to Meta, while retaining the name Facebook to refer to the app.

According to Gartner, "the metaverse is a collective virtual shared space, created by the convergence of virtually enhanced physical and digital reality; . . . think of a metaverse as the next iteration of the Internet."[15] While the hype about the "metaverse" as nomenclature dies down, the existence of virtual reality (VR), augmented reality (AR), and mixed reality (MR) and lots of human activity in and around them continues to develop in full force. Indeed, the metaverse is a network of interconnected virtual worlds that share several common characteristics. First, there is presence, meaning that you are virtually present in a virtual world. Next there is persistence, meaning that you are immersed in that world until you decide not to be. Immersion means that you literally are in a different world for the time being. And finally, interoperability is another common characteristic of the metaverse experience, where a wide variety of technologies interconnect. Among the key interconnected technologies are extended reality (XR), AR, AI and GenAI, blockchain and decentralized ledger technologies, neurotechnologies, optics, biosensing technologies, and more.[16]

A new term seems to be catching on to capture this emerging virtual world: "spatial computing," in which users wear wraparound lenses. In addition to Meta and its oculus devices, Apple is banking on this virtual space, where computing and related activities with others will be experienced via its Vision Pro headset, which is still very expensive. Ben Dickson of *PC Magazine* defines spatial computing as "a technology that enables computers to blend in with the physical world in a natural way. Apple is not the first company to delve into the space, but it believes this will be the next big thing for computing."[17] At the end of the day, spatial computing represents the convergence of various exponential and non-exponential technologies, including AR, VR, MR, the Internet of Things, 5G, AI, and GenAI. It is a space that is sure to continue to develop, and it should be useful especially for professional, entertainment, and industrial applications.

The Special Case of Quantum Computing

Quantum computers are able to solve certain types of problems faster than classical computers by taking advantage of quantum mechanical effects, such as superposition and quantum interference. Quantum computing relies on a different module—quantum bits or "qubits"—for the purpose of running and solving complex quantum algorithms. Some applications where quantum computers can provide such a speed boost include machine learning, optimization, and simulation of physical systems. Eventual use cases could be portfolio optimization in finance or the simulation of chemical systems, solving problems that are currently impossible for even the most powerful supercomputers on the market.[18]

What, you might ask, is quantum mechanics? According to the US Department of Energy, "Quantum mechanics is the field of physics that explains how extremely small objects simultaneously have the characteristics of both particles (tiny pieces of matter) and waves (a disturbance or variation that transfers energy). Physicists call this the 'wave-particle duality.'"[19] Because I am not a scientist (let alone a quantum physicist), if you, like me, have been left cold or confused or both by this definition, I turned to Perplexity AI to explain quantum computing to me as if I were a five-year-old. The response I received, highlighted in sidebar 6.1, was quite helpful.[20]

According to IBM, quantum computing is based on these four key principles:

- *Superposition*: Superposition is the state in which a quantum particle or system can represent not just one possibility but a combination of multiple possibilities.
- *Entanglement*: Entanglement is the process in which multiple quantum particles become correlated more strongly than regular probability allows.
- *Decoherence*: Decoherence is the process in which quantum particles and systems can decay, collapse, or change, converting into single states measurable by classical physics.
- *Interference*: Interference is the phenomenon in which entangled quantum states can interact and produce more- and less-likely probabilities.[21]

Because of its deeply complex attributes and technological challenges, quantum computing is not yet fully available, though there are companies like IBM and consultancies like Accenture that are way ahead of most in their development and plans for deployment. IBM, which has some of the most advanced quantum computing prototypes and research and development, further states: "By taking advantage of quantum phys-

---

Sidebar 6.1
Perplexity AI's Explanation of Quantum Computing to a Five-Year-Old

Imagine you have a magical box of toys. In this box, you have regular blocks and special blocks. The regular blocks can be either red or blue, just like how regular computers use bits that can be 0 or 1. But the special blocks in your magical box can be both red and blue at the same time! These special blocks are like the "qubits" in a quantum computer.

Now, let us say you want to build a tower with your blocks. With regular blocks, you can only put one block on top of another, one at a time. But with your magical box, you can use the special blocks to build many towers at once! This means you can try lots of different ways to build your tower really quickly.

Quantum computers, like your magical box, can solve certain problems much faster than regular computers because they can try many possibilities at the same time. This makes them super powerful for solving really tricky puzzles!

Source: Author's query to Perplexity AI.

---

ics, fully realized quantum computers would be able to process massively complicated problems at orders of magnitude faster than modern machines. For a quantum computer, challenges that might take a classical computer thousands of years to complete might be reduced to a matter of minutes."[22]

However, lest we think the adoption of quantum computing is either imminent or easy, McKinsey has enumerated these challenges to rolling out quantum computing for the general business community and public:

- *Lack of shared approaches.* There are no shared generally accepted approaches to assessing and comparing qubit technologies.
- *Difficulty in comparing qubit technologies.* Currently, there are five major qubit technologies under development but no way to consistently compare them: photonic networks, superconducting circuits, spin qubits, neutral atoms, and trapped ions.
- *Fidelity at scale.* Fidelity is intimately connected to quantum

computing's defining hurdle, which is increasing qubit count and computational power for complex algorithms while maintaining high levels of qubit quality (in other words, high fidelity).

- *Computation speed.* Individual qubits can retain their quantum state—what is called "coherence"—for only a limited time. To compensate, gate operations (a quantum gate is a basic quantum circuit operating on a small number of qubits) should occur quickly enough to make complex computations possible before qubits in the system lose coherence.
- *Multiqubit networking.* The more qubits that can be linked to one another to perform gate operations, the more readily they can implement quantum computing algorithms and the more powerful the resulting quantum computer would be.
- *Control over individual qubits at scale.* Control over individual qubits is critical to quantum computing. As the number of qubits in a quantum computing system increases, control over individual qubits becomes increasingly complex.
- *Cooling and environmental control.* For most qubit technologies, the required scale of the cooling equipment in terms of both size and power is beyond the feasibility of currently available equipment.
- *Manufacturing.* Some qubit designs use existing production technology, while others require new manufacturing techniques. The production of eventual full-scale quantum computers will require automated manufacturing and testing for components at scale.[23]

Once the logistical and physical challenges are solved or overcome, the exponential nature of quantum computing will be obvious and overwhelming, as its speed and capacity will obliterate that of most other forms of computing. This will be especially so when dealing with cryptography and encryption, rendering much of what we do today to protect confidentiality and encrypt information and asset access useless—in every sector and in every walk of life, whether banking, defense, cybersecurity, health, and beyond.

It is in the cybersecurity space where this becomes most immediately dramatic. According to Accenture, a leading consulting firm in the quantum space: "Quantum also offers the power to identify secret cryptographic keys in an extremely efficient way. This could potentially expose businesses to threat actors globally—and all at once. This disruption eclipses the diligent planning and deep investment that went into Y2K preparations. It is an immense, high-impact event that will override existing cryptography methods and make current infrastructure and application protections irrelevant."[24]

There are already important preparations that are taking place in both business and government circles getting ready for that day when quantum computing obliterates current forms of encryption. Accenture has been developing programs and frameworks in collaboration with other quantum tech experts as well as the US government. Advice from it to businesses and other organizations is to (1) assess their quantum risk and create a strategic plan; (2) launch a full-scale effort to find where all the vulnerable encryption exists within their systems (networks, applications, partners, clouds, devices, etc.); (3) create a new cryptographic architecture that not only resists quantum attacks but also manages the quantum defensive resources; and (4) pay attention to the governmental resources that are being developed. While these preparations appear daunting, most companies and their technology and information security executives and teams should consider their organization's specific glidepath on this inevitable future event by enlisting internal and external experts to create an action plan before it is too late.

In the United States, those government resources include the National Institute of Standards and Technology's new quantum security resources, which are being developed and starting to gain real traction. According to the quantum security expert Tom Patterson: "We're now in that 'suddenly' moment in time. After 10 years and hundreds of attempts, this National Institute of Standards and Technology–led group has agreed on the new set of algorithms that will make up the PQC [post-quantum cryptography] standards. This is critically important for humanity. This standardization is the starting bell for most organizations around the world that have been waiting for 'the answer' before they begin 'their journey.'"[25] Knowing Tom's unique expertise and experience in this space, I would seriously heed his advice.

A Detour into the Metaverse

As mentioned earlier in the chapter, although the metaverse was not yet the next big thing that Mark Zuckerberg thought it was when he changed the name of his company to Meta, he was smart enough to pivot to the rise of GenAI with Llama and a broad and deep investment in a wide variety of GenAI capabilities. Meta is now one of the most successful GenAI players in the marketplace.

Despite the financial and technological challenges to the development of the metaverse, such as the few returns yielded by Meta's heavy investment in Reality Labs and the industry's pivot to GenAI in 2022, the metaverse economy is projected to grow significantly, with estimates suggesting it could be worth $400 billion by 2030.[26] There are three areas of great interest to those developing this technology—consumer branding in digital worlds, employee collaboration in work-from-anywhere scenarios, and the meshing of physical and digital more closely in asset-intensive industries. Examples of metaverse or immersive applications in the industrial context include the increasing use of digital twins, where virtual replicas of physical assets, systems, or processes are deployed for a variety of efficiency, quality, and productivity purposes, including getting real-time data and analytics, monitoring performance, predicting outcomes, and optimizing operations. Nvidia is at the cutting edge of the deployment of digital twins for its own work and for that of its customers, including scientific computing operations such as its ForCastNet model, which predicts extreme weather events, energy systems related digital twins for Siemens to simulate heat-recovery steam generators, and automotive and telecommunications systems digital twins for BMW and Ericsson for factory operations and network management, respectively, using Nvidia Omniverse digital twin technology.[27]

Whether the metaverse becomes integrated into how we live and work remains an open question at this time; but given the relatively large investments expected over the next half decade, I would bet on its emerging, probably through the lens of what we now call spatial computing instead of what we called the metaverse during Zuckerberg's fever dreams a few years ago. Here is a list of a dozen metaverse platforms to know about in 2025:

- Decentraland
- Fortnite
- Metahero
- Meta Horizon Workrooms
- Microsoft Mesh
- Mozilla Hubs
- Nvidia Omniverse
- Roblox
- Rooom
- Sandbox
- Second Life
- Somnium Space[28]

The metaverse is not child's play. As the US Government Office of Accountability, known for its important research work (before the second Trump administration), has stated: "We surveyed 23 civilian federal agencies on their use of and plans for immersive technologies. Most of the agencies use them, often for training. For example, the Department of Homeland Security uses simulators as part of law enforcement training on the use of force. It used these technologies to train nearly 10,000 employees in a variety of areas in [fiscal year] 2022. 15 agencies planned to increase use. Challenges cited included meeting cybersecurity requirements and high costs."[29]

There are a number of unique, and real-world, aggravated risks associated with this domain, including identity and authentication issues, content moderation and harassment, data governance and regulations, mental health and well-being, economic risks, and liability risks, not to mention a serious array of security and privacy concerns for tracking behaviors and instilling stakeholder trust. Additionally, there are economic and scaling challenges and obstacles to making immersive technologies mainstream, including hardware and software improvements, particularly for AR devices, to enable more miniaturization and weight reduction, make devices more durable, and growth in the breadth of user needs is still questionable, and whether immersive reality will have any effects on the remote or hybrid workplaces, all remain important and debated topics.[30]

An intriguing, related concern is one identified by the Unanimous AI CEO Louis Rosenberg in a paper and speech called "The AI Manipulation Problem." It has to do with consumers unwittingly engaging in real-time dialogue with predatory AI agents that skillfully persuade them to buy particular products, being fed misinformation, or fooling them into revealing sensitive personal data through the deployment of agenda-driven virtual spokespeople who will be highly persuasive through real-time adaptive influence.[31]

Last but definitely not least, it is deeply important to bear in mind the risks of the use of immersive technologies by children and vulnerable populations. An array of concerns arises in this context. XRSI, a global nonprofit focused on safety and ethics in the metaverse, is dedicated to analyzing and providing solutions dealing with human rights, governance, and the ethical use of the metaverse. Its five principles are

1. *A privacy and safety initiative,* where XRSI has developed a comprehensive Privacy and Safety Framework that incorporates regulations from GDPR and COPPA aimed at creating baseline protections in the metaverse and in spatial computing.

2. *A child safety initiative* to create safe and inclusive experiences for children using immersive tech, including developing standards, awareness programs, and guidance for families, educators, and policymakers.

3. *A diversity and inclusion effort* promoting just that within the immersive context, including human rights and equity considerations.

4. *A Medical XR Advisory Council*, where the intersection of health care and medical technologies is explored for the purpose of creating frameworks to provide safety and efficacy of medical solutions.

5. *A global standards development initiative* that focuses on the development of international standards for emerging tech, including neurotechnology (a central consideration in immersive tech) with an emphasis on human rights, ethics, and inclusion.[32]

Strategic and Leadership Considerations
for Exponential Computing

Once again, key strategic and leadership takeaways coming from this expansive exploration of exponential computing lead me to one place, asking one of the central questions that this book addresses: How does an effective and ethical leader manage the exponential nature of some of these cutting-edge computing developments taking place and accelerating into the future to maximum stakeholder benefit and minimum stakeholder harm? We will explore tools and ideas to help with these considerations in parts III and IV of this book.

7

AUTONOMY

From Killer Robots to Smart Cities

Autonomy is another huge area of growth in exponential technology. As we have done before, we will level set first with definitions, and then look at the huge growth of autonomous and semiautonomous vehicles and the variety of additional related robotic, and even humanoid, developments as well as peer into the world of smart cities and robotaxis and of automated warfare and killer robots.

An Introduction to "Autonomy"

The etymology of the word "autonomy" goes back to ancient Greek, where the word "autonomia," which means independence or "freedom to use its own laws," has two parts: "auto" means self; and "nomos" means custom or law. While the original purpose of the word fit its times and was designed to refer to self-government and political governance, the word "autonomous" has passed the test of time and is useful for us today—for example, "autonomous vehicles" and a few additional contemporary and futuristic inventions like drones, robotaxis, and killer robots.

The Caterpillar company provides a helpful definition of the distinctions between automation, semiautonomous, and autonomy that are especially useful for understanding advances in the heavy manufacturing, transportation, and mining sectors:

- *Automation:* This noun refers to a set of related functions performed automatically by equipment. Automation assumes that the operator performs any requirements before or after the automated sequence in order to complete the task. Multiple automation sequences are required to enable equipment to work semiautonomously or autonomously.
- *Semiautonomous:* This adjective describes multiple automated sequences that a machine can perform without human input that result in a task being completed. Semiautonomous machine operation assumes that the operator performs some tasks.
- *Autonomy:* This noun refers to a state of equipment in which it can perform the programmed operations under defined conditions without human input or guidance. When we talk about this type of equipment, we use the adjective, autonomous. For example, some mines run autonomous trucks.[1]

Because California is the locus of Silicon Valley and many of its inventions, including the self-driving car, it is useful to look at the definitions developed by the California Department of Motor Vehicles, because we can see the beginnings of interesting regulatory treatments:[2]

- *Autonomous technology:* Technology, including a combination of hardware and software, remote and/or on-board, that has the capability to drive a vehicle without active physical control or monitoring by a human operator.
- *Autonomous mode:* The status of vehicle operation, where autonomous technology performs the dynamic driving task, with or without a human actively supervising the autonomous technology's performance of the dynamic driving task. An autonomous vehicle is operating or driving in autonomous mode when it is operated or driven with the autonomous technology engaged.
- *Autonomous test vehicle:* A vehicle equipped with autonomous technology that, when engaged, performs the dynamic driving task. An

autonomous test vehicle requires a human test driver or a remote operator to continuously supervise the vehicle's performance."

What Is "Exponential Autonomy"?

While no such term as "exponential autonomy" is currently used in the field of autonomy (at least not yet), an argument can be made in favor of such a term for certain autonomy technologies that are moving fast and furious with assistance, especially when GenAI capabilities are married to autonomous vehicles. We might include space vehicles like the Mars Rover, military drones like those being used in the war in Ukraine, agricultural equipment like autonomous tractors, and robotic police dogs, which were recently introduced in (and rapidly removed from) New York City. Some of these technologies are autonomous and others are semiautonomous, but all include attributes discussed earlier in this book. Exponential autonomous technologies are at the cutting and bleeding edge of technology from the standpoint of velocity, volatility, uncertainty, asymmetry, and interconnectedness.

To wit, if we consider humanoid robots, they display *velocity*—thanks to their *interconnectivity* to GenAI and the exponential advances in materials science going to the increasingly smaller chips used throughout their construction. Moreover, because GenAI is deployed so deeply in robotics, there are also *uncertainty* and potentially uncontrollability about how these autonomous entities will operate. There is also great potential for *asymmetric* deployment, for good and bad, in that a rogue state, criminal gang, or other nefariously minded person or group could quite easily deploy a drone or robot to cause asymmetric chaos or harm—such as drone warfare or biological terror. Here is a sampling of the wide variety of autonomous vehicles and robotic devices already being deployed:

- Self-driving cars
- Autonomous trucks
- Autonomous buses and shuttles

- Autonomous drones
- Personal delivery devices
- Autonomous underwater vehicles
- Industrial robots
- Collaborative robots (cobots)
- Medical robots
- Service robots
- Agricultural robots
- Remotely operated vehicles
- Exoskeletons and wearable robots

From Robots and Drones to Exoskeletons and Humanoids

Drones—in many shapes and sizes, and for many purposes—have taken the world by storm. They are a form of robotics, as a helpful guide from the Institute of Electrical and Electronics Engineers, summarized in table 7.1, shows us. There are robots that span the various environments where we operate—terrestrial, aerospace, and aquatic—and those designed for specific purposes—delivery, disaster response, industrial and military. There are robots that are autonomous and others that are semiautonomous. And there are robots that serve specific themes—educational, entertainment, research, service, social, and telepresence. But as the Institute of Electrical and Electronics Engineers states, "It's not easy to define what robots are and it's not easy to categorize either. Each robot has its own unique features, and, as a whole, robots vary hugely in size, shape and capabilities."[3] Table 7.1 provides an overview of some of the robots and their creators that dominate the transportation sector (aerospace, aquatic, and terrestrial), disaster recovery, and military spaces.[4]

As table 7.2 shows, there are also robots that are more consumer and industrial oriented as well as human-like, mimicking, or extending human physical qualities. Among them are exoskeletons, which are partial wearable robotic devices that humans can wear, and then there are humanoids—a whole other kettle of fish, as it were.[5]

The differences between robots and humanoids revolve especially

Table 7.1 Types of Robots and Their Creators: Transportation, Recovery, and the Military

Aerospace robots make up a diverse category that includes robots that fly and robots for space applications.	SmartBird, Raven, Curiosity, Perseverance, Ingenuity Mars helicopter
Aquatic robots are used to gather environmental data about the world's oceans, perform surveillance missions, and inspect and repair infrastructure.	Wave Glider, ACM-R5H, Aquanau
Autonomous vehicles are robotic cars equipped with cameras, lidar, GPS, computers, and other sensing and navigation systems that enable them to drive fully autonomously.	Boss, Stanley, Waymo, Locomotion
Delivery robots transport items like food, groceries, and medical supplies from one point to another.	Starship, Relay, Zipline
Disaster response robots perform dangerous jobs like searching for survivors in the aftermath of an emergency.	PackBot, Kobra, Quince, Elios
Drones are flying robots that let you capture data and images from an elevated vantage point. Drones come in a variety of sizes and shapes.	Anafi, Skydio, Global Hawk
Military and security robots include a broad range of tough, rugged robotic systems that can perform surveillance and other missions that may be dangerous for humans to carry out.	Packbot, AlphDog, Raven, BigDog, Cobalt

Source: Institute of Electrical and Electronics Engineers.

around whether a robot displays human behaviors and characteristics. Humanoids are a subset of robots, just as unmanned drones are a subset of robots. Robots are machines generally able to execute a series of actions and tasks automatically with both precision and speed, and they frequently do not have any resemblance to humans. Humanoids, conversely, are specifically designed to look like humans and act in human-like ways.

Humanoids are a subset of robots that are specifically designed to mimic human behavior and appearance. There can also be other bioforms that a robot can resemble; the most commonly seen already in public are robot police dogs. Here is an excellent definition, from Jacob Biba, writing for Built In: "Humanoid robots are robots that resemble and act like humans. Typically engineered to imitate authentic human expressions, interactions and movements, these robots are often outfitted

Table 7.2 Types of Robots and Their Creators: Consumer, Industrial, and Humanoid

Consumer robots are robots you can buy and use just for fun or to help you with tasks and chores.	Roomba, Tertill, Aibo, LOVOT, Vector
Educational robots include a variety of hands-on robotics modules and kits. You can find them in classrooms, STEM programs, and homes.	Cubelets, Dash and Dot, Root, Lego
Entertainment robots are designed to evoke an emotional response. They make us laugh, or feel surprise, or wonder.	RoboThespian, Partner, Lucie, Telegarden
Exoskeletons are wearable robotic suits equipped with electric motors that help move the user's body. Some powered exoskeletons can even give the wearer superhuman strength.	Ekso, HAL, Guardian XO
Humanoid robots have a mechanical body, with arms, legs, and a head like that of a person's, and they can often walk and manipulate objects much like we do.	Asimo, Atlas, Geminoid
Industrial robots perform repetitive tasks like picking, moving, and assembling parts, plus cutting, welding, painting, polishing, packaging, and other jobs typically found in manufacturing.	Unimate, Titan, Quattro, YuMi, Proteus, Spot, Digit
Medical robots are a broad category of robotic systems designed to assist people in hospitals, clinics, rehabilitation centers, and, in some cases, at home.	daVinci, MPL, HAL, Ekso, QTrobot
Research robots are experimental machines born in universities and corporate research labs.	Cassie, Armar, Chico, Slothbot
Service robots perform useful tasks like cleaning, greeting visitors, or making deliveries.	Whiz, Colossus, Relay, Cobalt
Social robots are designed to interact and communicate with humans, assist us with daily tasks like grocery lists and calendar events, or simply keep us company and make us smile.	Pepper, Jibo, Kuri, Vector
Telepresence robots allow you to be present at a place without actually going there.	QB, Vita, AVA, Beam, Temi

Source: Author.

with an array of cameras, sensors and, more recently, AI and machine learning technologies."[6]

There are a number of humanoid experiments taking place around the world. Among them is a humanoid robot called "Sophia," which was developed by Hanson Robotics and was created in 2016. Sophia has fifty facial expressions, can hold a conversation with a human, and, most surprisingly, was granted Saudi Arabian citizenship in 2017.[7] Another humanoid robot called "Ameca" is unique in that its United Kingdom–based creators, Engineered Arts, were focused on creating a humanoid robot with facial expressions so it can interact in a more human-like manner with humans. Most humanoid robots so far have not had that ability to express themselves facially to facilitate human interaction.[8] One of the best-known humanoids is "Atlas," created by Boston Dynamics, known for its athletic prowess and turbocharged, human-like physical capabilities, including its famous backflips. Its longer-term intended purposes are to help with search-and-rescue operations and the ability to enter challenging physical terrains.[9] Another cutting-edge robotic development is the T-HR3, created by Toyota, which is a humanoid robot designed as an avatar that mirrors the movements of a human operator. Most of its applications are for remote health care and assistance.[10]

The field of robotics is vast and growing, and it is part of the bigger economic, geopolitical, and military picture. Drone warfare has become the latest and potentially most revolutionary change for military, police, and national security. It is part of the big power competition between China and the United States, and it is part of the military confrontations and wars we are currently witnessing, most markedly in Ukraine but also in the unending confrontations and violence taking place in various parts of the Middle East. Drones are being used for surveillance and for military targeting, assassination, and bombing operations. We have already seen some of the terrible consequences of either out-of-control autonomy (without sufficient humans in or on the loop) killing innocents in war zones along with surgical strikes through drones targeting enemy leaders. Where this all goes remains one of the most important and potentially existential set of questions facing humanity.

Key Risks and Opportunities of Exponential Autonomy

Given the potentially exponential nature of many autonomous and semi-autonomous vehicles, robots, and devices, it is important to pause and consider both the risks and the opportunities of deploying autonomous and semiautonomous things into the world—whether we have control or not.

Key Risks Associated with Exponential Autonomy:
Killer Robots

On the most concerning end of the spectrum is the unpredictability of autonomous weapons, which is rooted in the complexity of interactions within machines between algorithms and dynamic and frequently unpredictable real-world operational contexts in which entities are deployed.[11] Even autonomous vehicles that are not weapons per se (e.g., a self-driving Tesla) can become weapons if there is not enough responsible human control in the loop or, what is worse, if cyberhackers deploying increasingly sophisticated GenAI for their attacks are able to disable, manipulate, or take over vehicles on the roads—or planes in the sky.

Another risk with autonomous weapons has to do with speed and scale. The risk of an autonomous or semiautonomous vehicle accident escalating and broadening a conflict is real. Related to this concept is the fact that robots or drones are easily produced and are not human, which somewhat perversely lowers the barrier to initiating or escalating a conflict. The recent drama in the Middle East involving remotely exploding pagers, drone surveillance, and targeted assassinations speaks to these concerns.

There is always the danger of physical security and cybersecurity hacks, violations, and vulnerabilities being exploited remotely, leading to a variety of other potentially damaging scenarios. Serious intended or unintended mistakes and consequences can also transpire when the humans in or on the loop are not paying sufficient attention (they are negligent, or grossly negligent) and collateral damage ensues in the form of innocent lives lost.

In all this, there are very serious ethical, legal, and international human rights concerns, which a number of governmental, intergovernmental entities, and nongovernmental organizations have been working on for a while, raising awareness and providing solutions. Among them is the United Nations Group of Governmental Experts on Lethal

Autonomous Weapons Systems, which in late 2023 issued a news release stating that "an algorithm must not be in control of decisions involving killing."[12]

So far, more than 100 countries support an international legal instrument on autonomous weapons systems, including all of Latin America; 31 African countries; 16 Caribbean countries; 15 Asian countries; 13 European countries; 8 Middle Eastern countries; and 2 countries in Oceania. After ten years of discussions at the United Nations Convention on Certain Conventional Weapons, many countries have expressed support for a two-tier approach to autonomous weapons, which, on one hand, would prohibit systems designed or used in a way that is not understood, predictable, or explainable. On the other hand, this approach would also regulate other systems with sufficient human control, which "might look like control over the types of targets, and duration, geographical scope and scale of use."[13]

The most notable nonprofit effort in this space comes from an organization called the Campaign to Stop Killer Robots, which represents a global coalition of 160 organizations, including Amnesty International, Human Rights Watch, and many others, which advocates for the full ban of fully autonomous weapons.[14] Their campaign ultimately calls for the creation of an international law that governs autonomous weapons systems. Other significant efforts are being led in the sector that includes think tanks and nonprofits, including the Future of Life Institute, Human Rights Watch, and the International Committee of the Red Cross, which are hyperfocused on finding solutions similar to those under way in other arenas, like the use of bioweapons and mining operations.[15]

Key Opportunities Afforded by Exponential Autonomy: Smart Cities and Sustainability

At the other end of the spectrum of autonomy are potentially many and broad benefits. The most promising involve industrial applications, personal vehicles, and assistance. Autonomous technology has already made great strides in the areas of efficiency and safety. For example, digital twin technology allows for a safer, human ability to be inside remote and sometimes dangerous locations through a virtual simulated environment to perform critical tasks, such as mining audits, data collection, and risk assessments in the ordinary course of events and also in crisis situations.

Another advantage provided by autonomy can be seen in large industrial settings for manufacturing and logistical activity. For example, automated guided vehicles and automated tow tractors are being used in mining, agricultural, and other environments to carry out challenging and even dangerous logistical operations.

In the health care sector, digital twin technology once again is enabling predictive modeling and personalized medicine. It is being deployed to track large-scale health events like disease outbreaks and also individualized treatments to track tumors subject to radiation therapy, for example.

Another angle through which to understand advances in autonomy is its interconnection with natural-language processing (NLP). There are a variety of ways in which this interconnectivity will provide enhanced human–machine interaction when machines are able to better understand human language instructions directly. NLP and autonomy together will also improve situational awareness, allowing systems to anticipate and potentially mitigate safety and security concerns by gathering and interpreting data from various sources. We already have the benefits of multilingual capabilities deployed on our smartphones—that represents another marriage of NLP and autonomy, allowing humans to communicate in real time in different languages. And generally speaking, this interconnectivity allows for much more data interpretation and decision-making in real time, efficiently and in an informed manner.

Many of the technologies and exponential technologies we discuss in this book, including autonomy, come together in the case of smart cities. According to experts at the University of Central Florida, who are partnering with the city of Orlando to convert it into a smart city: "The concept of a smart city is broad, but in general it means you integrate technology to remove the negatives of daily life. . . . No congestion. No sanitation issues. No excess air pollutants. No problems with reliable power or water. A smart city uses foresight to improve livability, sustainability and resilience so residents can enjoy today while preparing for the uncertainties of tomorrow."[16] According to IBM, a smart city "is an urban area where technology and data collection help improve quality of life as well as the sustainability and efficiency of city operations. Smart city technologies used by local governments include information and communication technology . . . and the Internet of Things."[17] Among the most important technologies that are part of the smart city constellation are the ones outlined by the Forbes Technology Council in July 2024:[18]

1. Autonomous vehicles
2. Cognitive cities technology
3. Geolocation data
4. Context-aware computing
5. Air taxis
6. AI-powered public transit
7. Smart storage
8. Flexible workplaces and "pilot labs"
9. GenAI-powered, natural-language service models
10. Proactive data security
11. Support for the gig economy
12. Community health-tracking systems
13. Intelligent waste management
14. Automated public transit payment systems
15. Intelligent traffic management systems
16. Integrated health- and safety-tracking platforms
17. Smart parking systems
18. 24/7 maintenance services carried out by robots
19. Micromobility hubs

What makes these cities smart and sustainable is the interconnectivity of data collection and deployment for purposes of smooth, efficient, and continuous operations, such as in public transportation, energy delivery, crime detection and public safety, waste management, and more. Robots will increasingly play an important role in waste disposal, for example. Experts predict that in addition to robotaxis, autonomous vehicles, and public transportation, we may also see fully automated trash removal and self-guiding delivery drones, among other robot-based services.

A word on the use of autonomous vehicles in cities—especially robotaxis. A big push for robotaxis has already been taking place for a while in several markets, mostly in the United States (Phoenix, Los Angeles, Las Vegas, and San Francisco) and China (Beijing and Shanghai). There have been some setbacks, which have affected the rollouts, especially in the United States, where there was a pedestrian fatality in 2022. Meanwhile, Saudi Arabia has invested in the Chinese robot taxi firm Pony.AI to bring robotaxis to Neom, its future megacity in the desert, which is already under major development, and Abu Dhabi and Dubai are competing to become the first in the Middle East to run robotaxis on their streets.[19] And if Elon Musk has his way via Tesla's planned robotaxi, we will probably see an even broader push for robotaxis throughout the United States, though much of this will be subject to regulatory oversight and rule-making, both locally and nationally.

Finally, there is the huge connection and overlap between smart cities, advanced technologies, and progress on sustainability initiatives. Great sustainability improvements can be made through the deployment of smart technologies. Among the "smartest" cities in the world are New York City, Singapore, London, Amsterdam, and Dubai. Among the most sustainable smart cities are the first four already listed and Copenhagen, Oslo, Washington, Berlin, Tokyo, and Paris.[20] If planned properly, the combination of objectives can create real progress for cities and their populations from the standpoint of climate change, social pressure, and governance. Indeed, given that urban areas globally consume approximately 78 percent of the world's energy and produce over 60 percent of its greenhouse gases, it is critical that cities increasingly and continuously adopt renewable, low, and zero-carbon technologies.[21] Smart cities are a critical pathway to success. Based on my own work and experience in this space, I believe that these two concepts—sustainability and technology—have a deeply positive and synergistic relationship and hold vast promise for win/win solutions to some of the greatest challenges of our times.

Let us put it this way: It pays to be prepared for better, cleaner, more efficient, healthy city living because demographic studies are pointing in only one direction: a robust increase in urban populations the world over where, by 2050, 68 percent of the world's population is expected to live in cities, according to the UN's 2018 projections.[22]

Strategic and Leadership Considerations
of Exponential Autonomy

How does an effective and ethical leader manage the exponential nature of autonomy to maximum stakeholder benefit? In the context of the technologies described in this chapter, it is a heady and high-impact question, especially for government policymakers at every level—cities, counties, states, provinces, nations, and in the global commons. The exponential impact that autonomous vehicles, robots, and weapons could have at the local, regional, and global levels is not hard to imagine. So policymakers, technologists, civil society and businesses need to assume great care for the responsible development of these wide-ranging outcomes with a potentially deep impact—for people, for environments, and most certainly for and through good governance.

III

SURVIVING AND THRIVING IN THE AGE OF PANDORA

Developing the Exponential Governance Mindset

8

LEADERSHIP

Turbocharging 360 Tech Governance

Part III addresses how to survive and thrive in the Age of Pandora using the five key elements of the exponential governance mindset. This chapter focuses on the first element: good to great leadership to ensure integrated and holistic overall governance and a tech-specific governance approach at every level of an entity. This first element underscores the need for tech governance to be seamlessly integrated—from the bottom up (staff and the subcontractor ecosystem), from the middle out (management and expertise at all levels), and from the top down (C-suite, executive management, and the board). Hence, we use the "360" moniker to describe the ideal end state or objective of tech governance—as a whole-of-entity undertaking. The single most important driver of 360 tech governance success is that it needs to be turbocharged from the top of the house—the board or oversight body and the executive leader and management of the organization. Without this critical ingredient, everything else becomes potentially more complicated, convoluted, inefficient, ineffective, challenging, or impossible. In other words, seamless, well-done 360 tech governance is borne from good overall entity governance.

Successful tech governance is about having clarity on the technology rules of the road, a direct connection to entity mission and vision, freedom from material conflicts of interest, and a holistic, all-of-entity approach to integrating tech governance into overall governance. The idea of successful tech governance applies to any and every type of entity—for profit, nonprofit, governmental, and so on. The crux of successful tech governance is whether technology within an entity is governed consciously and proactively or is ignored, neglected, or discombobulated. Or what could be worse, if tech governance is purposefully mismanaged. In other words, is the entity's tech governable, reformable, or ungovernable?

The reality of 360 tech governance is about a synchronous, integrated governance culture from the top down, from the bottom up, and radiating from the middle out. While we will discuss the criticality of the "responsible tech culture" in the next chapter, suffice it to say here that it starts and ends with the general tenor of the board and management—whether it has a disciplined approach to governance generally that also extends to its handling of tech. Or is it more mediocre governance that muddles through? Or is the approach to governance generally (and by association to tech governance), fast and loose, less governance and more guardrail window dressing or tech governance-washing (to extend the "green-washing" metaphor to tech governance)?

In this chapter, we explore several definitions and examples and then turn to questions stakeholders should ask about the tech governance at their entity. We conclude with a few critical, potentially low-hanging, action items leaders should consider immediately and a leadership-based thought experiment to push you to think further about this topic.

Levels of Tech Governance

Let us begin with an understanding of pertinent governance at several levels—the governance of technology per se, entity or organizational governance, ecosystem or sector governance, and regulatory or government-incentivized governance. For perspective, see figure 8.1.

(Actual) Technology Governance

In today's technology-infused and -permeated world, the governance of technology itself must always be an organizational priority. This means that various key functions—like information technology, information security, finance, risk, compliance, legal, audit, operations, and even physical security—work together to explain what is in place from a technology

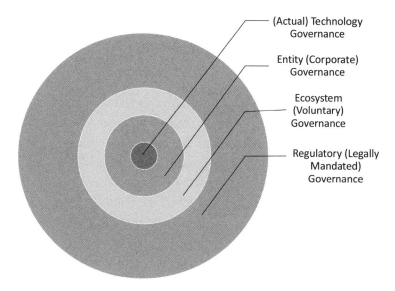

Figure 8.1 Levels of Tech Governance
Source: Author.

perspective, and what is needed to achieve business goals and strategy, do a gap analysis, and then fill the gaps.

Reaching these objectives requires a concerted, cross-disciplinary effort to choose, upgrade, or sunset technology processes, products, and services, with appropriate budgets and resources, all presented as a cohesive and coherent business plan to management and the board. For entities that are developing new tech—including exponential tech like GenAI, quantum computing, or synthetic biology—this means integrating governance at every level of development of actual tech—from design, inception, and testing to adoption, troubleshooting, and decommissioning.

At the most granular level, the OpenAI saga points to the critical importance of tech governance at the inception and earliest stages of developing new technology. This requires the right tone from the top and empowered interdisciplinary teams. According to news sources, OpenAI has been plagued by bad reports (including anonymous complaints from insiders), layoffs and resignations concerning purportedly insufficient activity, or improper guardrails and security.[1] Given that OpenAI is developing some of the most aggressive and opaque GenAI (with the aim of achieving AGI), this should trouble their leaders—board and executive management—not to mention stakeholders—internal (employees) and external (users and regulators)—who are using their services and deploying their products to their own personal or professional activities.

It is important to recognize that tech governance is not just for producers, creators, and innovators of exponential technology. Tech governance is also for adopters and purchasers of technology. Tech governance at its best involves smart people talking with each other at every stage of not only tech development but also of tech purchase, adoption, and integration and being properly incentivized to do so through a systematic and purposeful performance incentive structure. Sidebar 8.1 summarizes the key steps and questions one might ask, not only in the development of exponential cloud and AI products and services but also in their adoption, acquisition, and use. How is an organization to best govern—both from the bottom up and from the top down—its usage and deployment of these cutting-edge technologies? This sidebar gives ideas from a piece I co-wrote with cloud and AI expert, founder, and technologist Vishwas Manral.[2]

These internal technology development and deployment guardrails are applicable to all types of entities and all kinds of technologies, whether they use edge computing, synthetic biology, metaverse/immersive technologies, autonomous vehicles, or robotics. It applies to the data ingested and produced, the algorithms acquired or developed, and the product- and service-specific governance developed internally and through externally obtained benchmarks, audits, and best practices.

Entity (Corporate) Governance

Entity governance means organization-level governance, such as for a company/nonprofit like OpenAI. For its first few years of existence starting in 2015, OpenAI was a nonprofit with a laudable societal mission: that "AGI benefit all of humanity." By 2019 it was receiving large investments from for-profit entities like Microsoft through a convoluted governance structure. These investments underscored the internal mission and vision confusion at OpenAI, as to whether it was truly a nonprofit

---

Sidebar 8.1
Key Steps to Consider in Governing Cutting-Edge,
Exponential Technology

1. Understand the existing state of governance and gaps in the company's technology adoption by doing a governance risk assessment.
2. Prioritize the biggest risks and benefits. Organizations need to start with guardrail-level governance as the first step to help run workflows.
3. Map, monitor, and measure against the guardrail state continuously, and update policies, tools, and personnel based on changes.
4. Start automation where gaps can be automatically discovered and fixed.
5. Have a clearly expressed corporate or organizational technology governance charter that has an integrated, top-down approach. This governance approach will require integrating the top objectives with actual low-down metrics. This may require having an integrated view of the various systems, not a siloed view.
6. Map, monitor, and measure against organization goals and objectives and automate the change process. This requires continuous assessment to move toward organizational goals and the target state.
7. Produce a management-and-board dashboard that summarizes the approach to continuous bottom-up and top-down tech governance with qualitative and quantitative measurements that are subject to periodic updating, presentation, and monitoring.

Source: Vishwas Manral and Andrea Bonime-Blanc, "Cutting Edge Technology: Continuous and Holistic Governance of Cloud and AI," *Directorship Magazine*, February 14, 2024, www.nacdonline.org/all-governance/governance-resources/directorship-magazine/online-exclusives/2024/february/cutting-edge-tech-continuous-holistic-governance-cloud-AI/.

---

or a stealth for-profit start-up—or possibly both. This internal tension blossomed into public view during and after those five turbulent days in November 2023, when Sam Altman, OpenAI's CEO, was fired and rehired over a weekend and the old board configuration changed dramatically, from primarily a nonprofit to primarily but still an unofficial for-profit.[3] Clearly, the internal, undelineated mix of for-profit and nonprofit entities and missions, and of safety-focused versus growth-minded cultures within the same organization, was not only confusing but also potentially combustible—and continues to this day in the latest iteration of OpenAI's governance structure announced in mid-2025, in which the nonprofit continues to "control" a newly created for-profit public benefit corporation (PBC), emulating what some other forward-thinking tech companies have already done (as discussed below).[4]

Some tech companies have already developed novel, entity-level tech company governance solutions—a third way, as it were. Consider the long-standing example of Mozilla, operator of the Firefox web browser, where a nonprofit foundation owns the for-profit business. This model has met with mixed results—on one hand, more transparency, clarity of mission, and stakeholder engagement; on the other hand, some governance confusion, financial sustainability issues, and other challenges. The effort has not gone unnoticed in Silicon Valley, with OpenAI having recently adopted the PBC alternative corporate governance structure.

Another company in the GenAI space, Anthropic (in which Google is a major investor), is organized as a PBC and describes its mission and governance, which consists of a standard board of directors and a long-term benefit trust, as follows: "Anthropic is incorporated in Delaware, and Delaware corporate law expressly permits the directors of a public benefit company to balance the financial interests of the stockholders with the public benefit purpose specified in the corporation's certificate of incorporation, and the best interests of those materially affected by the corporation's conduct. The public benefit purpose stated in Anthropic's certificate is the responsible development and maintenance of advanced AI for the long-term benefit of humanity. This gives our board the legal latitude to weigh long- and short-term externalities of decisions—whether to deploy a particular AI system, for example—alongside the financial interests of our stockholders."[5]

The bottom line on good entity or organizational governance—whether you are a for-profit, nonprofit, nongovernmental organization, or government agency—is the same: as a member of a board, you must focus on making sure your mission and vision are clearly and strictly aligned with your purpose so that your stakeholders (whether shareholders, users, or citizens) know that their interests are being considered, that the governance of the entity is transparent, understandable, and ad-

Table 8.1 "NACD Technology Governance Report 2024": Overall Guidelines for Corporate Boards

Guideline	Details
Strengthen oversight	Revise board processes, practices, and structures to oversee how technology will affect the way the company creates value. The board's work to strengthen oversight reinforces its role as a thoughtful management adviser and authority.
Deepen insight	Gain a more robust understanding of complex new technologies and managers' plans to take advantage of them. Deeper insight enables the board to have fuller, context-driven dialogues with managers about technology opportunities and risks.
Develop foresight	Pressure test assumptions about beliefs, plans, and investments related to technology, and dedicate resources to forward-looking discussions. This practice allows the board to form a trusted partnership with managers in their joint discovery of new technology opportunities and outcomes.

Source: "NACD Technology Governance Report 2024."

dresses the rights, responsibilities, and benefits of stakeholders in a way that stakeholders should expect.

More specifically, what does good-to-great entity technology governance look like? The National Association of Corporate Directors (NACD) issued a groundbreaking report on the board's role in technology governance, providing three overall guidelines and ten key takeaways.[6] The three overall guidelines are summarized in table 8.1, and the related ten takeaways are illustrated in figure 8.2.

Ecosystem (Voluntary) Tech Governance

This type of governance could also be called "best practices peer pressure" governance. It is the type of governance driven by third-party pressure that moves entities to either become looser in their entity governance or stricter. There is a great example from long ago and far away in a different sector—the US defense industry (think GE, Lockheed, Martin Marietta, and many others). They got into repeated trouble with the US government on a variety of foreign bribery and domestic fraud issues in the 1970s and 1980s. Concurrently with a major congressional inquiry (the 1985 Packard Commission), and to preempt new laws and stricter regulation, GE's

Ten Recommendations for Technology Leadership in the Boardroom

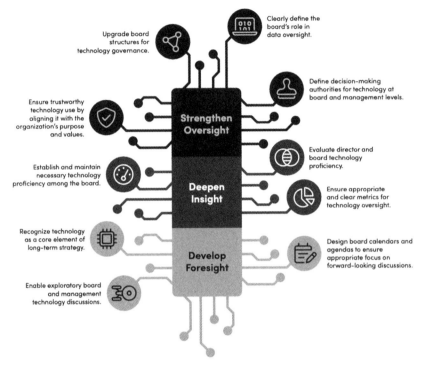

Figure 8.2 Ten Recommendations for Technology Leadership in the Boardroom

Source: *Report of the Blue Ribbon Commission on Technology Leadership in the Boardroom: Driving Trust and Value.* © 2024 National Association of Corporate Directors. All rights reserved; www.nacdonline.org/all-governance/governance-resources/governance-research/blue-ribbon -commission-reports/BRC/2024/tech-leadership-in-the-boardroom/. Reprinted by permission.

CEO, Jack Welch, convinced a dozen of his peer defense company CEOs to launch the "Defense Industry Initiative" on ethics and compliance. It became the originator of what is now a broadly accepted set of voluntary ethics and compliance program standards adopted by businesses (and other types of entities in government and civil society), and also used by regulators and prosecutors, to judge whether a company has an effective ethics and compliance program.[7]

We have already seen some movement toward ecosystem governance best practices in some of the technologies we have been discussing in this book. There are multiple sector and global efforts—some led by governments (in the European Union and the United States under President Joseph Biden), others by international bodies like the United Nations, and many of them public–private collaborations—to put arms around the unbridled development of exponential tech of all kinds and to protect stakeholders in the process. We are also seeing numerous professional associations, think tanks, and international organizations organized primarily around other issues (human resources, audit, privacy, etc.) developing major initiatives around GenAI and other exponential tech, making it part of their own agenda—examples include the International Association of Privacy Professionals, the Ethics & Compliance Initiative, the Society for Human Resources Management, the Association of Chartered Certified Accountants, and the American Bar Association, just to name a few.

While the ecosystem governance approach does not always work or even happen, it is a reflection of public, societal, and private pressures that may drive a sector to adopt better practices in the absence of clear or consistent regulatory guidelines or laws. That may yet come to the tech sector, given the monumental impact that exponential tech products and services are already having—we have seen quite a few national and international efforts at voluntary governance frameworks—for example, through the Bletchley Initiative launched in the United Kingdom in late 2023 and UN-based initiatives. However, these voluntary initiatives, while powerful in their own way, do not carry the carrot-and-stick approach that regulatory frameworks and laws carry. That is why there is one more level of governance—regulatory (legally mandated) governance—to consider in our evaluation of 360 tech governance.

Regulatory (Legally Mandated) Governance

There is legal and regulatory governance at the local, state, provincial, federal, national, regional, and international levels, including through international bodies—such as the Organization for Economic Cooperation and Development, the United Nations, and the European Union—that work on treaties, conventions, and best practices in governance that later translate into national or local laws and regulations. The most recent and dramatic example of regulatory international cooperation occurred on March 13, 2024, when the European Parliament adopted the EU AI Act, the first risk-based AI legal and regulatory framework ever enacted, which will no doubt have both dramatic effects within the EU and reverberations around the world. The EU AI Act is focused on fostering "trustworthy AI in Europe and beyond, by ensuring that AI systems respect fundamental rights, safety, and ethical principles and by addressing risks of very powerful and impactful AI models." We discuss this in greater detail in chapter 11.

Beyond the EU AI Act, other laws and/or initiatives that are intended to become law are under way. Table 8.2 provides a snapshot in time of such developments as of late 2024.[8]

An example of an unsuccessful US state-level AI regulatory effort was the California AI Act (SB 1047). This potential law was deeply debated and contested in 2023–24, with hard positions taken by members of the tech glitterati (pro and con), along with politicians of various stripes. The key issue: whether the proposed law went too far in regulating AI risks

Table 8.2 Jurisdictions Around the World with AI or GenAI Regulations/Frameworks Approved or under Development, as of August 2024

International Organization	Status
Group of Seven	AI regulation mandates member state compliance with international human rights law
United Nations	New draft resolution on AI encourages member states to implement national regulations
Organization for Economic Cooperation and Development	AI recommendations encourage member states to adopt trustworthy AI
Council of Europe	Developing new Convention on AI to safeguard human rights, democracy, and the rule of law in the digital space covering governance, accountability, and risk

continued

Table 8.2 *continued*

Region/Country	Status
Australia	Voluntary AI Ethics Principles
Brazil	Under development
Canada	At federal level expected, not provincial yet
China	Interim AI Measures approved targeting specific, administrative regulation of GenAI services
Czech Republic	Enacting EU AI Act nationally
European Union	EU AI Act approved in 2024
France	Participates in EU AI Act, plus looking at sector-specific laws
Germany	Evaluates AI specific legislation needs
India	National frameworks inform approach to AI regulation
Israel	Promotes responsible AI innovation through specific policies
Italy	Evaluates AI-specific legislation needs
Japan	Adopts soft law approach to AI governance, but hard law advancing in legislature
Kenya	National AI Strategy and Code of Practice expected to set foundation of AI law
Nigeria	Draft National AI Policy under way to pave way to comprehensive national AI strategy
Norway	Position paper informs approach to AI, sector-specific legislative amendments
Saudi Arabia	Relying on guidelines for now
Singapore	AI frameworks guide ethical and governance principles, sector specific regulations
South Africa	In process of obtaining inputs for a draft National AI plan
South Korea	AI Act to be consolidated body of AI law once approved by National Assembly
Spain	Creates Europe's first AI supervisory agency, active in EU AI Act
Switzerland	National AI Strategy aims to finalize AI regulatory proposal in 2025
Taiwan	Draft laws and guidelines under consideration
Turkey	Multiple guidelines on use of AI in various sectors
United Arab Emirates	Several decrees and guidelines, some related to data protection laws
United Kingdom	Flexible framework with sector-specific laws
United States	Relies on presidential executive orders federally, some state legal developments

Source: Author, based on a White & Case Memorandum 2024.

(some of which may be far-fetched), thereby stifling innovation. It was approved by the California legislature but was ultimately vetoed by Governor Newsom, under pressure from big tech.[9]

Actors on the Tech Governance Stage

 To get a sense of the main groups of actors playing in the tech governance world, I have broken them down into three main categories: the "tech masters of the universe," the "tech enablers and worker bees," and the "tech guardians of the universe." Let us take a look at each group.

"Tech Masters of the Universe": Founders, Investors, CEOs, and Their Boards

It is truly mesmerizing what the largest global tech companies and their sometimes mercurial but always interesting leaders have been achieving over the past few years—from Zuckerberg at Meta, Musk at Tesla, and Bezos (and now Jassy) at Amazon to Nadella at Microsoft, Cook at Apple, Pichai at Alphabet, and Huang at Nvidia. And then there are the other tech "masters of the universe," the money men, as it were (because there are hardly any women): Andreessen, Horowitz, and many others who run incubators, private equity firms, and venture capital firms.

Any way you look at it, there is a "Tech Masters of the Universe" class who are critical actors on the tech stage and by dint of that on the tech governance stage—with outsize influence on how their entities and investments conduct entity governance. Some of the greatest business and innovation minds, wealth, and power the world has ever seen seem to be concentrated in the hands of a very small, elite, powerful group of private individuals and their companies, mostly located in the United States and mostly in Silicon Valley—all men and mostly white, with a few notable racial background exceptions. Table 8.3 names some of these individuals and their associations.

As a critically important component of entity governance, the gender and diversity disparity of tech always was and continues to be gaping. Hence the tech world is dominated by the mostly white, mostly billionaire

Table 8.3 A Smattering of Tech Masters of the Universe and Their Companies

Who	Associated Companies
Marc Andreesen and Ben Horowitz	Founders of a16z (US)
Jeff Bezos	Founder of Amazon (US)
Tim Cook	CEO of Apple (US)
Daniel Ek	Cofounder and CEO of Spotify (Sweden)
Bill Gates	Founder of Microsoft (US)
Reid Hoffman	Founder/partner at LinkedIn / Greylock Partners (US)
Jensen Huang	Cofounder and CEO of Nvidia (US)
Jack Ma	Cofounder and former CEO of Alibaba Group (China)
Pony Ma	Cofounder and CEO of Tencent (China)
Strive Masiyima	Founder and executive chairman of Econet Group (Zimbabwe / South Africa)
Elon Musk	CEO of Tesla, Starlink, X, xAI, and others (US)
Satya Nadella	CEO and chairman of Microsoft (US)
Narayana Murthy	Cofounder of Infosys (India)
Sundar Pichai	CEO of Google (US)
Peter Thiel	Cofounder/partner, Palantir, PayPal, Founders Fund (US)
Masayoshi Son	Founder and CEO of Softbank Group (Japan)
Reng Zhengfei	Founder and former CEO of Huawei (China)
Mark Zuckerberg	Founder/CEO of Meta, Facebook, Instagram, WhatsApp (US)

Source: Author.

American males listed in table 8.3 and their mostly male funding, partnering, financial, and innovation ecosystems. In contrast, table 8.4 shows various statistics regarding women in tech, which are, bluntly speaking, astounding but in a negative way.[10]

And as a reminder, businesses with female CEOs and board members and companies with a more diverse executive team and/or board report higher likelihood of and actual above-average profitability, as we have been told for years, nay decades, by the likes of S&P Global, *Harvard Business Review*, McKinsey, Catalyst, the World Economic Forum, and others. For example, a recent such study conducted by Women Count and the Pipeline looking at the FTSE 350 showed a link between the presence of women board directors and profitability, in that corporations with more than a quarter of women on their executive committees realized a profit

Table 8.4 Selected Women in Tech: Gender-Based Statistics

Statistic	Percent or Number
Women as share of founders of start-ups generally	25
Women as share of high-growth start-ups	10
Women as share of overall tech workforce	33
Female founders' share of venture capital funding	2
Women in tech who identify as Black	3
Women in tech who identify as Latina	1.7
Share of women in tech reporting harassment and sexism	50
Black women CEOs' share of pay compared with white male CEOs'	62
Share of women in tech who leave their jobs by age 35 years	50
Share of executive, senior-level, and management positions in S&P 500	26.5
Share of software engineering jobs held by women	14
Average salary of women in tech is over $15,000 less than men	$15,000 less
Share of women over 35 in junior tech positions	30 (men are 5)

Source: Author.

margin of 16 percent—more than ten times higher than those with no female board members.[11]

Responsible tech governance is clearly not just about CEOs. It is also about boards of directors and who is on boards, and their relative independence, diversity, and other key governance considerations. Are board members of the "friends and family" variety, as we have seen on the boards that Elon Musk and Mark Zuckerberg have constructed at their companies? Or are they made up of savvy, independent, and diverse board members who will conduct decision-making largely independently from the powerful CEO and in the best interest of shareholders and other key stakeholders?

Tech Enablers and Worker Bees: Management, Staff, and Experts

Of course it goes beyond the right tone from the top, mood in the middle, and buzz from the bottom, as my friends in the ethics and compliance community have quipped over the years. It is about how each of these levels is interconnected—or not—to the others in a more or less seamless culture or ethos, something we will explore further in chapter 9.

Responsible 360 tech governance requires the right executive leadership—especially from the CEO or other entity leader and their management team—developing and implementing the best tech culture and strategy for the given entity and its stakeholders. Digging a little deeper into the organization, it is also about having the right, properly resourced, and empowered tech talent, teams, and team leadership conducting tech governance from the ground up, top down, and across the entity—in synchronicity with management technology strategy and board tech oversight.

And, finally, within an organization, key players are the expert staff—full-time, part-time, and subcontracted—who need to be not in silos but on the same tech governance page, appropriately and continuously trained for virtual upsides and downsides, social engineering threats, and innovation, and always interconnected through cross-disciplinary communications, teams, and projects.

Tech Guardians of the Universe: A Swath of Stakeholder Protectors

Social, community, research, regulatory, governmental, think tank, and university expert influencers make a huge difference in whether we have safety, ethics, transparency, security, and all those other good things that stakeholders need and want but that the Tech Masters of the Universe do not always think or care about (because it might slow them down from "moving fast and breaking things" and making tons of money). Thankfully, there is a wide array of leaders, influencers, and governance actors on the tech governance stage who play critical roles in developing acceptable tech governance standards. And believe it or not, there are some guiding lights in the business community as well, mainly within the leading big technology firms like Microsoft, Google, and Salesforce, where they have set up "independent" or otherwise semi-independent committees and/or review boards to focus on specific ethical concerns or issues. In this regard, Microsoft has what it calls its AETHER Committee (AI, Ethics, and Effects in Engineering and Research Committee) to advise its leaders on ethical challenges, and Google DeepMind has its Responsibility and Safety Council for AI development.[12]

Some Tech Guardians of the Universe are focused on pure entity governance at tech companies. Others are invested in how the technology gets made—the 360 life cycle, from inception and release to sunsetting—and yet others act more akin to watchdogs. Here is a list of important contributors to this tech protection that would qualify (in my humble opinion) as Tech Guardians of the Universe:

- Access Now
- African Observatory on Responsible AI
- African Union
- AI Now Institute
- Algorithmic Justice League
- All Tech Is Human
- Asia-Pacific Economic Organization
- Berkman Klein Center for Internet and Society at Harvard
- Brookings Institution
- Center for Artificial Intelligence & Digital Policy
- Center for Security and Emerging Technology
- Center for Democracy and Technology
- Carnegie Endowment for International Peace
- Center for AI and Digital Policy
- Center for Humane Technology
- Council of Europe
- Council on Foreign Relations
- Cyber Future Foundation
- European Union
- Future of Life Institute
- Group of Twenty AI Principles
- Harvard University, Berkman Klein Center for Internet and Society
- IIEE
- ISO
- Massachusetts Institute for Technology (various)
- Organization for Economic Cooperation and Development
- Partnership on AI

- RAND Corporation
- Stanford Institute for Human Centered AI
- Alan Turing Institute
- University of California, Berkeley, Center for Long-Term Cyber-security
- UNESCO
- Woodrow Wilson International Center for Scholars
- World Economic Forum, Digital Trust Initiative
- XRSI

The Tech Governance Landscape: Ungovernable, Reformable, Governable

The difference between responsible tech governance and governance that is derelict or even irresponsible is the difference between governance at Theranos (a now-defunct and infamous former biotech unicorn) and Microsoft—one of the most successful big tech companies in history, and why there may still be hope from a governance standpoint for OpenAI. But you may say that this is comparing apples and oranges, and that might be true. While Theranos was part of a different industry and based pretty much from its inception on fraudulent blood testing claims, OpenAI, for all its challenges, does not appear to be such a case. While some of its claims—mainly voiced through its CEO, Sam Altman—are grandiose, it is most definitely creating and selling GenAI services that are demonstrably useful and amazing. However, OpenAI would be wise to learn lessons from the Theranos case. Theranos's founder and CEO, Elizabeth Holmes, purported to have groundbreaking, potentially exponential, simple, easy-to-use, multipurpose blood-testing tools and services when the company did not. Theranos, at its CEO's instigation, had remarkably poor corporate governance and even worse stakeholder care—most significantly toward patients who unwittingly used its fraudulent blood test. Theranos soared for a few years, achieving a top valuation of $9 billion, but then started a fast descent and eventually crashed and burned when the fraud began to unravel, as journalists (most notably the award-winning *Wall Street Journal* reporter John Carreyrou, who went on to write a fantastic best-seller,

Bad Blood, chronicling the events) uncovered the story leading to Holmes and others being found guilty of criminal fraud. Holmes is currently in jail serving an eleven-year term.[13]

Governance at Theranos was all window dressing—with seven high-achieving, well-known, older men, including former secretaries of state, defense, generals, and a law firm partner—recruited to preside over the unicorn start-up. In addition to the absence of diversity of any kind, there was no one on the board versed in biotechnology or even science generally. But it gets worse—the board did not function as an informed, proactive oversight body that knew what questions to ask and whether and how to hold the CEO/founder accountable. It was the prototypical "friends and family," or perhaps better said, "famous names" type of board that we often see and that so often is ineffective or worse, intent on making money and rubber-stamping the founder's wishes.[14]

In the case of Microsoft since Satya Nadella took over in 2014, we have seen a marked improvement from its past under Bill Gates and Steven Ballmer in terms of entity governance. Such relatively good governance has been on display from the board itself (though, as discussed below, Nadella becoming both CEO and chairman of the board is not necessarily a best practice). Additionally, Microsoft has developed a series of governance innovations addressing new technological developments like AI and GenAI, including a pioneering responsible AI framework, and has broadly shared these good practices within the industry and beyond. This is why we should care—because good-to-great leadership, or even mediocre leadership that is willing to improve, plays an essential role in the success of a venture or other type of entity.

And that is why there is still hope for OpenAI. Let me explain. For five days in November 2023, technology observers had real-time, front row seats via social media and news media to something unique: the very public and dramatic unraveling and re-raveling of the Silicon Valley darling OpenAI. These developments laid bare the almost impossible governance task of harmonizing the original public nonprofit mission with the turbocharged, for-profit growth mindset.[15]

The new OpenAI Board was expanded in early 2024 to include sev-eral leading female corporate executives and founders as well as retired general Paul M. Nakasone, former head of the National Security Agency. These were clearly efforts at reforming overall governance at OpenAI with heavy-hitting and diverse board appointments. These governance changes, however, were not all "good." Sam Altman, the now-reinstated CEO, became a board member again, and other elements (which we explore in chapter 9) continued to underscore governance and cultural concerns within the organization. These concerns included the absence of whistleblower processes, the silencing of ex-employees through draco-nian severance agreements, and most concerning, the departure of key AI expert safety and security personnel. At the time of this writing, OpenAI had just announced its for-profit entity becoming a public benefit corpora-tion, which by definition requires it to serve the public interest in addition to its shareholders. The road to achieving this will no doubt be paved with challenges, obstacles, and litigation from a variety of interested parties, including cofounder Elon Musk, who has been very vociferous and liti-gious against OpenAI's various governance developments.

Thus, responsible 360 tech governance is also about a CEO, executive director, or president who is properly selected, accountable, and emotion-ally intelligent to his or her people. A leader who sets the tone from the top on how the rest of the organization is held accountable—with param-eters that come from the leader and which the leader lives up to every day. Enter someone like Jensen Huang, cofounder and CEO of Nvidia, who is widely considered to have exercised good management and governance practices since he cofounded Nvidia thirty-one years ago, or someone like Ilya Sutskever—cofounder, ex–board member, and chief scientist of Open-AI—who left when he had disagreements with Sam Altman about the safety and guardrails OpenAI was apparently not systematically placing on its development of GenAI and possible AGI. Let us keep an eye on these leaders of two very different companies at very different stages of development and success to see if and how they are able to maintain good-to-great governance.

Questions Stakeholders Should Ask about Turbocharging 360 Tech Governance

In this section, we lay out some of the key questions that stakeholders should ask regarding their entity's 360 tech governance. If you are an investor in a tech start-up, a retail shareholder in a magnificent seven stock, a concerned citizen worried about law enforcement's use of algorithms in robot dogs or street corner video surveillance, a citizen of the world wondering whether your country is sufficiently protected from critical infrastructure cyberattacks or concerted enemy drone attacks, you are a stakeholder. As a stakeholder, you may want to ask about how the leadership of these various entities—company, police department, national cyberforce—is organized and can live up to its real or apparent governance commitments to you as a stakeholder. The next four subsections explore questions to ask such leaders.

Who Is Currently on Your Board or Other Oversight Body in This Age of Pandora?

As a shareholder, employee, or citizen, depending on what entity you are querying, look at who is on the oversight body or board. Are they competent for the type of entity? Do they have the right diversity mix for this entity—experience, education, gender, race, geography, hands-on or other expertise—to be making the most important strategic decisions for this entity?

As a group, does this board function properly? Is there a chair who knows how to run a meeting—leading and empowering, with enough independence not to be conflicted, and enough emotional intelligence to navigate the complex issues and the challenging personal and personnel dynamics?

Does Your Board or Equivalent Body Have the Right Structure to Navigate the Age of Pandora?

How is governance structured at your entity? Is there a formal board with bylaws, a charter, a formalized structure for meetings, resolutions,

minute-keeping, and decision-making? Are there the appropriate committees for the business of this entity? The typical ones that are needed
or mandated such as audit, nominations/governance, and compensation?
But are there also other committees needed for this Age of Pandora—like
risk, technology, sustainability, digital transformation, or anything else
pertaining to the mission and vision of the entity? Is the CEO being held
accountable for good overall 360 tech governance? Is good governance
being deployed not just for risk management but also for opportunity and
value creation? The NACD "Technology Leadership in the Boardroom
Report of 2024" provides very helpful guidance on specific technology
governance designs that the board should consider.[16]

Do Your Executive Leader and Team Understand Technology and Exponential Technology? Do They Know How to Create Integrated 360 Tech Governance?

The Age of Pandora requires responsible, emotionally intelligent board
members, CEOs, and leaders. And that is a major task for the board or
other oversight body—to select, oversee, and incentivize the leaders—
both in management and its own ranks. And to ensure that the leader
cascades down the proper governance and incentive structure into the
entire organization. Is the current leader someone who understands the
technology deployed in, by, and from the entity to its stakeholders and
its other critical implications—culture, stakeholder impact, strategy, and
resilience creation? Does the CEO have the right people and talent advising them on such issues and helping to implement the vision of 360 tech
governance? Is the CEO and their team an education-first curious group
of people who are willing to learn? Do they have situational awareness—
that is, do they understand the world they live in and the effects on the
entity and its business and stakeholders?

Are Key Actors in Your Entity's Exponential Technology Loop Properly Incentivized?

In this Age of Pandora, we need accountable, emotionally intelligent CEOs
more than ever, but it is up to the board to provide the right carrots and

sticks and overall incentive structure. To paraphrase the late vice chairman of Berkshire Hathaway, the investor Charlie Munger: If you show me the incentives, I will show you the outcomes. And thus, the time has come for boards to incentivize CEOs and their teams to create 360 tech governance and to demand from those leaders how they are doing this. Indeed, if your incentive structure is structured to incentivize the wrong type of behavior, this could lead to serious technology-related aberrations like the rush to create products or services with poor-quality data, badly built algorithms, or worse. Once again, the NACD "Technology Leadership in the Boardroom 2024 Report" provides essential guidance on the connection of performance incentives and tech governance.[17]

These measures range from: How is the CEO paid? What is the balance of salary and stock, and what metrics are being used to measure performance? Are those metrics reasonable or unreasonable? Reachable or unreachable? Attainable or unattainable? Skewed in one direction or balanced? Financially driven or driven by other, more qualitative measures? Is the rest of the organization measured accordingly? Is the CEO's pay package a stand-alone one, or do similar measures trickle down to other members of management and/or staff? How good are the metrics, and are they evenly, periodically and properly enforced?

Actions Leaders Should Take to Create Integrated 360 Tech Governance

While exponential tech may help us find information and facts about leaders and may help to weed out rotten apples, as it were, it is up to each of us to choose the better leaders in the lot. Leaders and boards do not always have the tools to do so, and with the explosion of misinformation and disinformation, that task has become much harder. That should not stop leaders from understanding who they are as people—whether voting for someone locally or nationally or promoting someone within a team or recruiting a new board member for a Fortune 500 company. The character, emotional intelligence, and interconnected systems thinking of a leader—at any level—is the superpower of the future. And leaders need to train for it, look for it, deploy it, and reward it. Among some of the key actions we can take are:

- Recruit "renaissance" people—people with a wide range of knowledge, skills, and expertise across multiple disciplines, with curiosity and humility—into the highest leadership ranks, both at the board and management levels, and hold them accountable through proper incentive structures.
- Educate and promote leaders on continuous situational awareness and systems thinking.
- Adopt an integrated 360 tech governance organizational approach.
- Engage in intelligent and calibrated oversight board refreshment—bringing in new board members and new skills as needed.
- The CEO video must match the audio—a CEO who speaks one way and acts another is a CEO on the verge of cultural and governance trouble.
- The oversight body must always hold the CEO accountable for governance and culture.
- The board should adopt a new entity governance charter for this new Age of Pandora deploying the concept of integrated 360 tech governance.

"Leadership" Theme Thought Experiment

Because leadership (or the absence of good leadership) is at the crux of everything an entity does, as a concluding take, I would like to leave you with a thought experiment. If you are a shareholder or other key stakeholder in one of their companies (investor, employee, customer), knowing what you know about the governance styles of Elon Musk, Mark Zuckerberg, and Sam Altman in their companies (mainly Tesla, Meta, and OpenAI), on one hand, and those of Satya Nadella, Mustafa Suleyman, and Ilya Sutskever and their companies (namely, Microsoft, DeepMind / Inflection and Safe Superintelligence), on the other hand, ask yourself these questions:

- What is the state of overall entity governance? Solid? Middling? Poor?
- What is your entity doing to allow reporting of concerns by staff and contractors without fear of retaliation? Encouraging? Silent? Repressive?
- Does the board play a role in this?
- Is management ready and willing to stop the tech presses (as it were) if there is a serious concern?
- Is there a board worth its salt, independent, proactive about oversight, and willing to lean in?

While some of this information is not always readily or easily available, it is critical for key stakeholders—especially investors, shareholders, and employees—to have a sense of how good, mediocre, or poor the 360 technology governance of their organization is and where improvements may be needed. This was the situation OpenAI discovered in the spring of 2024 when a tsunami of anonymous and on-the-record whistleblower complaints concerned about the safety of their AI and GenAI products came flowing out of the company and actually led to a number of governance improvements.

9

ETHOS

Embedding Responsible Tech Culture

This chapter focuses on the tech culture—the ethos—that leaders create, nurture, enable, and disseminate within their organizations—consciously and unconsciously—and the resulting "great, good, bad, or ugly" tenor of this culture. Understanding how leaders use, integrate, and/or deploy technology and exponential technology within their organizations reveals a lot about their overall organizational culture and ethos. Are leaders fostering a healthy, retaliation-free, speak-up, follow-up, and problem-solving culture that puts tech responsibility, safety, and ethics first? An entity's internal tech culture also has both direct and indirect consequences for its reputation risk and/or opportunity for both internal and external stakeholders (as we will explore in greater depth in chapter 10).

Embedding a responsible tech culture is, first and foremost, the responsibility of the highest levels of organizational leadership: the board and management. What leaders say—but more important, what they do—is critical for how an organization "does" technology—a reflection of its tech ethos—and the success and ethicality (or failure and toxicity) of its internal and external use and deployment of tech.

Embedding a Responsible Tech Culture: What Is It, and Why Should We Care?

I spent many years of my almost two decades as a corporate executive acting as, or filling the role of, chief ethics, compliance, risk, and corporate responsibility officer (CECO/CRO) at four companies, ranging from Fortune 500s to start-ups. Sometimes I was the general counsel, other times I served as the CECO/CRO, but I almost always handled the creation, improvement, and/or implementation of an ethics, compliance, risk, and/or corporate responsibility program for my company. And I have continued to do this for more than a decade as a strategic adviser and board member for my own clients and boards. So, I have literally seen the 360 of what it means to build and run such programs and what makes them effective, ethical, and responsible or the opposite—ineffective, unethical, and/or irresponsible and toxic. Been there. Done that.

Enter the Age of Pandora. What does it mean to have an effective, ethical, and responsible culture or ethos in this time of explosive exponential technologies? What are the qualities of an ethical and responsible tech culture? Let us start with a few basic definitions. "Effective" means that you do your work in a way that is objectively successful per a variety of operational, strategic, and financial metrics that are deployed in your organization and sector.

So why also use the words "ethical" and "responsible"? Because both words connote that one cares about not just achieving results *effectively* but also *how* these results are achieved. And this "how" is measured by whether you do it in a way that is ethical, responsive, and responsible to your key stakeholders' needs, requirements, expectations, and aspirations. Let us look at a few more pertinent definitions:

- *Ethics:* "the principles of conduct governing an individual or a group"; "a consciousness of moral importance"; "a guiding philosophy."[1]
- *Responsibility:* "the quality or state of being responsible: such as moral, legal, or mental accountability."[2]
- *Responsible:* "liable to be called on to answer"; "liable to be called to account as the primary cause, motive, or agent"; "being the cause or explanation"; "liable to legal review or in case of fault to penalties"; "able to answer for one's conduct and obligations"; "trustworthy"; "able to choose for oneself between right and wrong."[3]

An ethos is built by people, not machines. Thus, people need to frame the ethos. And the people most capable and responsible for doing so in the first instance are leaders who must, in turn, solicit feedback from and always listen carefully to both internal and external stakeholders.

Very simply, leaders—whether the CEO, the ED, MD, or president and the Board of Directors or Trustees or similar oversight body—set the tone from the top: the ethos of the organization. Period. End of story. Yes, the mood in the middle and the buzz at the bottom are critically important pieces of the culture puzzle. But decision-making, budgets, resource allocations, and walking or not walking the talk are things that leaders do or do not do, and that have outsize effects and reverberations on the overall footprint and perception of the organization relative to almost anything else—effects on attraction and retention of talent, on turnover, on reputation, on brand value, and more.

A fascinating case in point can be seen in the cultural transformation that Microsoft underwent when Satya Nadella became CEO in 2015. Many longtime Microsoft employees and observers will tell you there was a pre-Satya, Ballmer-and-Gates-dominated culture—often described as ruthless, aggressive, winner-take-all, and, some would argue, tech irresponsible in its approach to strategy, products, and talent—before the Satya culture announced in his book *Hit Reset*.[4] The Satya culture has been borne out by countless cultural and business successes since he took over, including articles and profiles such as one in *Fortune* in 2024, which examines his decade-long cultural transformation.[5] Such accounts are also reinforced by some of the "best companies" lists that are annually assembled by the likes of Just Capital, Best Places to Work, Glassdoor, and others.

The Tech Culture Landscape: From Toxicity to Responsibility

This leads me to a discussion of the tech culture landscape, where we will review a variety of approaches that range from toxic to responsible. We start with what is going on in Silicon Valley—the epicenter of most major technology companies, financing, and what we call the "tech bros"—more recently bestowed with the collective moniker the "broligarchs"—as they have moved into the deeply polarized politics of American democracy and beyond and, since the advent of the second Trump administration in early 2025, have become part and parcel of the government ruling class (in addition to the economic one).

As I stated in one of my articles, in Silicon Valley with its start-up, "move-fast-and-break-things" mentality, where people rarely ask for permission and only sometimes ask for forgiveness, there is a notorious aversion to guardrails of any kind, notably by the tech bros, though there are exceptions. It is a mindset typical of innovators and technologists who do not have the time or inclination to worry about governance, risk, ethics, or stakeholders until there is a dire need. Then, the "grown-ups" enter the room—whether they are investors, partners, new management, board members, regulators, or, sometimes, government prosecutors.[6]

Whatever we call them, in one corner, we have the all-in technologists who are inventing, financing, and/or deploying GenAI and other exponential technologies. Among them are those who, like Marc Andreessen, call themselves the accelerationists who do not believe in putting any brakes on what they are doing in the name of innovation and the pursuit of ever-greater wealth. Check out these excerpts from Andreessen's widely lauded (or berated) "Techno-Optimist Manifesto," where he clearly and forcefully lays out his case for techno-optimism and techno-acceleration, while unapologetically berating those who do not agree:

> *The Enemy*
>
> We have enemies. Our enemies are not bad people—but rather bad ideas.
>
> Our present society has been subjected to a mass demoralization campaign for six decades—against technology and against life—under varying names like "existential risk," "sustainability," "ESG," "Sustainable Development Goals," "social responsibility," "stakeholder capitalism," "Precautionary Principle," "trust and safety," "tech ethics," "risk management," "de-growth," and "the limits of growth."[7]

And the diatribe goes on from there at great length.

In the other corner, we have the likes of Tristan Harris and Aza Raskin from the Center for Humane Technology, former technologists at major tech companies, who in 2015 founded the nonprofit for the purpose of "aligning technology with humanity's best interests."[8] Their mission is to protect humans from known and unknown technological aberrations—especially those coming from uncontrolled exponential tech—by raising concerns early and often. They first warned us of the dangers of social media in Jeff Orlowski-Yang's groundbreaking documentary *The Social Dilemma*.[9] Then they warned us of GenAI and its worst downside implications in the YouTube discussion "The AI Dilemma" in early 2023, on the heels of its ChatGPT release in late 2022.[10] And they have continued to raise these issues in the public square through their influential podcast "Your Undivided Attention."[11]

There are many others working around the world to minimize the adverse effects of frontier technologies on humanity and the planet—too many to count and discuss here. Suffice it to say that the toxic aspects of the tech culture wars being waged between those with deep pockets and vested interests to preserve and multiply their technology riches and those who would like to not only protect humanity from downsides but also include humanity in the upsides is marked and increasingly fraught.

Because of the political polarization in the United States between the tech accelerationists or bros and those representing various other stakeholders, we have seen serious effects on important initiatives. For example, some of the more vocal and wealthy accelerationists—often aligned with the extreme right wing of the Republican Party—have worked to shut down important initiatives. Case in point: the Stanford Internet Observatory, cofounded by Alex Stamos and led by Renee DiResta in 2020, two leading and widely respected experts on Internet-based disinformation and misinformation propagation, was forced to shut down in 2024 under severe conservative political pressure.[12]

Since the beginning of the second Trump administration and its elevation of numerous techno-accelerationists to positions of great power and influence—including J. D. Vance, a protégé of Peter Thiel and now the vice president of the United States; Elon Musk, the brief but impactful head of the so-called Department of Government Efficiency, or DOGE; and David Sacks, of PayPal mafia fame, now the White House's AI and crypto tsar—we have seen Trump's techno-accelerationists both systematically dismantle previous administrations' attempts to understand and/ or rein in exponential tech downsides and also bless and turbocharge unfettered frontier tech development, especially with regard to crypto.

The OpenAI Saga

OpenAI provides another example of the tech culture wars, or better said "civil wars," because it took place within the company itself. During the company's five days of drama in November 2023, two of its long-standing board members—Helen Toner and Tasha McCauley—were asked to resign after the OpenAI Board first fired and then rehired the CEO, Sam Altman. His firing was ostensibly for his "not being consistently candid" with the board. But then he was back and the two board members were gone.[13]

Cultural issues at OpenAI seem to have been deeper than the struggle over Sam Altman's leadership—and the ultimate removal of board members who were concerned about his leadership style. OpenAI's former chief scientist and cofounder, Ilya Sutskever (the brains behind ChatGPT), had advocated for stricter guardrails and helped to create a superalignment (safety) team within OpenAI focused on ensuring the safe development of artificial general intelligence (AGI). He was the board member who had delivered the firing message to Sam. But as the tide turned and Sam returned, Ilya was sidelined and so too was his superalignment (or safety) team. Sutskever then left OpenAI a few months later and started his own safety-first company called Safe Superintelligence in June 2024.

And it does not stop there—there have been numerous departures and vocal pronouncements—both anonymous and for attribution—by OpenAI employees and ex-employees as well as others in Silicon Valley voicing deep concerns about how OpenAI was treating the topic of Gen-AI and AGI governance and safety. Concerns include the inability to speak up without fear of retaliation and the disbanding of the superalign-

---

Sidebar 9.1
Selected Comments by Jan Leike, former Head of Safety and Superalignment at OpenAI

According to Jan Leike (on X), "I joined because I thought OpenAI would be the best place in the world to do this research. . . . However, I have been disagreeing with OpenAI leadership about the company's core priorities for quite some time, until we finally reached a breaking point." Leike writes that he believes much more of the company's bandwidth should be focused on security, monitoring, preparedness, safety, and societal impact.

"Building smarter-than-human machines is an inherently dangerous endeavor," he wrote. "OpenAI is shouldering an enormous responsibility on behalf of all of humanity. But over the past years, safety culture and processes have taken a backseat to shiny products."

Sources: Hayden Field, "Current and Former OpenAI Employees Warn of AI's 'Serious Risks' and Lack of Oversight," CNBC, June 4, 2024, www.cnbc.com/2024/06/04/openai-open-ai-risks-lack-of-oversight.html; author.

---

ment team under a leader who also openly voiced concerns and joined Anthropic, a company known for its greater focus on safety. Jan Leike, who had been OpenAI's head of safety/superalignment, wrote quite a few things upon his departure from OpenAI, as summarized in sidebar 9.1.[14]

There is also an open letter from mid 2024 (and a complaint filed with the US Securities and Exchange Commission shortly thereafter) from existing and former (both anonymous and for attribution) employees of OpenAI decrying a culture of repression, retaliation, and fear within the company and the dire need for an anonymous helpline/hotline for concerns to be aired without fear of retaliation. Current and former OpenAI employees published an open letter describing concerns about the AI industry's rapid advancement despite a lack of oversight and a lack of whistleblower protections. "AI companies have strong financial incentives to avoid effective oversight," the employees wrote. "OpenAI, Google, Microsoft and other companies are at the helm of a generative AI arms race—a market that is predicted to top $1 trillion in revenue within a decade."[15]

The OpenAI–Microsoft Connection

To put it bluntly, a responsible tech culture is about the ethos of an entity. It is about the culture that the oversight body, executive management, and, most significantly, the CEO or head of the entity imparts to the overall organization every day—through their actions, through their statements, with their incentive structures, and through their leadership in challenging times.

Is there a chasm between what the leader says on technology and what they do? Do they back up their statements with action when it comes to budgets, resources, and strategy regarding technology and ethics, risk, and responsibility to stakeholders? Is the CEO unwilling to allocate the needed budget for superalignment, or cyberdefenses, tech audits, or additional resources to provide quality control checks—for example, because there is not enough money to go around?

Why does this matter, and why should we care? OpenAI offers important indicia of a deeper and broader cultural malaise, with several ex–board members and key employees loudly and publicly leaving the company because of its culture of secrecy, apparent clamping down on internal speaking up and dissent about its safety practices, and the fact that there is so much polarized sentiment about its CEO, Altman, who is loathed by some, adulated by others.[16]

Whether in the end OpenAI becomes wildly successful financially, going private and or public, making a gazillion dollars for its founders, board members and others, is not the only indicator of success. Success will also be measured on how safely it deploys its GenAI and related tools—will AGI be reached and in a safe and responsible manner? Will the other non-AGI tools and programs be otherwise ethically built—with clean data inputs; properly vetted algorithms; and nondiscriminatory, non-hallucinatory, and clean information outputs?

This all remains to be seen, but the early stages of OpenAI from a tech ethos standpoint do not warm the heart. Perhaps the more recently acquired adults in the room—impressive board members and executives—will steer the company in the right direction. From the CEO oversight standpoint, the signs are not so good, as Altman continues to do what he did before, with many other investments and projects outside OpenAI under way, and his multiple and potentially conflicting roles. He is the CEO, he is a board member, and he is a member of the latest security and safety committee, plus he is pursuing myriad other non-OpenAI tech investments and projects all over the world. Though time will tell, time is not on our side, given the velocity, volatility, and uncertainty of techno change, the asymmetry afforded by its tools to potential wrongdoers, and its interconnectedness with other exponential tech. The need for techno-responsibility has never been greater.

Microsoft's Example

In its continuing relationship with Microsoft, OpenAI may learn a thing or two. Microsoft has, over the past decade, been at the forefront of large tech company good governance and responsibility. Under Nadella's leadership, it has been at the leading edge of establishing responsible AI and relatively secure cyberrisk management and oversight for years, establishing best practices copied by many.

However, in 2023 and 2024 Microsoft had several major setbacks, with cybersecurity events of great magnitude affecting both commercial and government clients. As *Wired* magazine put it: The "US government has a Microsoft Problem. . . . Microsoft has stumbled through a series of major cybersecurity failures over the past few years. Experts say the US government's reliance on its systems means the company continues to get a free pass." Indeed, the piece goes deeper: "The United States government kept buying and using Microsoft products, and senior officials refused to publicly rebuke the tech giant. It was another reminder of how insulated Microsoft has become from virtually any government accountability; . . . that state of affairs is unlikely to change even in the wake of a new report by the Cyber Safety Review Board, . . . a group of government and industry experts, which lambasts Microsoft for failing to prevent one of the worst hacking incidents in the company's recent history. The report says Microsoft's 'security culture was inadequate and requires an overhaul.'"[17]

And as responsible as Microsoft appears to have been on AI and related matters, it is certainly not immune to the rush and brutal competition to win the GenAI race among the biggest tech companies taking place right now. Indeed, Microsoft's lead negotiator with OpenAI during those intense few days in November 2023 when Altman's fate was up in the air, stated, "Speed is even more important than ever; . . . [it would be] an absolutely fatal error in this moment to worry about things that can be fixed later."[18] To which I would add the question: What about things that cannot be fixed later?

This is exactly what the debate at the bleeding edge of exponential technologies is all about. Are you a culture of "move fast and break things," of "don't ask for permission, ask for forgiveness" (which could be deadly when it comes to some of the exponential technologies we explore in this book). Or are you a culture of understanding risks as you find them and guardrail accordingly as you go along—of effective risk management, testing, auditing, transparency, and stakeholder care?

That said, among large tech companies, Microsoft continues to be a leader; in 2019, it adopted what it calls "responsible AI in action," which incorporated these six principles:

> *Fairness*, in which the central question is:
> - How might an AI system allocate opportunities, resources, or information in ways that are fair to the humans who use it?
>
> *Reliability and safety*, in which the central question is:
> - How might the system function well for people across different use conditions and contexts, including ones it was not originally intended for?
>
> *Privacy and security*, in which the central question is:
> - How might the system be designed to support privacy and security?
>
> *Inclusiveness*, in which the central question is:
> - How might the system be designed to be inclusive of people of all abilities?
>
> *Transparency*, in which the central question is:
> - How might people misunderstand, misuse, or incorrectly estimate the capabilities of the system?

Accountability, in which the central question is:

- How can we create oversight so that humans can be accountable and in control?[19]

Microsoft has also demonstrated its commitment to responsible AI when it hired Mustafa Suleyman to be the head of Microsoft AI. Suleyman, who cofounded DeepMind and Inflection AI, has become a leading public voice of exponential tech safety, through his book *The Coming Wave* and many podcast and video appearances. His hiring by Nadella to head up AI at Microsoft is a good sign for the continuation of a more responsible approach to exponential technology at the company.

Microsoft's continuing relationship with OpenAI could cast a bit of a pallor on the future of responsible AI at the company, given that OpenAI itself has not been a paragon of virtue on the topic of GenAI safety at least until now. If there is a major or catastrophic GenAI safety event through OpenAI, who will take the blame? Microsoft or OpenAI? Depending on the details and facts of such a hypothetical case, what would this mean to Microsoft?

Accenture's Blueprint for Responsible AI

Another example of a good culture of exponential tech responsibility can be found in Accenture's work. Accenture has seven principles for operationalizing responsible AI:

1. Human by design
2. Fairness
3. Transparency/explainability/accuracy
4. Safety
5. Accountability
6. Compliance / data privacy / cybersecurity
7. Sustainability[20]

Accenture's program applies not only to its operations but also to its clients' work—a telltale sign of taking responsibility for and understanding the needs of customers and other stakeholders. The "Accenture Blueprint for Responsible AI" begins with an understanding of AI's impact on humans, so it calls the first principle "human by design," focused on how effects are identified and managed. Second, it focuses on "fairness," meaning that all groups affected should be treated equally. "Transparency/explainability/accuracy" refers to making sure all AI use is disclosed, understood, and understandable for confident decision-making. "Safety" is the fourth principle, and it explains that it focuses on "evaluating potential concerns" and taking "action to mitigate harm when deploying AI." "Accountability" comes next, requiring the documentation of an enterprise-wide governance structure that includes clear roles, policies, and responsibilities. "Compliance / data privacy / cybersecurity," the sixth principle, revolves around ensuring legal compliance, AI cyber preparedness, and the protection of data. Finally, "sustainability," the seventh and last principle, focuses on effects on the planet and the need to deploy appropriate steps to mitigate them.[21]

The Athena Alliance Life Cycle Approach to Embedding Responsibility

Borrowing from a collaborative project I cochaired and coauthored at the Athena Alliance (where I serve on the advisory board and in which I am a small investor), embedding ethics in the tech culture must be achieved practically. What exactly does this mean? It means looking at your entity's product or service life cycle, breaking it down, and ensuring that the proper and necessary people, processes, and tools are imbued with ethical analysis and responsible choices—at every step of this life cycle. Here is an overview of the six phases of the Athena Alliance's "AI Governance Playbook" ethical product life cycle approach:

Phase 1: Product Strategy and Design
Phase 2: Data Collection and Preparation
Phase 3: Prompt Engineering, Model Training, and Evaluation (Prerelease)
Phase 4: Model Deployment and Monitoring (Postrelease)
Phase 5: Product Life Cycle Management and Transition Plan
Phase 6: End of Life/End of Service[22]

Phase 1: Product Strategy and Design

The integration of ethics and compliance at the outset of AI and other tech design is essential. This includes considerations about buying versus managing, and alignment with corporate strategy. Ensuring this integration requires a collaborative culture between several key functions, including ethics; diversity, equity, and inclusion; legal; privacy; and quality control experts, as well as engineers, data scientists, and software developers.

Phase 2: Data Collection and Preparation

The data collection and preparation stage should involve specialists responsible for overseeing data provenance, quality, and governance. Their role is to ensure that data handling practices align with ethical standards and regulatory compliance, setting a strong foundation for responsible AI development.

Phase 3: Prompt Engineering, Model Training,
and Evaluation (Prerelease)

Model training and prompt engineering should be done thoughtfully to ensure fairness, mitigate bias, and make good faith efforts to anticipate potential unintended consequences. The aim is to develop AI models that are not only effective but also align with ethical guidelines and regulatory expectations.

Phase 4: Model Deployment and Monitoring (Postrelease)

Once the model (product or service) has been deployed, embed continuous monitoring and feedback loops in the life cycle review process in key areas, including ethics, legal, and regulatory compliance, product safety, and production quality. This phase should also include scenario planning, risk identification, and mitigation and crisis management / incident planning.

Phase 5: Product Life Cycle Management and Transition Plan

Effective product life cycle management hinges on continuous adherence to evolving legal and ethical standards. The focus is on ensuring that the evolution of the AI product is both responsible and sustainable, keeping in mind the long-term implications for the organization, users, and society.

Phase 6: End of Life / End of Service

The end of life or service phase, particularly in cases of product obsolescence or defects, requires a strategic approach to data retention and model repurposing. This phase should include a comprehensive review of data retention practices from an ethical standpoint and explore responsible strategies for the decommissioning or transformation of the models. It should also include a review of affected workflows and downstream tools to ensure a smooth transition when AI tools are removed. This is a crucial stage for learning from past experiences and applying these insights to the future development of products and services.

Using Incentive Structures to Encourage Responsible Innovation

How to use incentive structures to encourage responsible innovation is an important topic that deserves the attention of leaders. I offer the policy ideas set forth in sidebar 9.2 as a conversation starter for organizations that are looking to integrate responsible tech in their management performance incentive structure.

Questions Stakeholders Should Ask About Embedding Responsible Tech Culture

So, with all that said—the ups and downs of a responsible or less-than-responsible tech culture—what are some of the key questions that stakeholders should ask about a company like OpenAI, Anthropic, Mistral, Microsoft, or Google or about how another business, nonprofit, or government agency with techno-responsibilities handles its technology? Here are a few ideas:

1. Does the entity have an effective ethics and compliance and/or corporate responsibility program tied to performance metrics? Do the entity's leaders walk their cultural talk?

Sidebar 9.2
Policy Ideas and Actions for Connecting Responsible Technology and Performance Incentives

- Pollution taxes: These encourage companies to develop greener technologies by making pollution more expensive.
- Low-carbon technology innovation subsidies: Government financial support helps companies developing environmentally friendlier technologies.
- Responsible innovation standards: These frameworks help companies demonstrate their commitment to responsible practices, potentially improving their reputation and investor relations.
- Research funding programs: Programs like the EU's Horizon 2020 support responsible research and innovation projects.
- Regulatory reform: Efforts to balance public safety with innovation allow beneficial technologies to reach the market faster.
- Public engagement requirements: These mandates for companies, which involve stakeholders and citizens in the innovation process, ensure that technologies align with societal needs.
- Carbon trading systems: These market-based mechanisms incentivize companies to reduce emissions through technological innovation.
- Innovation compensation: This high compensation is an incentive for employees of companies that successfully develop responsible technologies.
- Liability frameworks: These balanced approaches make firms responsible for downside risks while still allowing for useful experimentation.

Source: Author.

---

2. Do they apply these principles to their technology creation or deployment? Do they have a phased approach to developing or acquiring and deploying new tech that integrates an ethical and responsible lens into the process?

3. What is the nature of the entity's speak up / listen up / act up culture? Does it exist, is it merely wallpaper, or is it worse: a culture of silence and retaliation?

4. What is the entity's reputation in the marketplace? Good, bad, ugly? And does leadership care?

5. What is the role of the board or other oversight entity over the tech ethos of the entity? Proactive and serious? Laid back and passive?

6. Is the board proactive in overseeing technology? Has it commissioned any AI studies or asked about the integration of tech into the entity's ethics program? Does it understand the technology, let alone the intersection of ethics, responsibility, and technology?

Actions Leaders Should Take to Embed Responsible Tech Culture

Here are actions leaders should take to embed responsible tech culture:

1. The CEO and executive team ethics and responsibility video must match the audio—are these executives walking the talk?

2. Build an ethics code that is based on inclusive, adaptive, and practical behavior with a deep speak up, listen up, act up, and improve focus, and have a continuous feedback loop.

3. The oversight body must always hold the CEO accountable for a culture of responsibility through performance metrics, strategic milestones, and other measures.

4. It is critically important to embed ethics and responsibility in the techno–life cycle—to put ethics and responsibility in the tech loop.

5. Have a team of interconnected, interdisciplinary, multifaceted experts ensuring responsibility in the technology life cycle on an ongoing basis.

A Final Word on Ethos and the Exponential Governance Mindset

As we stated at the beginning of this chapter, establishing and maintaining a responsible tech culture, an ethos of ethics in your entity, is largely and primarily a core responsibility for an entity's leadership. We have seen countless examples of companies gone seriously wrong, and almost always the causation or at least correlation can be traced back to—who was the CEO/leader? What kind of an oversight board was there? And were the staff and others able to speak up freely without fear of retaliation? It does not matter what type of entity you are—nongovernmental organization, business, government agency—if your leader does not model ethics and responsibility, and your board or oversight body looks the other way or is simply subordinate to executive leadership, frankly all bets are off.[23]

It really is up to the Sam Altmans, Satya Nadellas, Elon Musks, Mustapha Suleimans, Marc Andreessens, and other leaders to set the right tone, not only for the tech culture of an organization but also for the overall ethos of the organizations they lead and the safety or fear they engender in their stakeholders. And it is up to their oversight boards to hold them accountable.

An Ethos-Themed Thought Experiment

If you are a shareholder, owner, or other key stakeholder in an entity and want to think further about its ethos and culture, I invite you to engage in this thought experiment: Is your organization embedding a responsible tech culture, or is it at least trying to? Consider these questions:

- How is your executive leader leading from a culture standpoint? By example? Not really? Or by the wrong kind of example—by not doing what he or she is saying?
- Are staff and contractors able to report safety and other concerns without fear of retaliation? Is there a program to promote reporting—including anonymous reporting—without fear of retaliation?
- Does the board hold the CEO and executive management accountable and responsible for more than revenues and profits—for actually taking concrete steps to embed a responsible tech culture?
- Does the board receive quarterly reports on ethics, culture, and performance-incentive metrics?

10

IMPACT

Integrating Stakeholders into the Tech Loop

This chapter focuses on the importance of leaders and decision-makers understanding and integrating key tech stakeholders and their primary interests into an organization's technology life cycle—from invention or acquisition to usage and deployment. To do this, we need to understand who our key tech stakeholders are. Concurrently, we also need to understand what their key issues are—whether economic, environmental, social, technological, or governance. Technology issues, risks, and opportunities interconnect directly and deeply with the domains of ESG (environment, society, governance) and SDG (the UN's Sustainable Development Goals). In my 2020 book *Gloom to Boom*, I coined the term "ESGT" to include technology directly with environment, society, and governance. Indeed, we have seen increasingly how leading practitioners, companies, and entities have integrated tech into sustainability and ESG considerations.

Now, in the Age of Pandora, with the explosion of new tech and exponential tech, the parameters of which are constantly metamorphizing, we urgently need to comprehend effects on key stakeholders. Think of the child in the metaverse without guardrails, or the social media content moderator viewing violence and death on the Internet, or the innocent civilian caught in the crosshairs of autonomous drone warfare or exploding pagers, or the enormous water needs to cool data centers in geographies suffering from droughts. These are, respectively, social, governance, and environmental effects on tech stakeholders—children, workers, communities, and the environment.

Exponential tech has effects in all sorts of ways—positive and negative, predictable and unpredictable, known and unknown—and that is why the onus is on those who invent, invest, deploy, and reap the benefits from such technologies to understand who their key stakeholders are and how such stakeholders in the tech loop are affected.

How entities manage their tech stakeholders will ultimately affect their reputation and trustworthiness. Whether key stakeholders are share holders, employees, customers, users, communities, citizens, or taxpayers does not really matter. What matters is that each entity and its leadership purposefully identify its top tech stakeholders, understand how an entity's tech deployment touches and affects its key stakeholders, and whether and how it takes responsibility to protect stakeholders from downsides and share in upsides.

What Is "Integrating Stakeholders into the Tech Loop" and Why Should We Care?

"Stakeholders in the tech loop" is a play on words to describe three concepts. First, in the world of technology, we are increasingly hearing about "humans in the loop" of new technologies, especially those that are unpredictable, volatile, uncertain, potentially, or actually dangerous. It will become increasingly important for all decision-makers to have the right stakeholders (and their interests represented) in the tech loop so we can understand and be empowered to make decisions. This becomes especially important in worse case scenarios, so that a human in or on the loop can flick the proverbial kill-switch. Second, knowing and understanding who the key stakeholders with a stake in your entity's tech are (including its strategy, talent, products, and services) is a critical element of success for any type of organization in this Age of Pandora. And third, I underscore the "tech loop" because the intent is to make sure that your key stakeholders' interests are in your particular technology use life cycle.

Humans In, On, or Out of the Loop

Having "humans in the loop" (HITL) is essential for a wide variety of checks and balances on the development of exponential technologies. Talking strictly about HITL, we are mostly talking about having human staff, subcontractors, experts, and others in the tech loop, as it were. We hear this concept frequently in the discussion of autonomous vehicles and autonomous weapons—that is, tech that can make its own decisions such as drones in war zones, but also increasingly drones for commercial and other nonmilitary purposes. This would include, for example, self-driving cars supposedly programmed to avoid hitting pedestrians but failing to do so.[1] To the extent these autonomous vehicles or robots end up "making decisions" that can affect the welfare and even life of living beings, we need to get "humans in the loop" to pull the kill-switch when and if needed, which, for example, if it is in an autonomous vehicle, might mean the driver/passenger.

The military and defense sector uses three concepts related to this theme of humans in the loop. They have a concept of "human *in* the loop," meaning that humans initiate and carry out actions regarding a weapon (which, in this case, is not fully autonomous) making decisions in real time. They have another concept called "human *on* the loop," meaning that humans involved in autonomous weapons management are able to react and abort an action. And then there is the scariest concept of all—"human *out* of the loop," which means that there are no humans in or on the loop of a truly autonomous weapon with zero human involvement, period.[2]

Moving into the civilian tech arena, according to Google Cloud, HITL is: "a collaborative approach that integrates human input and expertise into the life cycle of machine learning (ML) and artificial intelligence systems. Humans actively participate in the training, evaluation, or operation of ML models, providing valuable guidance, feedback, and annotations. Through this collaboration, HITL aims to enhance the accuracy, reliability, and adaptability of ML systems, harnessing the unique capabilities of both humans and machines."[3] From Google's standpoint, HITL refers to humans involved in the nitty gritty, frontline essential tasks of providing labels for training data, evaluating the performance of ML models, providing feedback to ML models, actively learning from data labeled by humans and reinforcement learning where ML models learn by trial and error with human inputs.

In an important critique of the concept of HITL regarding autonomous weapons, these concerns have been raised by Kobi Leins and Anja Kaspersen, as indicated by the noted categories:

1. You cannot have *"meaningful interaction"* with data or sensors, or actuators at the time of data collection and operation.
2. You cannot *"meaningfully interact"* with active code.
3. People get bored when working with autonomous systems.
4. The complexity, speed, and scale of many autonomous, and even automatic, systems do not allow time to challenge them.
5. If *"meaningful human interaction on the loop"* is remote, there are even greater risks.
6. The term "human" usually means a fairly narrow type of human, which is not representative of broader humanity or humankind.
7. Skills required to understand complex adaptive systems will be lost with increased automation.[4]

Although we are nowhere close to understanding how and what to do with these various "humans in / on / out of the loop" considerations, why make it even more complex by introducing the concept of "stakeholders in the tech loop"? It is very simple: For an organization operating in the Age of Pandora to build or deploy responsible exponential technology, it not only needs to understand how to integrate the human in/on the tech loop, such an entity also needs to understand and integrate the interests, perspectives, expectations, welfare, and health of its key stakeholders.

Know Your Tech Stakeholders

So who are your key tech stakeholders? Hopefully, most entities—whether in business, government, or civil society—know both intuitively and

Figure 10.1 An Array of Potential Stakeholders
Source: Author.

proactively who their most important stakeholders are. If that exercise has not been consciously carried out by management and the board—what are you waiting for? Figure 10.1 presents a wide array (not an exhaustive list) of potential stakeholders you can consider.

Beyond a simple exercise of understanding who an entity's primary stakeholders are based on the overall organizational footprint and purpose, every organization should go one step further to understand and consider who its most important *tech* stakeholders are. And, of course, such tech stakeholders will be different depending on the entity. If, on one hand, you are an average non–purely tech company or other type of organization, you are probably purchasing tech from the large tech companies and your tech stakeholders will not be that varied. You still need to know how the tech you are purchasing is incorporated into your products and services and thus, customers, consumers, and users must be among your tech stakeholders. On the other hand, if you are the creator and developer of tech from the smallest start up to the largest tech company, your key tech stakeholders will be broader and more diverse. Figure 10.2 provides an example of the latter.

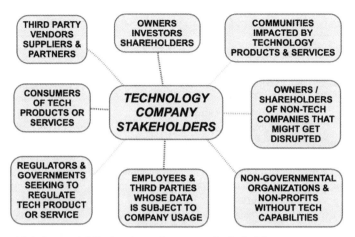

Figure 10.2 Potential Technology Company Stakeholders
Source: Author.

Know Your Stakeholders' Tech Issues, Risks, and Opportunities

Complementary to knowing your stakeholders (and knowing your tech stakeholders) is the critical corollary of knowing their key issues, concerns, risks, and opportunities. The importance of matching your top stakeholders to their key issues has never been more critical in this age of stakeholder capitalism and Pandora. A lot of work has been done in the world of sustainability, ESG/ESGT, and SDGs to help guide us, as shown in table 10.1.[5]

Just Capital's Stakeholder and ESG Issue Framework

Just Capital is a nongovernmental organization that assesses seventeen ESG issues affecting five key stakeholder groups by scouring the publicly available documents of close to a thousand publicly traded United States–based companies. It uses these data, among other things, to produce annual overall rankings. While in the larger global scheme of things this is a limited universe, it still provides useful insights and a methodology that illustrates my point about entities identifying their key tech stakeholders and matching them to their most important—even material—tech issues.[6] So it is useful to review what Just Capital has done. First, it

Table 10.1 A Sampling of ESGT Issues, Risks, and Opportunities

Environmental	Social	Governance	Technological
Climate change	Human rights	Corporate	Cybersecurity
Sustainability	Labor rights	governance	AI and generative AI
Water	Child labor	Leadership	Agentic AI
Air	Human trafficking	Culture	Data mining
Earth	Human slavery	Performance	Surveillance
Carbon emissions	Health and safety	metrics/incentives	Internet of Things
Energy efficiency	Workplace	Business ethics	Automation
Natural resources	conditions	Corruption and	Robotics
Hazardous waste	Workplace violence	bribery	Biotechnology
Recycling	Product safety	Fraud	Automated robotic
Clean tech	Fair trade	Money laundering	processing
Green buildings	Discrimination	Taxation	Misinformation
Biodiversity	Harassment	Anticompetition,	Disinformation
Animal rights	Data privacy	antitrust	Deep fakes
Pandemics	Bullying/mobbing	Geopolitical risk	Social engineering
	Diversity, equity,	Lobbying	Biometrics
	inclusion	Government	Wearables
		relations	Nanotechnology
		Regulatory	
		compliance	
		Conflicts of interest	

Source: Author.

defines five key stakeholder groups, weighting their importance in 2025 as follows:

1. Workers: measuring how a company invests in its employees (39 percent ranking weight).
2. Customers: measuring how a company treats its customers (26 percent ranking weight).
3. Shareholders and governance: measuring how a company prioritizes good governance (13 percent ranking weight).
4. Communities: measuring how a company supports its communities (13 percent ranking weight).
5. Environment: measuring how a company minimizes environmental impact (9 percent ranking weight).

Table 10.2 Just Capital's 2025 Seventeen Stakeholder Issues

Issue	Ranking Weight (%)
Pays a fair, living wage	11.6
Acts ethically at the leadership level	10.0
Protects workers' health and safety	9.8
Communicates transparently	7.7
Provides benefits and work/life balance	7.2
Supports workforce retention, advancement, and training	6.9
Treats customers fairly	6.3
Offers fair pricing	6.1
Creates jobs in the United States	5.6
Protects customer privacy	5.5
Addresses human rights in supply chain	4.6
Fosters an inclusive workplace	4.0
Minimizes pollution	3.6
Supports strong governance	3.2
Uses resources efficiently	2.9
Combats climate change	2.5
Gives back to local communities	2.5

Source: Just Capital, http://justcapital.com.

Just Capital then identifies seventeen key stakeholder issues on which it grades companies, ranking them once a year on the results. The issues and their relative ranking weights are summarized in table 10.2.[7] Almost every one of the issues it identifies—traditionally viewable as ESG or sustainability related issues—has an intersection with or connection to technology or technological effects. From the notion that workers need jobs created near them and need to be reskilled and educated for the new technologies to being treated with fairness, work/life balance, and privacy rights unviolated.

In case you are curious, table 10.3 provides the ranking for some of the leading publicly traded United States–based technology companies for 2025. It is quite a range when you consider the overall ranking of companies (there are 1000 on the list). Table 10.4 highlights the range of where the Magnificent Seven technology companies rank, and this range could not be any greater—from Alphabet at the top, at 19, all the way down to Tesla, at 756 (out of the 1,000 US companies that make up the US Russell 1,000 Index).

Table 10.3 Just Capital's 2025 Rankings of Top Ten US
Technology Companies

Company (Sector)	Overall Ranking
Hewlett Packard Enterprise Company (computer services)	1
HP Inc. (technology hardware)	2
Accenture (commercial support / technology services)	5
Applied Materials (semiconductors and equipment)	13
ServiceNow Inc (software)	16
Alphabet Inc. (Internet)	19
Advanced Micro Devices (AMD) (semiconductors and equipment)	23
Akamai Technologies (Internet)	29
Salesforce (software)	30
Intel Corp (semiconductors & equipment	36

Source: Just Capital, http://justcapital.com.

A special comment on Tesla and Meta is warranted, since they both received extremely low rankings in both 2024 and 2025 (in 2024 they were at the same level of 697th out of 937 companies analyzed by Just Capital). In the case of Tesla, the rankings suffered especially because of very poor stakeholder ratings from the customers, workers, and shareholders stakeholder groups. As Just Capital noted in a special commentary in 2024: "Tesla's vehicle technology, specifically its driver-assistance system, has been involved in a number of crashes. This year it was found that the amount of crashes and fatalities related to the system is far higher than previously reported which resulted in an investigation into possible fraudulent marketing, per reports Tesla recently recalled 2 million vehicles to address this technology specifically. Tesla will receive the Most Severe (III) treatment, resulting in the lowest score in the Shareholders Stakeholder due to the role of company leadership in this issue." Thus, quality, fraud, and leadership trust are all issues intertwined with Tesla's technology—some of it exponential.

In the case of Meta in 2024, its poorest stakeholder ratings by far came from the customer category. In fact, none of its other stakeholder ratings fell below the industry average, though the rating from shareholders was close to below average. Just Capital also made a special comment about Meta's low ranking in 2024—the company "faced growing reports

Table 10.4 Just Capital's 2025 Rankings of the "Magnificent Seven" US Technology Companies

Company	Overall Ranking
Alphabet Inc.	19
Nvidia	43
Apple	75
Microsoft	151
Amazon	267
Meta Platforms Inc.	412
Tesla	756

Source: Just Capital, http://justcapital.com.

of its involvement in the spread of misinformation, hate speech, and other discriminatory and incendiary content on its platforms." Indeed, Meta received one of the lowest scores of all 937 companies in 2024 (though it did a little better in 2025) because of the intertwining of these serious tech-enabled issues and risks and, critically, leadership trust issues.

In early 2025, coinciding with the return of the second Trump administration, Mark Zuckerberg announced a series of policies and pivots to a Trump-favorable corporate stance, including lifting critically important stakeholder safety guardrails, replacing safety and trust personnel with a "community notes" system akin to that implemented at X (formerly Twitter) by Elon Musk. These measures are likely to open up the floodgates of algorithms promoting misinformation and disinformation on that platform.[8] These tech company pivots to fewer instead of more guardrails to combat the disinformation tsunami do not augur well for the protection of users, especially vulnerable populations, and for the free flow and protection of facts over lies and manipulation, not just in the United States but worldwide.

Examples of Matching Tech Stakeholders to Tech Issues

In this section, we discuss how some important tech issues affect key stakeholders to illustrate the importance of leaders and decision-makers paying attention to these effects as well as the expectations of their stake-holders.

Tech Workers and Mental Health

When a social media company (e.g., Meta, X, Threads, and YouTube) hires employees or subcontractors in a country in the emerging world or Global South for content moderation roles that focus on scouring the media for inappropriate content (violence, sexual content, pedophilia, and other highly disturbing images and text), several things are going on at once. First, the company can claim that it has a diversified, international employee/subcontractor population. Second, the company is saving money because similarly skilled workers in the developed world are likely to be more expensive and have more legal rights from a labor standpoint.

Most important, however, Kenya-based employees in the case of Meta, for example, who are at the cutting edge of the most toxic social media feeds, witnessing some of the worst human behavior—some real, others manipulated via GenAI tools, and yet others pure misinformation and disinformation—are getting paid relatively little to do potentially psychologically traumatizing work with little or no job security or benefits.[9] This one example shows the effects of a tech company's products/services on key stakeholders—in this case, employees and contractors.

Precrisis Blockchain-Based Payments Distribution in Nepal

In Nepal, the company Rahat (winner of digital currency company Circle's 2024 "Unlocking Impact Pitch Competition") employs blockchain and smart contracts to ensure rapid, accurate aid payouts to individuals in disaster-prone regions before a crisis strikes—enabling them to receive payments directly on mobile devices, even in low-tech environments. Rahat can be used in low-tech environments, with SMS- and USSD-based features for beneficiaries without smartphones. Beneficiaries can spend their USDC (Circle's US-dollar-backed digital currency) at participating vendors to easily buy goods and services or cash out for local currency. This system supports financial resilience and demonstrates how technology can bolster disaster response.[10]

Drivers and Surveillance

Another example of effects on a key tech stakeholder, not from a tech company but from an insurance company that has adopted tech tools, looks like this: When an insurance company deploys AI and telematic tools on its insured population—for example, to track a driver's driving habits in an insured car—that insurance company gathers a ton of data about that driver (or drivers of that car), much of which may be intensely private. Both the insurer and the insured in this case are deploying and being subjected to technology tools—mostly AI- and GenAI-driven surveillance and data collection.[11] The insured in this case is not only a stakeholder (as a customer) but also a tech stakeholder (as the subject of surveillance and data collection). Why? Because, by deploying surveillance software and other AI or GenAI into a person's car, that person has become a tech stakeholder, and the insurance company has become an exponential tech operator.

Children in the Metaverse

One of the most serious concerns in immersive technology—including the metaverse, augmented reality, virtual reality, and what we are now calling spatial computing—is the need to safeguard everyone, especially vulnerable populations who participate in such environments. Just as in the "real" world, harassment, discrimination, and even virtual sexual assaults have unfortunately occurred, and increasingly so in these immersive environments. But the worst effects can happen to children who, as with social media and the Internet generally, can be seriously harmed in the metaverse because their brains have not yet fully developed. XRSI, a nonprofit dedicated to helping build safety and inclusion in the emerging tech ecosystem, has published numerous publications over the years on safety in the metaverse, including reports focused on children. Its recent recommendations include the right to experiential authenticity, the right to emotional privacy, the right to behavioral privacy, and the right to human agency.

Additionally, and based on work done in Australia developing safety-by-design standards, XRSI has been advocating for such standards at the inception of the technology.[12] Australia was the first country to adopt strict social media laws to prevent children younger than sixteen years from accessing social media. The Online Safety Amendment (Social Media Minimum Age) Act of 2024, which is being implemented in 2025, applies to accounts on certain social media platforms and is part of a broader national strategy to create safer digital spaces for everyone.[13]

Data Centers in the Desert

Two other key tech stakeholders all over the world are the environment and communities, which are bound together by the issue of energy and water consumption by ever-expanding data centers deployed by large tech companies to service the insatiable hunger for compute power. Compute requires not only energy and power needs—much of which the more responsible large tech companies are trying to meet with renewable and other (nuclear) energy sources—but also a disproportionate quantity of water is needed to cool these energy intensive centers.

Take, for instance, the impact of the exponential growth in GenAI tools, products, and services on the consumption of energy. In the International Energy Agency's Electricity 2024 forecast, they project that data center electricity consumption in 2026 will be double to that of 2022, reaching the equivalent of Japan's total consumption—about 1,000 terawatts. This increased consumption directly affects corporate carbon emissions—indeed, Microsoft reported in 2024 that their carbon emissions were up almost 30 percent from 2020 because it built additional data centers to process its GenAI development.[14]

In terms of water impact, the story is similarly a cause of concern. Sticking with the effects of large technology companies on water, it is estimated that Google's data centers consumed about 5 billion gallons of fresh water (or 20 billion liters) in 2022 for cooling purposes. According to a study, Google's data centers used 20 percent more water in 2022 than in 2021, and Microsoft's used 34 percent more.

Communities and the environment are critical tech stakeholders that present a series of issues, risks, and opportunities that technology companies must take into account. The good news is that there is a surge in the development and adoption of more sustainable technologies to help create data center cooling technologies, new cooling methods, and less-energy-intensive chips.[15] In late 2024, there was suddenly a huge push by some of the biggest tech companies—like Amazon, Microsoft, and Google—to develop and eventually adopt new forms of modular nuclear energy production as well, one of which is being considered for the Three Mile Island location, which had been shuttered since 2019. The most serious US nuclear reactor accident ever recorded happened at this location in 1979.[16]

Technologically Empowered *Favelas*

Accenture shares a case study of supporting economic empowerment of women in impoverished urban environments (*favelas*) in Brazil, where the company lent its technological expertise to a local nonprofit to create technological architecture and app development to address economic conditions locally. The project, called ASMARA, provides a way for women living in these urban environments to sell products door-to-door to generate income through a digital model that allows retail companies to donate and distribute a variety of their products to the *favelas*. This project was expected to support 15,000 women and their families in São Paulo in 2024 and involves the creation of a new program that collects data to create development programs including housing, urban renovation, and workforce inclusion.[17] Once again, here the tech stakeholders are local urban communities, specifically poor families and their heads of families, mostly women, who are benefiting from a three-way collaboration between a technology company providing the tech savvy, a local nonprofit providing the human resources, and the local business community providing materials and products.

Tech Materiality, Life Cycles, Reputation, and Trust

In this section, we review several additional considerations relating to impact that organizational leaders should consider in tackling the theme of this chapter—integrating stakeholders into the tech loop.

Building a Tech-Inclusive Materiality Matrix

Typically, a materiality matrix allows a business to plot key environmental, social, governance, and other business issues, risks, and opportunities on x/y axes to understand which of those issues are the most material to the organization on two fronts: the business and business model, on one hand; and key stakeholders, on the other hand. Figure 10.3 provides an example of such a matrix from a leading technology company—Advanced Micro Devices (AMD), which ranked highly on Just Capital's Rankings—9th in 2024 and 23rd in 2025 of top 1,000 publicly traded companies. Thus, it is not a surprise to see that it has engaged in this exercise.

A look figure 10.3 reveals that there are several key tech issues in AMD's materiality matrix. At the highest materiality level, the mostly tech-related issues they identify are "energy efficiency of products" and "responsible AI in product use." And at a medium materiality level, they identify "technology for social impact (digital impact)," "products security and data privacy," and "products as climate solutions."

Integrating Stakeholders into the Tech Product Life Cycle

Finally, once you have a good sense of who your key tech stakeholders are and what their most important tech issues, risks, and opportunities are, and you have plotted them on a materiality matrix, another important exercise is to integrate those key stakeholders in one form or another into your company's or entity's technology deployment life cycle. If we use a fictional government agency as our example, and the Athena Alliance AI Governance Playbook product and service life cycle model (which we already partly explored in chapter 9), we might consider the six phases discussed in the next subsections in integrating the interests of key stakeholders into the tech life cycle. This governmental agency example is that much more poignant at the time of this writing as the effects of the Trump administration's Department of Government Efficiency takeover of federal departments and agencies seems to be wreaking havoc, chaos, and potentially long-lasting effects on government technology infrastruc-

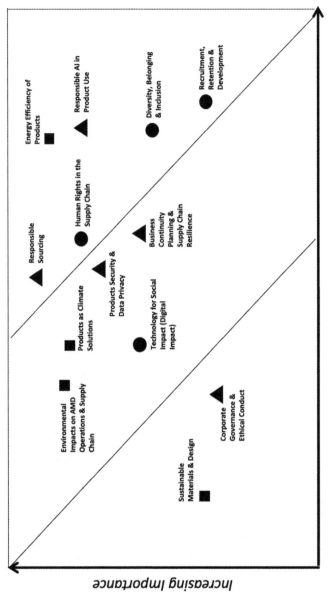

Figure 10.3 Sample Company Materiality Matrix: AMD

Source: AMD.

ture and software programs, underscoring the critical importance of what we share here, even more than before.

Phase 1: Product Strategy and Design

If you are a consumer of tech rather than a developer of tech, your responsibility as a government agency (or other entity) will be to evaluate the creator of the technology in the supply chain to ensure that ethics and safety are built into the tech (whether software or hardware).

Phase 2: Data Collection and Preparation

Continuing with the government agency example, to the extent that the government is collecting data or purchasing data, it needs to ensure that the data supplier or aggregator is doing so in compliance with applicable laws and regulations.

Phase 3: Prompt Engineering, Model Training, and Evaluation (Prerelease)

If the agency in question is actually developing software and algorithms—in other words, it has an engineering department—during the prerelease period, a conscious effort at understanding who the principal stakeholders are in the development of this policy should be introduced into the development of the product/service.

Phase 4: Model Deployment and Monitoring (Postrelease)

Likewise, in the postrelease period, a proactive approach to understanding the impact of the model on stakeholders must be made to ensure that no harm, no quality issues, and no other downsides occur.

Phase 5: Product Life Cycle Management and Transition Plan

Once the product or service—in this case, a government agency's policy implementation deploying technology solutions—is well embedded in practice, there should be periodic monitoring, auditing, and testing of the product/service; and to the extent it is running its course, preparation for sunsetting, always keeping in mind stakeholder effects in the process.

Phase 6: End of Life / End of Service

Finally, when it comes to sunsetting and terminating the life of a tech product or service, the government agency in question (or other entity) must consider the impact on the most directly involved stakeholders.

Know Your Impact: Reputation and Trust in the Balance

A final consideration that should always be part of management and the board's oversight of its organization's creation, use, or deployment of technology is to understand the reputational downsides and upsides and their trust implications. First, leaders and organizations need to understand that their mishandling or negligence on technology issues does not only have potential financial implications (in the forms of fines, lawsuits, and regulatory investigations), it most certainly can have reputational costs, which can last longer and be more costly than short-term financial costs. There are many cases of reputation risk gone wrong over the years and the long tail of consequences to an organization. Consider the example of the Boeing 737 Max crisis, which first erupted in 2018 with the firm's brand new jetliner plunging into the sea near Indonesia and the next one in 2019 near Ethiopia. The corporate response was weak and slow. Serious engineering and technical problems were uncovered, with the most important conclusion of all being that the engineering and quality culture at Boeing had taken a back seat to a culture of greed and profit-making above all.[18]

In today's world, where brands rely increasingly on intangible value—to the tune of up to 80 percent of their full valuation—it is critically important for leaders to consider what their reputation is for technological issues, risks, and opportunities as part of their overall reputation. Harris/Axios published an annual ranking of most reputable organizations in 2024, and the relevant rankings for tech companies include those displayed here:[19]

1. Nvidia
4. Sony

9. Apple

10. Samsung

16. Amazon

17. Google

18. Microsoft

20. IBM

32. Dell

63. Tesla Motors

68. OpenAI

95. TikTok

97. Meta

100. Trump Organization (including Truth Social)

Reputation is inextricably tied to leadership trust. While much has been written about this topic, I will leave the reader with this thought: the key connector between stakeholders and an entity is in the concept of leadership trust—trust in management, the executive team, and the board. As we saw earlier in this chapter, trust in leaders like Mark Zuckerberg of Meta and Elon Musk of Tesla was part of the reason their ratings were almost rock bottom under the Just Capital rankings for 2024 and not much better in 2025. I would also posit that part of the reason why several companies are at the high end of the Axios/Harris reputation rankings is because of their good-to-great leadership (think Satya Nadella of Microsoft and Tim Cook of Apple). In both the Nadella and Cook cases, we see leaders who have been in place for a lengthy period (Nadella succeeded Steve Ballmer in 2015, and Cook succeeded Steve Jobs when he died in 2011). In both cases, their companies have achieved high positions on rankings by Best Places to Work, Glassdoor, Just Capital, Harris/Axios, and others over the years, displaying a consistency of culture, employee satisfaction, benefits, and focus. And in terms of results, both companies under these two CEOs have been among the most financially and operationally successful of all global companies over the past decade.

As Warren Buffett is said to have stated many decades ago, a reputation is built over years and can be lost in days. Trust is also something that builds over years and can be lost overnight in our rapid-fire environment of social media, misinformation, and disinformation.

What Stakeholders Should Ask Relevant Organizations About Integrating Stakeholders into the Tech Loop

Stakeholders need to ask relevant organizations questions like these to integrate stakeholders into the tech loop:

1. Who is a stakeholder in your tech loop and why?
2. What is your oversight body / board doing about tech stakeholder effects—good, bad, ugly—and do they understand them?
3. What is management doing about tech development—inputs, process, outputs?
4. Is the management structure appropriate to properly gauge tech risk and opportunity effects on stakeholders?
5. Is there such a thing as a tech council, digital transformation body, or interdisciplinary team that is actually asking the right multifaceted questions about technology at your entity?
6. Is there something equivalent to a kill-switch—humans in the loop who can stop harmful effects?

Key Leadership Takeaways

These are key leadership takeaways:

1. Know your tech stakeholders—who are they, what are their expectations of you?
2. Make sure the issues that are near and dear to your tech stakeholders are included in your governance, risk management, strategy developments, and scenario planning.
3. Understand the impact of your products on your key stakeholders.

4. Connect the dots to the larger social, planetary footprint: the SDGs, your license to operate, the future of humankind, life on Earth (biodiversity, humanity).

A Closing Word on Impact and the Exponential Governance Mindset

Integrating stakeholders into the tech loop is one of the foremost responsibilities of organizational leaders in this Age of Pandora. Leaders must focus on first understanding and then including and integrating stakeholders' interests and expectations into the tech loop—from tech inception to tech sunsetting. It is a leader's responsibility to make sure that stakeholders are protected from tech downsides, on one hand, and that they fully benefit from these technologies' promises and upsides, on the other hand.

Leaders of an organization need to be hyperfocused on how exponential technologies that they have invented, acquired, developed, deployed, or managed affect their key stakeholders and whether the interests and expectations of such stakeholders are properly integrated into the entity's technology loop. Hence the term "stakeholders in the tech loop."

11

RESILIENCE

Deploying Polyrisk and Polycrisis Preparedness

What is resilience in the Age of Pandora? Put very simply, it means understanding that because we live in a "polyrisk" and "polycrisis" world, we need to be as prepared as possible to survive and thrive through it all. As the fourth element of the exponential governance mindset, resilience is about focusing on developing the personal and organizational resilience—polyrisk and polycrisis preparedness—that is needed in this age of rapid and often-dangerous challenge and change. It means that leaders must be continuously prepared for what is next and have the necessary tools to learn, mitigate, and/or deal with downsides while fully taking advantage of upsides. It is a process of continuous learning, analysis, monitoring, improvement, pivoting, and action.

Deploying polyrisk and polycrisis preparedness means that organizational leaders need to consider and integrate technology and exponential technology data and cases into their risk management, crisis readiness, business continuity, people, and asset security and protection—especially through scenario planning. It means that continuous polyrisk and polycrisis preparedness must be part of what executives, boards, and staff do normally and regularly, so that when (not if) the next crisis or polycrisis occurs, the organization and its people are ready to deal with it proactively and successfully.

In this chapter, we start with the big picture of risk and polyrisk by reviewing the larger interconnected and multifaceted global strategic risks identified by the World Economic Forum (WEF) in its work. The WEF is a global think tank founded over fifty years ago and headquartered in Geneva that is best known for its annual Davos conference of business, social, and political leaders but is also very well regarded for its numerous councils, research, and publications focused on what is next on the global agenda, especially technology, innovation, and sustainability. Next, we go a little deeper into an overview of the exponential tech risk landscape generally and then more specifically, looking at the universe of AI and GenAI risk; and reviewing several key resources and developments in governance, including the European Union's AI Act, the AI Risk Repository, and frontline risk examples. The chapter wraps up with a couple of interesting examples of polyrisk convergence—including digital twins and the coming together (or blurring of lines) between the physical and virtual in the world of cybertech.

Deploying Polyrisk and Polycrisis Preparedness: What Is It and Why Should We Care?

For an organization, it is no longer just about having good risk management and some form of crisis management and business continuity in place. It is also about having polyrisk intelligence and polycrisis preparedness. What does this mean, and why should we care? It means having appropriate components of preparedness for foreseeable and even unforeseeable eventualities—an enterprise risk management (ERM) system—in place and proactive risk governance from your board that is customized for your organization as well as the tools for crisis management (team and plan) and its aftermath and recovery period—business continuity. Polyrisk intelligence means understanding that we live in times with multiple, overlapping risks, including tech and exponential tech risks.

Just consider how you and/or your organization would manage under these scenarios:

- What do you do if you discover an AI deep fake video about yourself on Facebook or X?

- If there is disinformation in the form of viral social media about your company or one of your colleagues, what do you do?
- When a ransomware attack closes down your company's computers, do you have a backup plan that can be deployed offline? Have you backed up essential assets to remote, disconnected, siloed servers? Do you know how to interact with the ransom demanders?
- Someone in your organization receives an envelope with white powder falling out of it; are you ready to deal with this physical, possibly biological threat?
- You are in a robotaxi that gets lost and has an accident; what is your plan?
- A drone attack has bombed an industrial facility next to yours; what is your next move?
- You are the human in the loop of a semiautonomous robotic arm that has just gone haywire; do you know how to apply a kill-switch?

I use the term "polyrisk" because I think it is a necessary addition to our repertoire for understanding risk in the Age of Pandora. It is a useful and complementary consideration for the now-more-established term "polycrisis." We saw "polycrisis" pop up in the 2023 WEF "Global Risks Report." The term dates back to the 1970s and was more recently popularized by the historian Adam Tooze, who explained in an interview with Radio Davos that "it's an idea that was launched by a French theorist of complexity called Edgar Morin, and then it was picked up by Jean-Claude Juncker, the president of the European Commission, in 2016, to describe the experience of trying to govern Europe when you had to deal with the Greek debt crisis, Putin's first aggression against Ukraine and the rumblings of Brexit in the background, and the refugee crisis in Syria spilling over into Europe." And "If you're feeling confused and as though everything is impacting you all at the same time, this is not a personal, private experience; . . . this is actually a collective experience."[1] Indeed, according to the 2023 WEF "Global Risks Report," experts examining the short- and long-term challenges the planet is facing found the risk of polycrises "where disparate crises interact such that the overall impact far exceeds the sum of each part is growing."[2]

Similar to the meaning of polycrisis, my concept "polyrisk" is intended to represent the fact that no risk exists in isolation and that, in the rapidly changing risk landscape, we need a term that represents the idea of compound, multifaceted risk that is continuously evolving and overlaps other risks. Figure 11.1 represents the picture I asked ChatGPT4o to create for me by describing what I envisioned.

Think about each globe in figure 11.1 as manifesting one complex risk, like cyberinsecurity, which by definition has many different manifestations and facets—advanced persistent threats, ransomware, phishing, social engineering, misinformation, disinformation, and more. Then think of another globe representing geopolitical risk (which is also deeply multifaceted) and a third globe representing risk associated with autonomous weapons programmed with GenAI. Now put these all together, and the multifaceted polyrisk we might be talking about is the war in Ukraine, where cyberwarfare and semiautonomous weapons—both propelled in great part by GenAI-based algorithms—have presented complex polyrisk and are an intrinsic part of the geopolitical polycrisis unfolding there.

Consider, similarly, the polyrisk presented by tensions between the United States and China in Taiwan. In this case, we would have this cluster of polyrisks: (1) geopolitical risk, in that tensions are high between Taiwan and China and if they boil over could lead to contained or uncontained hostilities and/or regional or even global kinetic and or virtual war; (2) cyberrisk and virtual risk, in that cyberweapons, surveillance, and spycraft are or may be deployed; and (3) global economic risk, in that medium to severe hostility by China against Taiwan could cause anywhere from a global economic recession to a depression disrupting local, regional, and global transportation, energy, supply chains, and so much more—especially affecting global chip production and supply chain since Taiwan currently produces about 90% of the world's high-end chips, central-processing units, and graphics-processing units.

I have been working in the risk, crisis management, and business continuity space for three decades developing and deploying risk, crisis,

Figure 11.1 Polyrisk as Multiple Overlapping Multifaceted Risks

Sources: Author's request to ChatGPT40 to create a picture of what she envisioned.

and business continuity plans and teams through a wide variety of crises, including Y2K; planning the construction of a power plant in a South American country's guerrilla war zone; the aftereffects of the September 11, 2001, terrorist attacks on the United States for a multinational company with a global footprint; preparing another global company with its headquarters in Times Square, New York, right after 9/11; and deploying and implementing a crisis plan during the East Coast Blackout of 2003.

What we have come to experience in the first two decades of the twenty-first century are more numerous, complex, deeper, faster crises globally—whether they were primarily caused by or correlated with climate change, pandemics, wars, crimes, cyberattacks, or nation-states' actions. And now we have relatively new and sometimes mind-boggling risks (and of course opportunities) associated with exponential technologies. Hence, the importance of using the terms "polyrisk" and "polycrisis."

The Tech Risk Universe in a Polycrisis World

While the debate on tech-existential versus tech-normal risk continues, it is important to place the risks that come with exponential technologies within the context of how we typically look at risk, with two observations. First, we need to make sure that the new tech-risk knowns and unknowns are fully understood and integrated into risk management, ERM, and risk governance. Second, we need to deploy tools using these new technologies—most notably, GenAI—for which a wide gamut of enterprise risk, risk management and governance, and compliance software programs and tools are being created or reengineered to deploy more efficient data and analysis that only GenAI can provide, including service providers like Archer, OneTrust, ServiceNow, IBM, and MetricStream. In other words, we need to think outside the typical box, look around corners, and look ahead; and we need to find and deploy the best tech tools to assist us with improved tech risk analytics, including predictive analytics and sophisticated scenario planning.

The Big Polyrisk Picture: Global Strategic Risk

A lot of time and effort has been devoted (or spilled, some would say) over the last few years on whether the new technologies like GenAI and SynBio or autonomous weapons pose existential risk to humankind and the planet. On one side, the likes of Elon Musk and Geoffrey Hinton— very different people, admittedly—have argued that if we do not maintain an ever-vigilant attitude toward the implications of GenAI from a risk management and guardrail standpoint, we may find ourselves with unexpected, unpredictable, and potentially dire consequences. Hinton, called the "godfather of AI" for his groundbreaking machine learning work, and who was recognized with a Nobel Prize in 2024, gave a *60 Minutes* interview in June 2024, in which he appeared much more concerned than before about the more immediate advent of scary, uncontrolled AGI.[3]

On the other side of this debate are the "move fast, break things" crowd who are happy to seek progress no matter what because the existential risk that others talk about is exaggerated and unlikely (and/or their survival plans and bunkers are ready). In this corner of the debate are Meta, with its principal spokespeople, Mark Zuckerberg, and his chief scientist Yan LeCun, and also, sometimes, Elon Musk, depending on what day it is and which one of his companies he is thinking about. If it is his relatively new GenAI company, xAI, well, all is good. But before Musk launched xAI and it was all about OpenAI and its scary approach to AGI, then maybe some guardrails would be in order.

And somewhere in between are most of us, trying to figure out practically what the most serious or severe downsides may be and how soon they will occur. Take the open letter from both anonymous and on-the-record existing and ex-employees of OpenAI. In June 2024 they penned a public piece beseeching OpenAI and others in the AI field to enable workers and employees to have safe speak-up mechanisms—free of threats or retaliation—to be able to point out concerns, problems, dangers, and failures.

Focusing now on the big picture of global strategic risk, including tech risk, one of my favorite go-to resources is the annual WEF "Global Risks Report," which is published every January and provides a thorough and comprehensive analysis of five big risk buckets: economic, environmental, geopolitical, societal, and technological.[4]

Figure 11.2 presents a snapshot of current risk for 2025, highlighting the most severe risks for the coming year. Included in the top fifteen risks are three technological risks: (1) misinformation and disinformation, at fourth; (2) adverse outcomes of AI technologies, at thirteenth; and (3) cyberespionage and warfare, at fourteenth.

One of the disturbing findings in the 2025 "Global Risks Report" (which has not been present in recent reports) is that for both 2025 and the two-year severe risk outlook, there are two new geopolitical strategic risks that are closely interconnected with technology issues: (1) "state-based armed conflict," coming in at first for 2025 and third for the next two-year outlook; and (2) "geoeconomic confrontation," listed as third in 2025 and ninth for the two-year outlook. The presence of these two geopolitical risks at the top of the severity ranking is a clear reflection of the turbulent geopolitical times we live in. It also underscores how technology breakthroughs have played a critical role in exacerbating or supporting (depending on your perspective) warfare, civil conflict, and trade wars.

Another critical risk—societal polarization—also shows up in the WEF's top ten severe risks for 2025 (at fifth), the two-year outlook (at fourth), and the ten-year horizon (at eighth). Societal polarization is also deeply interconnected with technology, with the rise of social surveillance and social media tools and techniques, and with the spread of rampant misinformation and disinformation.

Environmental risks continue to be the most prevalent type of severe risks; they are present in all three time horizons that the WEF "Global Risks Report" examines, with five of the top ten most severe risks in the ten-year outlook. Once again, the intersection between climate risks and technology is critical to keep in mind, as climate tech and other global and local initiatives may offer solutions for combating our unfolding planetary climate challenges and disasters. Table 11.1 provides a detailed look at the two-year and ten-year horizons and underscores the continuing importance of technology strategic risk, with three making the ten-year forecast in the top ten risks—"misinformation and disinformation," at fifth; "adverse outcomes of AI technologies," at sixth; and "cyberespionage and warfare," at ninth.

As in previous years, the WEF "Global Risks Report" once again provides a detailed, data-driven Risk Interconnectedness Map showing the interconnections of the five large buckets of strategic global risks.[5] Suffice it to say that there are many and multiple connections and interconnections between these buckets of risk, and certainly within the technology category between the six named technology risks.

Among the strongest interconnections involving technology risks are these:

- Between technology risk "misinformation and disinformation" and:
  - Societal risk, "societal polarization"

Table 11.1 The World Economic Forum's 2025 Global Risks, Ranked by Severity, Short and Long Terms

Short Term (2 Years)	Long Term (10 Years)
1. Misinformation and disinformation (T)	1. Extreme weather events (En)
2. Extreme weather events (En)	2. Biodiversity loss / ecosystem collapse (En)
3. State-based armed conflict (G)	3. Critical change to Earth systems (En)
4. Societal polarization (S)	4. Natural resource shortages (En)
5. Cyberespionage and warfare (T)	5. Misinformation and disinformation (T)
6. Pollution (En)	6. Adverse outcomes of AI technologies (T)
7. Inequality (S)	7. Inequality (S)
8. Involuntary migration or displacement (S)	8. Social polarization (S)
9. Geoeconomic confrontation (G)	9. Cyberespionage and warfare (T)
10. Erosion of human rights and/or civic freedoms (S)	10. Pollution (En)

Source: WEF Global Risks Report 2025. Legend: En = environment; S = societal; T = technological; G = Geopolitical

- ○ Geopolitical risk, "intrastate violence"
- ○ Societal risk, "erosion of human rights"
- • Between technology risk, "cyberespionage and warfare," and:
- ○ Geopolitical risk, "geoeconomic confrontation"
- ○ Economic risk, "illicit economic activity"

Exponential Tech Risk in the Polyrisk Landscape

Once you understand the risk big picture for the present and into the future, the next step is to understand the risk profile of the technologies that you are inventing, purchasing, integrating, and/or deploying in your organization, and your products, services, and their impact on your stakeholders. So it is important to know the risks of the technologies and exponential technologies you are creating and/or using. Table 11.2 provides a high-level overview of some of the key risks within each type of exponential technology that we examine in this book. It is also critical that as we review these risks, we always consider the reverse side of the risk coin—that embedded in every risk and its multiple facets are opportunities—in their multiple manifestations.

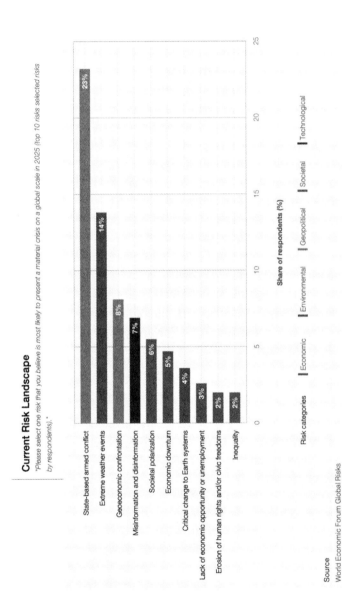

Current Risk Landscape

"Please select one risk that you believe is most likely to present a material crisis on a global scale in 2025 (top 10 risks selected risks by respondents)."

Source
World Economic Forum Global Risks
Perception Survey 2024-2025.

Figure 11.2 The Global Risk Landscape in 2025

Source: World Economic Forum, "Global Risks Report 2025," 13, January 2025, https://reports.weforum.org/docs/WEF_Global_Risks_Report_2025.pdf. Reprinted by permission.

Table 11.2 Tech Risks and Opportunities in Several Exponential Tech Domains

GenAI	SynBio	Autonomy	Materials	Computing
Cyberinsecurity	Unintended	Out-of-control	Harmful	Cybersecurity
Hallucinations	genetic	robots	materials	Encryption
Misinformation	modification	Out-of-control	Pollution	Blockchain
Disinformation	or mutations	weapons	Biological conse-	Compatibility
Deep fakes	Synthetic life	No proper kill-	quences	Complexity and
IP violations	forms	switch or human	Materials'	integration
Algorithmic	Environmental	in or on the loop	toxicity	Maintenance
discrimination	damage	Data security	Aquatic ecotox-	Cost
and bias	Genetic diversity	Incompatibility	icity	Ethics
Environmental /	loss	Faulty program-	Product safety	Reputation
climate / energy	Accidental release	ming and	Insufficient	Operational
impact (elec-	Toxicity	maintenance	regulation	Dependence on
tricity, carbon,	Allergenicity	Environmental	Supply chain	advanced mate-
water)	Unethical	impact	disruption	rials and tech
	manipulation	Overdependence	Ethical	Environmental
	Bioterrorism	Cybersecurity	implications	impacts

Source: Author.

In reviewing the lists of exponential tech risks (and opportunities) given above, it is also possible to find cross-cutting or shared bigger buckets of risks and opportunities that apply across most exponential technologies. Table 11.3 provides this more aggregated and simplified overview.

The AI and GenAI Risk Canvas

Let us now turn to a tighter lens on risk in the exponential tech world: on AI- and GenAI-specific risk. We look at an excellent resource from the Massachusetts Insititute of Technology (MIT) called "The AI Risk Repository," which maintains an ever-evolving risk taxonomy and typology collecting new information in real time as an open source resource. So far, it has collected over 1,600 AI-related risks. Also in this section, we take a look at GenAI on the front lines through the results of a Google DeepMind study as well as a review of the first publicly traded US company reporting on AI risk.

The AI Risk Repository

First launched in the summer of 2024, the MIT-based global "AI Risk Repository" is an open source, publicly available resource focused on providing

Table 11.3 Big Buckets of Risk across Most Exponential Technologies

Overall Risk	Specific Risks
Individual and societal	Privacy, data collection
	Talent skilling, reskilling, job loss
	Unequal access, inequality
Ethical and moral	Unfairness, bias, discrimination
	Unauthorized, repressive, authoritarian surveillance
	Unethical or illegal human exploitation
Governance	Ignorant, ineffective boards and governance bodies
	Ineffective, slow, backward regulations
	Toxic, unbridled leaders and innovators
Safety and security	Cyberinsecurity
	Intrusive, unknown surveillance
	Misinformation, disinformation, and information weaponization
	Fake news, deep fakes
Economic	Wealth concentration
	Fraud, scams, corruption
	Market disruption, antitrust
	Intellectual property theft and violations
Environmental	Excessive resource consumption (including water)
	E-waste and pollution
	Carbon emissions
	Energy transition
Geopolitical	Big power competition
	New, uncontrolled, uncontrollable weapons development
	Turbocharged cyberinsecurity
	Political polarization, undermining of human rights and democracy

Source: Author.

industry, policymakers, academia, and the public in general with an up-to-the-minute big picture overview of AI risk.[6] It is a truly impressive, comprehensive, living, breathing repository of all things AI risk.

Based on deep and broad research and sources, this repository identifies seven domains of AI risk in their taxonomy: discrimination and toxicity; privacy and security; misinformation; malicious actors and misuse; human–computer interaction; socioeconomic and environmental harm; and AI system safety, failures, and limitations. This overall taxonomy also contains twenty-four subdomains, as laid out in table 11.4, which also provides percentages that the particular AI risk domain represents of the overall AI risk database.

The domains with the highest collective percentage of risks were,

Table 11.4 AI Risk Database Coded with Domain Taxonomy from the AI Risk Repository

Domain	Subdomain	Percentage of Risks (Overall)
1. Discrimination and Toxicity	Unfair discrimination and misrepresentation	16
	Exposure to toxic content	
	Unequal performance across group	
2. Privacy and security	Compromise of privacy by obtaining, leaking, or correctly inferring sensitive information	14
	AI system security vulnerabilities and attacks	
3. Misinformation	False or misleading information	7
	Pollution of information ecosystem and loss of consensus reality	
4. Malicious actors and misuse	Disinformation, surveillance, and influence at scale	14
	Cyberattacks, weapon development or use, and mass harm	
	Fraud, scams, and targeted manipulation	
5. Human–computer interaction	Overreliance and unsafe use	8
	Loss of human agency and autonomy	
6. Socioeconomic and environmental harm	Power centralization and unfair distribution of benefits	18
	Increased inequality and decline in employment quality	
	Economic and cultural devaluation of human effort	
	Competitive dynamics	
	Governance failure	
	Environmental harm	
7. AI system safety, failure, and limitations	AI pursuing its own goals in conflict with human goals or values	24
	AI possessing dangerous capabilities	
	Lack of capability or robustness	
	Lack of transparency or interpretability	
	AI welfare and rights	
	Multi-agent risks	

Source: AI Risk Repository.

not surprisingly, at 24 percent, seventh, AI system safety, failures, and limitations; at 18 percent, sixth, socioeconomic and environmental harm; and at 16 percent, first, discrimination and toxicity. Interestingly, the top five specific subdomains with the highest percentage of risk were these:

- At 9 percent—*lack of capability or robustness* (under seventh, AI system safety, failures, and limitations);

- At 8 percent—*AI pursuing its own goals in conflict with human goals or values* (under seventh, AI system safety, failures, and limitations);
- At 8 percent—*unfair discrimination and misrepresentation* (under first, discrimination and toxicity);
- At 7 percent—*compromise of privacy by obtaining, leaking, or correctly inferring sensitive information* (under second, privacy and security); and
- At 7 percent—*AI system security vulnerabilities and attack* (under second, privacy and security).

Finally, the MIT "AI Risk Repository" divides its risk taxonomy into a domain taxonomy and a causal taxonomy, as summarized in tables 11.4 and 11.5, respectively.

For those interested in engaging more deeply, the "AI Risk Repository" also contains a treasure trove of academic and nonacademic research papers and databases that are stunning in their variety and comprehensiveness.

UNESCO's Nine AI Regulatory Programs

In a fascinating working paper, UNESCO provides an overview of what it calls nine potential regulatory approaches to AI. Table 11.6 provides a summary.[7]

The European Union's AI Act

The reason for mentioning the European Union's AI Act in the same breath as we speak about AI risk is that it happens to be the first, most comprehensive, regulatory, multinational framework that has become law in the world, focusing heavily on ensuring the safe and ethical development and use of AI. While this is certainly true for the twenty-seven nations in the EU, the EU AI Act also has major reverberations for and applicability to global business, for virtual domains, and for people almost everywhere. The EU AI Act is focused like a laser beam on a risk-based approach to managing AI; it breaks down risk into four categories: unacceptable risk, high risk, limited risk, and minimal risk. The first category,

Table 11.5 Causal Taxonomy of AI Risks from the AI Risk Repository

Category	Level and Description
Entity	Human: The risk is caused by a decision or action made by humans AI: The risk is caused by a decision or action made by an AI system Other: The risk is caused by some other reason or is ambiguous
Intent	Intentional: The risk occurs due to an expected outcome from pursuing a goal Unintentional: The risk occurs due to an unexpected outcome from pursuing a goal Other: The risk is presented as occurring without clearly specifying the intentionality
Timing	Predeployment: The risk occurs before the AI is deployed Postdeployment: The risk occurs after the AI model has been trained and deployed Other: The risk is presented without a clearly specified time of occurrence

Source: AI Risk Repository.

unacceptable risk, is banned; and the second, high risk, is heavily regulated.[8] Table 11.7 provides descriptions of each category of risk.

Additional aspects of the EU AI Act that are important to note include the extraterritorial reach of the act, which applies to "AI systems and outputs used in the EU regardless of where the provider is located" and severe potential sanctions for noncompliance, to the tune of up to €35 million or 7 percent of global turnover of a company, depending on the violation. Finally, and notably, the EU AI Act is not only about regulations and sanctions; it also creates incentives and structures for innovation. One of the widespread criticisms of the EU AI Act—mainly from the tech business community inside and outside the EU—is that the law impedes or puts severe brakes on innovation, something about which EU policymakers and bureaucrats are quite sensitive.

AI and GenAI Risk on the Front Lines: Google DeepMind Research

Going yet a little more deeply into the exponential tech polyrisk and polycrisis world, let us take a look at some of the analyses that are being done on this front. Google DeepMind conducted an investigation of how GenAI

Table 11.6 UNESCO's "Consultation Paper on AI Regulation: Emerging Approaches Across the World—Nine AI & Governance Regulatory Approaches"

Principles-Based Approach: Offer stakeholders a set of fundamental propositions (principles) that provide guidance for developing and using AI systems through ethical, responsible, human-centric, and human-rights-abiding processes.

Standards-Based Approach: Delegate (totally or partially) the state's regulatory powers to organizations that produce technical standards that will guide the interpretation and implementation of mandatory rules.

Agile and Experimentalist Approach: Generate flexible regulatory schemes, such as regulatory sandboxes and other testbeds, that allow organizations to test new business models, methods, infrastructure, and tools under more flexible regulatory conditions and with the oversight and accompaniment of public authorities.

Facilitating and Enabling Approach: Facilitate and enable an environment that encourages all stakeholders involved in the AI life cycle to develop and use responsible, ethical, and human-rights-compliant AI systems.

Adapting Existing Laws Approach: Amend sector-specific rules (e.g., health, finance, education, justice) and transversal rules (e.g., criminal codes, public procurement, data protection laws, labor laws) to make incremental improvements to the existing regulatory framework.

Access to Information and Transparency Mandates Approach: Require the deployment of transparency instruments that enable the public to access basic information about AI systems.

Risk-Based Approach: Establish obligations and requirements in accordance with an assessment of the risks associated with the deployment and use of certain AI tools in specific contexts.

Rights-Based Approach: Establish obligations or requirements to protect individuals' rights and freedoms.

Liability Approach: Assign responsibility and sanctions to problematic uses of AI systems.

Source: UNESCO.

can be deployed for malicious purposes and reported accordingly. The key takeaways include the observation that most GenAI misuse currently involves simple, low-tech tactics that do not require advanced technical skills. Moreover, GenAI misuse falls into two main categories—exploiting capabilities (exemplified in scams) and compromising systems (e.g., through data poisoning, where fake data are injected into a legitimate data set via a cyberattack). While Google DeepMind identified eighteen tactics, multiple tactics are often used in one effort. They then mapped those

Table 11.7 The European Union AI Act's Categories of Risk

Unacceptable-Risk AI Systems: They are prohibited and include systems that manipulate human behavior, exploit vulnerabilities, deploy certain biometric ID systems publicly or engage in "social scoring."

High-Risk AI Systems: References effects on health, safety, fundamental rights, and the environment within the critical infrastructure, education, employment, law enforcement, and medical devices sectors and require strict regulation, including risk assessments, data governance, humans in the loop, and cybersecurity.

Limited-Risk AI Systems: Are less-risky AI systems that nevertheless must meet transparency obligations, such as providing users with relevant information like the fact that they are interacting with an AI chatbot or deep fake.

Minimal-Risk AI Systems: Usually refer to video games and spam filters; do not have specific regulatory frameworks that apply to them but are expected to abide by general principles, such as fairness and nondiscrimination.

Source: European Union.

eighteen tactics to eight strategies to explain how such actions unfold and found that one of the core qualities of GenAI—its multimodality—makes it far easier to launch certain attacks and manipulate human likeness, thus creating more realistic presentations. Google DeepMind concluded that there is a need for both technical and nontechnical measures that are constantly evolving to meet the always-morphing threats to combat this malicious use of GenAI, including public awareness campaigns.[9]

In addition to the malicious use of GenAI, here are several quick examples of new or evolved risks GenAI can present to individuals and organizations:

- *Hallucinations, confabulation, and invention:* These occur when GenAI makes up information from either incorrect or corrupted data, or from other unreliable sources of information. For example, GenAI is deployed at a financial institution to make investment recommendations, which are submitted in a report and acted upon by the customer. This can lead to an investment going south, with negative financial and/or reputational consequences for both the customer and the company.
- *Manipulated content, misinformation, and disinformation:* These

occur when data provenance and quality are wanting and GenAI chatbots are deployed and trained on such questionable, corrupted, or purposefully manipulated data. The consequences can include incorrect or offensive responses, leading to unhappy or antagonized customers and other third parties.

- *Algorithmic bias*: This occurs if a company uses a biased GenAI model to filter and select candidates for job interviews; the model may perpetuate existing gender or racial biases, targeting mostly white men to hire. This will result in a less diverse workforce and legal action by candidates who unfairly missed out.[10]

AI and GenAI Risk on the Front Lines:
Public Company Disclosures

We are starting to see public companies reporting on AI and GenAI issues and risks. As the *Financial Times* reported in August 2024, "More than half of the US's biggest companies see artificial intelligence as a potential risk to their businesses. . . . Overall, 56 per cent of Fortune 500 companies cited AI as a 'risk factor' in their most recent annual reports, . . . a striking jump from just 9 per cent in 2022. By contrast, only 33 companies of the 108 that specifically discussed generative AI . . . [saw it as] as an opportunity."[11]

Among the AI risks reported by these companies were greater competition; concerns that proprietary technology will be exploited by others; and being blindsided by unknown, new entrants into the tech marketplace. Other risks include reputation risk, operational concerns, and "becoming ensnared in ethical concerns about AI's potential impact on human rights, employment, and privacy."[12] Among industries most concerned about AI are entertainment (90 percent) and software and technology groups (86 percent). "Over two-thirds of Fortune 500 telecommunications companies and more than half of health care, financial services, retail, consumer, and aerospace companies gave the same warning to investors."[13] Table 11.8 presents several actual statements by Fortune 500 companies in their public reports, as laid out in the Arize AI report, on which the *Financial Times* reporting was based.[14]

The Polyrisk and Polycrisis Convergence of the Virtual and Physical Worlds

The virtual and physical worlds are converging in a number of ways, and so are related risks. A perfect example is a "digital twin." As explained by Amazon Web Services, "A digital twin is a virtual model of a physical object. It spans the object's life cycle and uses real-time data sent from sensors on the object to simulate the behavior and monitor operations."[15] It provides the user with predictive capabilities, remote monitoring, improved performance, and an accelerated production time. In a piece titled "Digital Twins Are Fast Becoming Part of Everyday Life: Welcome to the Mirror World," the *Economist* offered this scenario: "When visiting a doctor a few years from now, you can be accompanied by a virtual version of yourself. This so-called twin will be a working model of your body that can be summoned on your physician's computer screen. Updated with your latest vital signs, it will help your doctor make an accurate diagnosis."[16] While this has not happened yet, we are definitely inching closer. Just think about your current doctor visits, which can now also be virtual and where the doctor has a lot of the digital data she already needs about you.

There are other examples quickly coming into play, including digital twins of jet engines that monitor their health on airplanes, Uber has digital twins monitoring their network of cars, and Amazon uses digital twins in its vast supply chain, which allows retailers to forecast sales—several years ahead![17] Of course, there are deep risks associated with all this—on personal and institutional levels—including the rise of digital doppelgangers, privacy, and data rights theft; the need for enormous additional sources of energy to power these twins; and a whole host of malicious and malevolent activity with which we are becoming too familiar.

A Convergence Paradigm for Cyberinsecurity and Infrastructure

One fact that has been clear to cyber experts for a while but is now becoming abundantly clear to everyone in this Age of Pandora is that the physical and virtual worlds are coming together, converging and/or

**Table 11.8 Public Comments Reported by Selected Fortune 500
Companies about AI and GenAI Risk**

Motorola: "AI may not always operate as intended and data sets may be insufficient
or contain illegal, biased, harmful or offensive information, which could negatively
impact on earnings and reputation."

Salesforce: "Its adoption of AI 'presents emerging ethical issues' around data collection and privacy. It said its profit margins could be affected by 'uncertainty' around
emerging AI applications."

Viatris: This pharmaceutical group, which was spun out of Pfizer, warned that the use
of AI solutions by employees or suppliers "could lead to the public disclosure of
confidential information" along with "unauthorised access" to personal data relating
to employees, clinical trial participants, or others.

In general: "Legal, regulatory, and cybersecurity AI risks were also a common theme
among Fortune 500 companies."

Source: *Fortune.*

influencing one another in deep and new ways—both risky and advanta-
geous. Nowhere does this fact manifest itself more than in the evolving
cyberinsecurity space, where government and business are increasingly
collaborating because of the magnitude of the threats involved. They are
doing so perhaps less out of choice and more out of necessity, given the
deeply daunting known cybersecurity challenges along with the unknown
consequences of how GenAI and eventually quantum technology are turbocharging cyberinsecurity.

Let us step back for a moment and take a look at a side-by-side comparison of physical and cybersecurity domains, which have already begun
to converge or at least overlap in various ways. Many of these categories
of activity are beginning to blur and manifest in both physical and digital
ways; see table 11.9.

A number of risks exist in both the physical and virtual worlds and
are converging. For instance, data corruption lives in both worlds, such
as when biased algorithms applied to a mortgage application result in the
rejection of persons of color. Likewise, the arrest of the wrong person because of poorly designed, biased facial recognition software is a cross-over
between the virtual and the physical. The social engineering of reception
staff at a remote location of an electric power utility can translate into
physical perpetrators surreptitiously adding malicious code to computers

onsite and causing a power blackout or ransom action later. Among the areas where we are seeing the convergence of physical and virtual security risks are these:

1. Data and synthetic data corruption
2. Misinformation, disinformation, deep fakes
3. Privacy and data privacy
4. Physical security and cyberinsecurity
5. Social engineering
6. Intellectual property theft, leaks
7. Surveillance overreach
8. Intended or unintended bias, discrimination
9. Third-party security risks

In response to this intertwining of known and unknown risks and threats to critical infrastructure, several developments in the United States under the Biden administration were designed to beef up the country's GenAI cybersecurity readiness in the seventeen categories of critical infrastructure that have been identified as requiring extra care and readiness. The Cybersecurity and Infrastructure Security Agency (CISA), part of the US Department of Homeland Security, had made great strides in bridging the previous gaps with the business sector. CISA had opened a wider dialogue with the private sector and made available and deployed a wide variety of tools, data, and policies to assist in combating what is one of the greatest threats to US national security and its socioeconomic well-being—cyberattacks (in many different forms) from nation-states, criminal gangs, and other malign actors, especially affecting the seventeen critical infrastructure sectors. Under the second Trump Administration's DOGE cost-cutting initiatives, CISA had its budget slashed, with consequences yet to be determined but possibly severe.[18]

A key for AI-related programs was the rollout by CISA of "CISA AI," through which it provides the public with a wide variety of CISA use cases, tools, training, and more. As it states on its website, "See how CISA is using Artificial Intelligence (AI) responsibly to improve its services and cybersecurity on several fronts, while maintaining privacy and civil liber-

Table 11.9 The Two Converging Domains of Physical Security
and Cybersecurity

Types of Physical Security	Types of Cybersecurity
People security (locations, travel, workplace safety)	Cyberattack simulation, training, awareness
Data protection and privacy	Vulnerability assessments
Enhanced surveillance systems	Endpoint security and monitoring
Synthetic data generation for training	Synthetic data generation
Predictive threat analytics	Predictive analytics
Deepfake detection and countermeasures	Biometrics, voice, and image recognition
Security robotics and drones	Contextualized security monitoring, reporting
Crowd management and behavior prediction	Supply chain and third-party risk management
Intelligent access control systems	Digital forensics and incident analysis
Optimized staffing plans	Automated patch management
Property image enhancement	Phishing detection and prevention
Improving workplace safety	Unpredictable behavior of GenAI

Source: Author.

ties. The use cases below offer current examples of efforts that are under way."[19]

Indeed, CISA published the "CISA Roadmap for AI," which provides guidance for all manner of entities on how to deploy AI and GenAI for cybersecurity. The road map has five lines of effort—responsible use of AI to support its mission; assurance of AI systems; protection of critical infrastructure from the malicious use of AI; collaboration and communications on key AI efforts with government and international partners; and public, expanding AI expertise in the workforce.[20]

CISA is not alone among US government agencies that are focusing on the need for experience and expertise in the converging areas of cybersecurity and GenAI. The well-known and well regarded National Institute of Standards and Technology (NIST), which is part of the US Department of Commerce, has been at the forefront of developing broadly used and internationally respected technology standards, metrics and tools, including in the fields of cybersecurity and infrastructure, and, recently, adding AI to its repertoire.

NIST conducts research, engaging stakeholders and producing reports on the characteristics of trustworthy AI. In the process, it has developed the "Trustworthy and Responsible AI" initiative, whose main building blocks are "Validity and Reliability, Safety, Security, and Resiliency, Accountability and Transparency, Explainability and Interpretability, Privacy and Fairness, with Mitigation of Harmful Bias."[21] NIST also partners with other organizations to support initiatives on trustworthy AI. These include a partnership with the National Science Foundation on the Institute for Trustworthy AI in Law & Society.[22] Finally, NIST created a new agency, the US AI Safety Institute, whose focus was to "pursue a range of projects, . . . includ[ing] advancing research and measurement science for AI safety, conducting safety evaluations of models and systems, and developing guidelines for evaluations and risk mitigations, including content authentication and the detection of synthetic content. As the technology and world changes, additional projects will likely be necessary."[23] However, under the new Trump Administration, the AI Safety Institute was renamed the Center for AI Standards and Innovation (CAISI), rebranded to downplay safety.

Here is a list of these case studies, which the original AI Safety Institute under Biden had made available for companies (or any other type of organization) to deploy internally:[24]

1. AI Scoring & Feedback (AS&F)
2. Automated Indicator Sharing (AIS) Automated PII Detection
3. Advanced Analytic Enabled Forensic Investigation
4. Advanced Network Anomaly Alerting
5. AI Security & Robustness
6. Critical Infrastructure Anomaly Alerting
7. Cyber Incident Reporting
8. Cyber Threat Intelligence Feed Correlation
9. Cyber Vulnerability Reporting
10. Malware Reverse Engineering
11. Operational Activities Explorer
12. Security Information and Event Management (SIEM) Alerting Models

Building Your Organizational Polyrisk and Polycrisis Resilience Systems

To mitigate all these converging risks, here are several suggested approaches companies and other entities can take to mitigate the physical risks and cyberrisks related to the adoption of GenAI:

- Data governance—bottom up, across, and top down—data quality controls
- Overall good governance
- Good enterprise risk management integrating data, cyber, and security issues
- Great cybersecurity
- Great data ethics, compliance, and transparency
- Good interdisciplinary coordination between ERM, risk management, information security, legal, security, business continuity, crisis management, and data protection
- Predictable, effective lines of communication with executive management, the C-suite, and boards
- Predictable, effective reporting of incidents for regulatory and legal purposes
- Training and awareness for everyone—beginning with the C-suite and board
- Zero trust
- Constant situational awareness information gathering, interpretation, and adaptation

A closing word on the connection of all this new exponential tech risk with existing risk, crisis, and resilience systems. These new risks can only be addressed by already-robust ERM, crisis, and business continuity management, as well as board-level risk, crisis, and business continuity governance. Without these foundational building blocks—which can only come from top management and the board—there really is no hope for an entity to understand, let alone conquer, the universe of new tech risk that is already suffusing all of us. Suffice it to say here that for a successful future-forward strategy that leads to effective foresight, an entity must systematically consider and integrate its tech issues, risks, and opportunities into its strategy.

In this chapter, we have focused on all manner of risks, starting with the largest and most strategic ones (WEF), then reviewing exponential tech risks, and then homing in on AI and GenAI risks, including the convergence of the physical and virtual worlds. Risk, of course, can lead to crises and polyrisks that are often part of a crisis. Plus, as we discussed above, we live in a polycrisis world—where multiple crises occur simultaneously, sometimes affecting each other in unexpected ways. Add exponential tech risk to this equation and we find ourselves in a complex world in dire need of resilience solutions as well as full of opportunities for deep, unexpected innovation and transformation, such as through the energy transition and the development of climate tech.

As a final, positive example of the more constructive side of the risk equation, I would like to share an overview of the UN's Sustainable Development Goal 9, "Industry, Innovation, and Infrastructure," because it brings together the risk and opportunity of innovation through resilience and diversity. Indeed, its longer definition is to "build resilient infrastructure, promote inclusive and sustainable industrialization, and foster innovation."[25] This list shows the eight targets developed for SDG #9. The first five targets are "outcome" targets, and the next three are "implementation" targets:

Outcome targets
1. Develop sustainable resilient and inclusive infrastructures.
2. Promote inclusive and sustainable industrialization.
3. Increase access to financial services and markets.
4. Upgrade all industries and infrastructure for sustainability, enhance research, and upgrade industrial technologies.

Implementation targets
5. Facilitate sustainable infrastructure development for developing countries.
6. Support domestic technology development and industrial diversification.
7. Universal access to information and communications technology.

Finally, as a tip of the hat to those who work so tirelessly in the back offices and assurance functions of organizations, I would be totally remiss to not address (see table 11.10) some of the key audits and tests that management and the governance body of any organization should implement in an ongoing and periodic manner regarding AI, GenAI, and other technologies deployed at the organization. While all this is a work in progress, we need to accentuate "progress" and resilience, working together on common human objectives, including safe and inclusive innovation.

Questions Stakeholders Should Ask about How Leaders Deploy Polyrisk and Polycrisis Preparedness

To close, here are some questions stakeholders of entities should be asking about how their management and boards are deploying polyrisk and polycrisis preparedness:

- Is the preparedness approach in place makeshift, modular, unfinished, tentative, or reactive? If so, what is needed to shift its performance upward?
- Does an entity have a risk management or ERM system in place and, if so, what type of system is it—static, dynamic, or forward, comprehensive, or limited?
- Does the preparedness approach integrate exponential technology risks into ERM?
- Is there a continuous tech improvement program that investigates the aspects of the crisis that have exponential tech characteristics?
- What technologies is an entity deploying to understand its risk profile—does it have a governance, risk, and compliance system in addition to ERM and other AI-driven software, and how does the board or equivalent oversight institution review and understand it?
- What specifically is in place for the day after the crisis? Are there proper digital back-up plans, asset protections, and siloed servers?
- Is there a comprehensive, interconnected preparedness approach

Table 11.10 Additional Polyrisk and Polycrisis Tools, Techniques, and Exercises to Risk-Manage Exponential Technologies

Tool	Specific Aspects
Algorithm audits	Regular reviews of algorithmic logic, input data, and outputs for bias, fairness, and ethical compliance.
	Examples: Audits for bias in machine learning models or explainability assessments.
Data audits	Verifying the quality, integrity, and provenance of data used for training algorithms.
	Tools: Data quality management tools (e.g., Talend, Informatica).
Change management audits	Reviewing version control logs to ensure proper documentation and accountability for algorithm updates.
	Tools: Git, SVN, or other version control systems with detailed change logs.
Third-party and vendor assessments	Auditing external vendors providing algorithms or AI solutions for compliance with organizational standards.
	Frameworks: Vendor risk assessment questionnaires or ISO 27001 standards.
Red teaming exercises	Third party tests to gauge harms that AI can cause if pushed to their limits.

Source: Author.

in place for known and unknown risks, crises that will come, the business continuity that will be necessary, and the stakeholder protections that will be required?

Actions Leaders Should Take to Deploy Polyrisk and Polycrisis Preparedness

Here are a few action items leaders should consider to achieve organizational resilience through the successful deployment of polyrisk and polycrisis preparedness:

- Require continuous enterprise learning.
- Have crisis readiness—team, plan, and scenario planning.
- Have business continuity—team, plan, and scenario planning.
- Deploy continuous monitoring, auditing, and lessons learned.
- Encourage continuous invention and improvement.
- Continuous care and upgrading.

A Final Word on Resilience and the Exponential
Governance Mindset

In the Age of Pandora, resilience needs to be part of every entity's planning and strategy. What this means exactly for each entity may be a little different. But one thing is clear: Risk management, crisis management, business continuity, and an overall approach of understanding technology risks and opportunities need to be part of this preparedness. Some organizations have created a new role—chief resilience officer—to encompass these various disciplines and practices. Not everyone will or should do this; but one thing is crystal clear for the rest of the twenty-first century: Resilience will be central to every organization's survival and success (or lack thereof). Every organization's leadership must define resilience for itself, based on its mission, footprint, purpose, and relevant relationships, stakeholders, and third parties. At a minimum, this means understanding and guardrailing for polyrisk and polycrisis. Doing anything less opens the door to serious harm, irrelevancy, and/or reputational loss.

12

FORESIGHT

Unleashing a Future-Forward Tech Strategy

This chapter is about how leaders develop strategy and foresight for their organization in this Age of Pandora—including, specifically, tech foresight. Leaders need to understand how to be prepared for what is next, both in terms of risk and opportunity, incorporating them into strategic planning. How can you best do that? By understanding and adopting situational awareness, systems thinking, effective risk, and opportunity management, and by conducting targeted and effective scenario planning. Foresight entails understanding and integrating many of the things we have discussed in this book and developing a holistic strategy that fits into the reality of our exponential future, taking into consideration such major megatrends as the rise of stakeholder capitalism and the ongoing geopolitical instability that are part of this Age of Pandora.

What Is "Unleashing a Future-Forward Tech Strategy" and Why Should We Care?

In today's hypercomplex environment, it is critical for any entity's business strategy to incorporate tech considerations for a holistic, inclusive, and situationally aware approach. And this is true regardless of whether the entity is a company, government agency, nongovernmental organization, or other type of organization. "Unleashing" means that the entity's leaders must purposefully and consciously develop and implement a holistic, integrated, and future-forward business strategy that takes into account exponential tech and other applicable risks and opportunities pertinent to the organization, its footprint, and stakeholders, calibrated to play out in the short, medium, and long terms. "Future-forward" means what it says: a forward-facing business strategy that understands trends and megatrends, where they are going, and how they might affect the entity and its strategy.

There are five components to developing "foresight" and "unleashing a future-forward tech strategy." Figure 12.1 illustrates these components, and here are shorthand descriptions:

1. *Actionable situational awareness*: Knowing the overall trends and megatrends that are relevant to your entity's footprint and business plan. We delved into these megatrends in detail in chapter 1.

2. *Systems thinking*: Understanding the systems within which we operate and that are deeply interconnected with our tactical and strategic work. Such systems may include sustainability, digitalization, ethics, polycrisis, polyrisk, and others that may be generic or particular to your organization's footprint and that intersect with your organization. Aspects of this systems thinking are covered in several chapters, including 2, 3, 4, 9, 10, and 11.

3. *Tech-risk intelligence*: Understanding how strategic global risk, enterprise risk management (ERM), and risk governance are part and parcel of organizational success. This theme is covered throughout this book, but in greatest detail in chapter 11.

4. *Tech-opportunity readiness*: Understanding the transformative power of tech-turbocharged opportunity, innovation, and value creation. Tech opportunity is a pervasive theme of this book and thus is significantly discussed in practically every chapter, but in greatest detail in all the chapters in parts II and IV.

5. *Interdisciplinary scenario planning*: Adopting targeted, interdisciplinary, scenario planning and exercises is a key part of developing strategy and strategic foresight. This theme is discussed mostly in this chapter and in chapter 11.

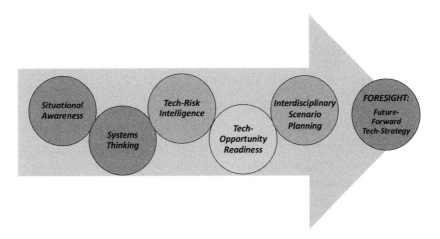

Figure 12.1 Foresight: Unleashing a Future-Forward Tech-Strategy
Source: Author.

Why should leaders care about unleashing a future-forward tech strategy? At the risk of stating the obvious, the reason is because tech strategy at every level affects each and every one of us on Earth—our well-being, our health, our safety, our security. It is in everyone's interest that all entities in every sector everywhere be serious about developing responsible tech strategies, and it is incumbent on organizational leaders—whether managers or board members—to pay close attention to strategic foresight.

Strategy in the Context of Foresight

Before we delve into each of the five elements of foresight, let us level set on what constitutes a "strategy." Focused more on business, here is Michael Porter's definition of strategy: "a broad formula for how a business will compete, what its goals should be, and what policies will be needed to carry out those goals."[1] Here are the key considerations that might go into the development of a well-crafted generic strategy:

- Vision
- Mission

- Values
- Objectives and goals
- SWOT (strengths, weaknesses, opportunities, threats) analysis
- Competition analysis / benchmarking
- Research and development
- Growth pathways (mergers and acquisitions, etc.)
- Resource allocation—budgeting
- Talent planning
- Tactical and operational delivery
- Measurement and analysis
- Performance metrics
- Stakeholder awareness/engagement
- Customer focus
- Innovation
- Risk management / ERM
- Risk governance

Here are some key questions to ask about strategy from a master on the subject, R. Edward Freeman, who first formulated the idea of "stakeholder capitalism" in the 1980s:

- Strategic direction: What is the direction or mission of the organization?
- Strategic program formulation: What paths or strategies will achieve such a mission?
- Budgeting: What resource allocations or budgets must be made for the strategies to be implemented?
- Control: How can we be sure the strategies are on track or in control?
- Structure and systems: What are the macro systems and structures necessary for implementation?[2]

In this Age of Pandora, we need to turbocharge our thinking about strategy. In addition to the traditionally important aspects of strategy, it is more important than ever for strategy to be grounded, first, in proper context—situational awareness, as discussed in chapter 1; and second, in "foresight," as explained in this chapter. More than ever before, strategy must be truly forward thinking, not just paying lip service to the future. Strategy must include scenario planning that is relevant not only to the world we live in but also the future world we are facing. We need to deploy the best human brains and the best tech tools—for example, predictive AI, with humans in the loop, to plot, understand, and delineate the scenarios before us, and with this understanding, to develop the strategy that unleashes our greatest potential.

The Five Elements of Foresight:
A Future-Forward Tech Strategy

As the title of this chapter hints, the purpose of unleashing a "future-forward tech strategy" is for leaders to gain "foresight." For example, if one looks at the contrast in results from two global chip-making giants over the past decade—Intel and TSMC—one could very well comment that business strategy foresight would account for the enduring success of one (TSMC) over the other (Intel). Indeed, while TSMC and Intel are both major chipmakers, they have different business models and strategies: TSMC is a contract chipmaker that manufactures chips for other companies, while Intel is an integrated device manufacturer that designs, produces, and sells its own chips. TSMC's success is based on its manufacturing excellence, technology leadership, and customer partnerships. Intel's strategy includes developing new chip technologies, such as glass substrate materials and co-packaged optics that are higher risk. TSMC has about 59 percent of the third-party chip manufacturing market, while Intel's share is minimal. TSMC's revenue comes mainly from smartphones and high-performance computing. Intel's revenue comes mainly from its personal computer and data center central-processing units. TSMC benefited from the AI boom because it manufactured Nvidia's graphics-processing units. Intel's revenue declined in the post-pandemic market because its central-processing units were not as essential as Nvidia's graphics-processing units for processing AI. All this is to say that the long-term business strategy model (and foresight) of the TSMC leadership team was clearer, more diversified, and steadier than Intel's.[3] With that said, let us discuss the five key elements of a future-forward tech strategy, or "foresight."

Element 1: Actionable Situational Awareness

Strategy is too often only about short-/medium-term planning and is not really strategic (long term) at all. It is more like a one-year plan that takes into account limited and contemporary information and data. As such, context and situational awareness of some of the bigger, multiyear trends and megatrends is not always part of what is called strategy. At a time technology is advancing so rapidly, it is critical for strategic decision-makers to consider the historical roots and current context in which we live and operate—that is, it is necessary for them to gain and maintain situational awareness.

Situational awareness is a leadership imperative in this Age of Pandora; as we discussed in great detail in chapter 1, we live in a world where several global, multiyear megatrends are affecting our daily lives and work in direct and indirect, predictable, and unpredictable ways. This is true whether it is the avalanche of technological innovation, discovery, and change, or the dire need to find tech solutions to the mounting climate crisis that affects us all. Or whether it is the reverberation of a series of deep geopolitical tectonic changes affecting (or being affected by) supply chains, migration patterns, or the energy landscape. Or whether it is the very tenor of capitalism—how countries and corporations manage through market or state capitalism, forms of socialism, or the new borderless global tech oligarchy, leadership trust remains one of the key issues and challenges facing all of us everywhere.

These megatrends correspond to what I would call the big picture of strategic situational awareness. And then there is what I call more tactical situational awareness. The term "situational awareness" was originally coined in a military context. According to the 2004 US Army Field Manual, situational awareness is "knowledge and understanding of the current situation which promotes timely, relevant and accurate assessment of friendly, competitive and other operations within the battlespace in order to facilitate decision-making. An informational perspective and skill that fosters an ability to determine quickly the context and relevance of events that are unfolding."[4] As the Army Field Manual states, "the emphasis is on understanding actionable situational awareness." As is clear from this definition—we could easily transpose it to different, nonmilitary contexts like business, nonprofits, and civilian government agencies.

Here is a helpful example of situational awareness in the context of health care. In it, the author shares a list of existing stand-alone systems and programs that are not always integrated (and perhaps require further integration). See table 12.1 for this example.[5] Practical, actionable situational awareness can only be achieved by leaders and decision-makers understanding and considering both the bigger picture megatrends or strategic situational awareness and the more directly relevant tactical situational awareness depicted by the example given above.

Without such situational grounding, how can the CEO of an AI startup like Perplexity AI, or the chief scientist of a genetic engineering biotech company like Epi One, or the chief AI officer of a government agency like US-based CISA, or board members of an established technology company like Microsoft—or frankly any other non-tech company or organization that by virtue of living and operating in today's hyperdigital world have become tech companies—even begin to provide the necessary, practical, and actionable inputs needed to develop an effective, longer-term, and successful tech-integrated strategy for their organization?

Actionable situational awareness requires the presence and participation of relevant internal and external experts to create a data-rich, deeply informed strategic picture. Professionals with geopolitical expertise, sustainability experience, or other relevant and specific technological know-how should be tasked with producing pertinent trend and megatrend reports and analysis to be fed in a timely manner to decision-makers at least quarterly, but preferably on a rolling basis. In a polycrisis world that will continue to be complex and fraught for the foreseeable future, we all need to adopt the "situational awareness" perspective of the military

Table 12.1 Example of Systems and Programs Supporting Health Care Situational Awareness in the United States

Disease Detection and Surveillance
BioWatch (the US government system to detect certain bioterrorism agents in the air)
BioSense (the US government system to gather syndromic surveillance data from hospitals)
Other state and local syndromic surveillance systems, such as RODS, ESSENCE, AEGIS
Centers for Disease Control and Prevention's (CDC's) multiple influenza surveillance systems (e.g., ILInet, Emerging Infections Program)
World Health Organization's Global Influenza Surveillance Network (GISN)
Traditional public health disease surveillance, case investigation, and contact tracing
Laboratory reporting systems

News and Web Trawling
ProMED (distributes disease reports submitted from around the world)
Global Public Health Intelligence Network (GPHIN) (mines global news for disease reports)
Google Flu Trends system

Alerting
Health Alert Network (sends messages from the CDC and state health departments to clinicians)

Bed Tracking
Many home-grown or off-the-shelf systems within hospitals
Many systems for reporting bed data to local, state, and federal governments

Patient Tracking
Many systems to track patients within hospitals
Many systems to track emergency medical services patients

Incident Command Systems
Web emergency operations centers and others

Electronic Health Records
Within hospitals or clinicians' offices

Source: Eric S. Toner, "Creating Situational Awareness: A Systems Approach," National Institutes of Health, https://www.ncbi.nlm.nih.gov/books/NBK32848/.

when it comes to planning ahead for our organizational battles—whether in business, civil society, or the public arena, always integrating the best interests of our key stakeholders as our north star.

Element 2: Systems Thinking

Next in line to develop effective foresight is the need to incorporate systems thinking and relevant systems into strategy formulation. As Freeman hints in his set of questions explored earlier in the chapter, strategy is very directly related to systems, and I would add ecosystems, especially in today's world of digitalization, sustainability, convergence, interconnectivity, and rapidly moving exponential tech.

The next subsections give snapshots of several systems that are directly relevant to developing a future-forward tech strategy: digitalization, the UN Sustainable Development Goals (SDGs), the concepts of ESG and ESG plus T (ESGT), and enterprise risk management. These are but a few examples of systems in a world full of systems, subsystems, and ecosystems—some that are independent and unrelated to one another, and others that are related, overlapping, or even converging. Suffice it to say that a decision-maker who is not thinking in systems and ecosystems concepts is a tactician disguised as a strategist.

Digitalization and the Rise of Digital Trust Systems

Focusing on the technological aspect, there are major developments that can only be described as systemic, borderless, and explosive in their impact. One is the worldwide adoption of the Internet. Another is the globalization of social media and increasingly powerful, even exponential, communications technologies. Yet another one is the development of web 3.0 and blockchain technologies. Another is the digitization of just about everything. And, of course, as we have been exploring in this book, the rise and explosion of AI and GenAI is yet another. Reacting to these systemic developments, a wide variety of responses (specific and general, local, national, and international) are being developed by cross-sector organizations to help govern, manage risk, and deploy solutions in the digital world. We explore a few of these developments in greater detail in the final chapter of this book, which is devoted to governing the global commons.

For now, let us delve into digital trust and how digital trust systems are permeating our daily work and play. The waves of digitalization and digitization that have occurred over the past few decades have only accelerated and represent "systems" in and of themselves. Gartner provides two useful definitions of the related terms "digitalization" and "digitization":

- "Digitalization is the use of digital technologies to change a business model and provide new revenue- and value-producing opportunities; it is the process of moving to a digital business."[6]
- "Digitization is the process of changing from analog to digital form, also known as digital enablement. Said another way, digitization takes an analog process and changes it to a digital form without any different-in-kind changes to the process itself."[7]

The first definition is more all-encompassing and strategic, while the second is more tactical and particular. Let us also look at Gartner's definition of another key concept: digital trust: "Digital trust underpins every digital interaction by measuring and quantifying the expectation that an entity is who or what it claims to be and that it will behave in an expected manner. CIOs who lead digital business initiatives need to learn how digital trust differs from traditional trust models."[8] Examples of creating digital trust range from having a robust and adaptable cybersecurity program and staff, including details such as conducting periodic training phishing exercises; protecting assets with digital tools, tests, and audits; and ensuring that the highest echelons of the organization—the C-suite and the board—are regularly briefed, trained, and updated on digital and cyber matters and develop a digital governance approach.

In chapter 14, we will examine one of the leading digital trust frameworks created so far, which was developed by the World Economic Forum in collaboration with a variety of leading tech consultancies.[9] For now, it is useful to simply consider their definition of digital trust: "Digital trust is individuals' expectation that digital technologies and services—and the organizations providing them—will protect all stakeholders' interests and uphold societal expectations and values."[10]

Sustainability, the SDGs, and Digitalization

One of the pervasive systems we all touch on daily is the concept of sustainability. The United Nations has had a long and profound connection to this theme, contributing many important milestones for decades, including the formulation of the ubiquitous Sustainable Development

Table 12.2 Examples of the United Nations' Digital Projects for Its Sustainable Development Goals

Sustainable Development Goal	Project Description
1: No Poverty	Creating digital IDs with bank and mobile money accounts to improve the delivery of social protection coverage to beneficiaries
3: Good Health and Wellbeing	Novel, platform-based vaccine technologies and smart vaccine manufacturing techniques
6: Clean Water and Sanitation	Deployment of digital tech in precision irrigation and leakage management systems based on the Internet of Things
14: Life Below Water	Providing satellite imaging and machine learning to help find and collect trillions of pieces of plastic trash in the ocean

Source: UN Sustainable Development Goals, https://sdgs.un.org/goals.

Goals (SDGs) issued in 2015 and due to be met in 2030.[11] The UN first defined "sustainability" in its Brundtland Commission Report of 1987: "Sustainability (is) . . . meeting the needs of the present without compromising the ability of future generations to meet their own needs."[12]

The seventeen SDGs issued in 2015 cover a variety of environmental, social, and governance issues—all of which intersect in one way or another with technology and digital issues. As I explored in my book *Gloom to Boom*, each and every one of the SDGs overlaps in the digital world in one way or another. Indeed, the UN maintains a deep and broad public/private program and record demonstrating how digitalization overlaps the seventeen SDGs. Table 12.2 provides just a few of their many great examples.[13] We also saw in chapter 11 that one particular SDG—9: "Industry, Innovation, and Infrastructure"—is keyed to the issue of technological and digital development.

ESG and ESGT

ESG is the practice of incorporating environmental, social, and governance considerations into business, finance, and the assessment of such issues, risks, and opportunities in the development of strategy. The term "ESG" was coined back in 2005 via a public/private dialogue culminating in a UN publication called "Who Cares, Wins."[14] The term continued to grow and then skyrocket in importance, use, and visibility in the late 2010s and early 2020s, when it became synonymous with making money through green funds and other financial vehicles. And then the backlash began. Not only were instances of greenwashing expanding, but ESG became the subject of deep political polarization—especially in the United States—where the far-right wing of the Republican Party adopted a politicized anti-ESG (also called by some anti-woke) strategy that has led to the serious degradation of the term's meaning.

Despite all these twists and turns, the term "sustainability," which is somewhat different in tone and content, has continued to survive the slings and arrows of the ESG wars. Indeed, a term called "greenhushing" has been coined to describe the fact that businesses continue to deploy ESG strategic and tactical considerations but are talking about them less publicly, mostly for fear of attracting the wrong kind of polarized political attention. And thus, we are seeing much more use of the term "sustainability" and a discussion of the SDGs as part of a company's business strategy.

And then, of course, there are those who have continued to work with the ESG nomenclature in different ways. In my 2020 book *Gloom to Boom*, I extended the ESG concept to what I call ESGT, and thus to include technological issues, risks, and opportunities that businesses and all types of organizations need to consider in developing their strategy. To further address how these topics all fall under the overall nomenclature of sustainability, I was fortunate to be the coauthor of a piece on this topic that was included in a groundbreaking book—*Sustainability, Technology and Finance*, edited by Georg Kell, Herman Brill, and Andreas Rasche—on the interconnections of ESG and technology.[15]

Element 3: Tech Risk Intelligence

To build a future-forward tech strategy—foresight—it is critical that a solid risk management and governance system be in place, to which I already alluded. As we explored in detail in chapter 11, decision-makers must have a profound understanding of how strategic global risk, enterprise risk management, and risk governance are part and parcel of their organizational success. Suffice it to say for the purposes of this chapter that the element of tech risk intelligence is a critical component of foresight.

Element 4: Tech Opportunity Readiness

Likewise, understanding the transformative power of tech-turbocharged opportunity, innovation, and value creation is central to every entity's mission and vision. In chapter 11, we explored the centrality of resilience for developing the exponential governance mindset. In addition to tech risk intelligence, no company, government agency, nonprofit, or university can be ready to take full advantage of tech opportunities without that solid base of resilience (crisis readiness, business continuity), as we discussed in detail in chapter 11.

As I am writing this chapter in the summer of 2024, the tech titans from several of the so-called Magnificent Seven (Alphabet, Apple, Amazon, Nvidia, Meta, Tesla, and Microsoft), in reaction to mixed earnings news on the current "success" indicators for GenAI products and services, were reported in Axios to have made statements.[16]

Meta stated: "AI will improve 'almost every' existing Meta product and 'make a whole lot of new ones possible,' Meta CEO Mark Zuckerberg said on his call Wednesday." "So, it's why there are all the jokes about how all the tech CEOs get on these earnings calls and just talk about AI the whole time. It's because it's actually super exciting."

Microsoft stated: "As for doubts about the wisdom of plowing so many billions into 'capex' [capital expenditures] to build AI capacity, Microsoft CEO Satya Nadella said the company is carefully tuning into the 'demand signals' from customers. Those signals—like massive growth in use of GitHub Copilot, which is now a bigger business than GitHub itself was when Microsoft acquired it in 2018—are flashing green," Nadella said.

Executives also argued that if they overbuild data centers and buy more servers than the AI buildout ultimately needs, the companies will find other good uses for that infrastructure. Alphabet stated: "When you go through a curve like this, the risk of underinvesting is dramatically greater than the risk of overinvesting for us here, Google CEO Sundar Pichai told analysts last week."

The thread that runs through these statements by these publicly traded US tech giants is that they are making a huge long-term bet on the success of AI, GenAI, and other exponential technologies associated with these technologies—robotics, advanced materials, biotech, climate tech, health tech, fintech, education tech, and so on—that have already begun to be deployed and will be deployed further and become ever more interdependent on these advances. And they are doing so in a marketplace that rewards short-termism, that bets daily, hourly, even by the second, on stocks. But investing in exponential technology development is not a short-term play. The tech titans know this (and can afford this) better than anyone else, and that is why they are willing to take the shorter-term slings and arrows and make the longer-term multi-billion-dollar investments today.

Tech opportunity readiness also manifests itself in the evolving tech talent and skills equation. While there is good reason, on one hand, to be worried that certain jobs and skill sets—like coding—may no longer be needed because GenAI and agentic AI will do it, on the other hand, a raft of new, redesigned, and different jobs emerging will likely replace the ones lost. While this may not always be easy for a particular individual to face because they do not have the opportunity or ability to reskill—or their employer or ex-employer did not assist properly with retraining— one of the most important things leaders must do and bake into their future-forward tech strategy is an innovative and continuous approach to talent design, skilling, reskilling, and redeployment.

Take for example the emergence of the "chief AI officer" role. This position is being deployed in business and governmental contexts as AI and GenAI permeate almost all aspects of life and business. The role was required by the US government for its own top departments via its "Executive Order on the Safe, Secure, and Trustworthy Development and Use of Artificial Intelligence," issued on October 30, 2023, but rescinded by the Trump Administration upon his taking office.[18] In it, there was a requirement that all top government departments and agencies (including the White House) establish such a role. The role was required to focus on the "coordination, innovation, and risk management for their agency's use of AI" and to develop a "deeply interconnected strategy" with other key functions, including human resources, information technology, cybersecurity, data, civil rights, and customer experience. Even with the Trump Administration's cancelation of this requirement within the federal government, these developments continue to ring true in other business and NGO contexts.

Element 5: Interdisciplinary Scenario Planning

A final element of foresight is adopting targeted scenario planning and exercises as a key part of developing strategy development in our poly-crisis world. One of the best ways to be prepared for the future is to run well-designed, targeted, and relevant scenario planning exercises within your organization. The scenarios should be chosen from your entity's risk and opportunity profile—in other words, from issues, risks, and opportunities that are relevant to your organization's business footprint and strategy, geography, personnel profile, and products and services. In the real world, this translates into four aspects.

The first aspect is the team. Interdisciplinary members of management and staff should take charge of the design and execution of these exercises periodically, often with the help of outside experts. These team members should be creative, informed, and proactive. And they must have the visible support of top management as well as the necessary resources and budget. The team needs to be interdisciplinary so that the major relevant issues to the business of the entity are included in the exercises, such as technology, legal, governance, sustainability, geopolitical, supply chain, and other relevant matters.

The second aspect is exercises. The core team and outside experts must scan the ERM results, the headlines, and the relevant situational awareness findings to design a creative, potential, and even imaginative but relevant exercise, such as:

- If you are the Olympics Organizing Committee for the 2028 Los Angeles games, some of the issues you would want to integrate into scenario planning would be GenAI turbocharged cyberinsecurity, physical security (of public, of athletes, of dignitaries), location security, misinformation, disinformation, social media reputational harm, the possible deployment of bioterror, and more. And, sadly, in view of the unprecedented destruction by the January 2025 wildfires in the Los Angeles area, uncontrollable droughts and even arson-driven wildfires that can potentially have a serious destructive and health impact on the Olympic Games, the athletes, visitors, and, of course, the local population.

• If you are OpenAI, right now some of the issues you would want to include in scenario planning would be governance reputational harm, product safety, data provenance integrity, intellectual property violations, hallucinations, and confabulations affecting key stakeholders and potential infighting and anticompetitive retaliation by technology leaders (e.g., Musk) closely associated with the Trump administration.

• If you are an electric utility in Taiwan, Japan, or the Philippines, your company (together with public/private entities) should run periodic scenario exercises contemplating a Chinese invasion or protracted and material damage to Taiwan, including potential issues like AI-turbocharged cyberattacks; drone attacks; transportation and supply chain disruption, including maritime disruption; back-up power to served populations; safety of personnel; and more.

The third aspect is participants. The relevant people engaged in such exercises should be at all levels—from the board to the front line and from headquarters to far away offices or sites. They should include mixed groups and experts—both internal and external.

The fourth and final aspect is lessons learned. This is a critical piece of this particular puzzle—the collection of actionable lessons that can be fed back into the relevant parts of the organization—whether it is further exercises, education for the employee population or targeted group, or continuous improvement of processes, people, and policies. And more.

The UK cybersecurity authority has a helpful website with cybersecurity scenario planning suggestions; see sidebar 12.1.[19]

Sidebar 12.1
The UK Cyber Security Centre's Guidance for Using Cybersecurity Scenarios to Manage Risk

1. *Discussion-based exercises.* These are inexpensive, require the least amount of planning, and can be run easily, including on a semi-impromptu basis. They are often used to develop awareness of a plan that has already been formulated, or for scenarios that are difficult to test in practice (such as a ransomware attack impacting every end point within an organization).

2. *Tabletop exercises.* These are table-based and involve a structured activity (including role play and games) as a focus for the scenario. These are usually held in an informal setting, with no hands-on practice or field work. They aim to generate discussion about the scenario to enhance awareness, develop, validate, or stress-test plans. Games can be effective at highlighting decision-making during an incident, and problems with the sequencing of postincident recovery actions (participants often highlight interdependencies between actions).

3. *Functional exercises.* These are the most immersive, and involve the technology, people, and processes being exercised. They can disrupt normal work, are expensive, and demand detailed planning. They provide greater insight about how your organization will react and reveal unforeseen results more effectively than tabletop exercises. They can vary in scale from a single department to a group of organizations.

Source: National Cyber Security Centre, "Using Cyber Security Scenarios," www.ncsc.gov.uk /collection/risk-management/using-cyber-security-scenarios.

Questions Stakeholders Should Ask Leaders About Foresight

Stakeholders need to ask leaders these questions about foresight:

1. Does management and the board engage in understanding their environment on a continuous basis—is there a team assigned to develop and maintain actionable situational awareness?

2. Do decision-makers consciously and proactively understand and

integrate relevant systems—like the SDGs, sustainability, and digital trust—into their development of business strategy?

3. Do decision-makers—at both the management and board levels—integrate risk intelligence, including tech risk intelligence, into the development of business strategy?

4. Do decision-makers—at both the management and board levels—integrate tech opportunity readiness into the development of business strategy?

5. Do management and the board actively encourage the use of interdisciplinary scenario exercises, planning, and continuous improvement as key components of developing strategy and strategic foresight?

Actions Leaders Should Take to Unleash Foresight

To unleash foresight, leaders should take these actions:

1. Investigate whether you are already using some of the five elements of the future-forward tech strategy, and if so, pull them together into a holistic approach.

2. Deploy the five elements of the future-forward tech strategy.

3. Seriously consider incorporating continually evolving, interdisciplinary scenario planning exercises into your management, executive, and board activities.

A Final Word on Foresight and the Exponential Governance Mindset

When we talk about "foresight" and "unleashing a future-forward tech strategy," we are talking about a business strategy that is inclusive, situationally aware, open, inventive, risk-intelligent, opportunity-smart, and forward-biased. This means that any and all cutting-edge, exponential technologies that are under development, bought, deployed, possible, and/or the subject of the competition, stakeholders, and allies need to be factored into the unleashed, future-forward, systemic, and systematic tech strategy.

A future-forward tech strategy is one in which the leadership of an organization—mainly management under its principal leader (CEO, MD, ED, president)—leads the charge every year and throughout the year to align business planning, budgeting, resources, and situational awareness with business purpose, both short-term and long-term mission, and vision. It is about looking to the future—short, medium, and long term—to ensure that necessary considerations, resources, people, and technology are aligned with action and operational plans. But it is also about considering how the governing body plays a critical oversight role that ensures that management is on the case, being holistic and systematic about understanding the role of emerging and exponential tech in its business planning, footprint, and forecasting. But this, of course, requires a governance body that is made up of the right people who have the needed experience and foresight. Let us see what this means by turning to chapter 13, where we explore how we, as people and as professionals, can futureproof ourselves and our organizations for this Age of Pandora.

IV

FUTUREPROOFING IN THE AGE OF PANDORA

Deploying the Exponential
Governance Mindset

13

FUTUREPROOFING OURSELVES AND OUR ORGANIZATIONS

Tips and Typologies

What does it mean to lead in exponential times, to futureproof ourselves, our organizations, and the global commons in a responsible way? As we have explored throughout this book, there are many exponential tech subjects, areas, branches, subbranches, offshoots, and developments far beyond anything we can fully capture here—many of them are extraordinary, revolutionary, and game-changing; others are certainly ephemeral, flashes in the pan, here today, gone tomorrow.

Deploying the Exponential Governance Mindset, Responsibly

With such a barrage of multifaceted change comes the need for more responsibility—education, vigilance, alertness, and the ability to identify and discern issues, risks, and opportunities. Thus there is a need to forecast and prepare for the known and unknown, certain and uncertain, predictable and unpredictable—faster and more successfully than ever before. As we examined in chapters 1 and 2, with the rise, intermingling, and sometimes convergence of these technologies, we may indeed have entered the Fifth Industrial Revolution or, more aptly, perhaps the First Postindustrial or Virtual Revolution. Are we ready to deal with these outsize developments responsibly?

In part I, we offered the big picture—the global tech megascape (megatrends landscape)—to understand the context of the Age of Pandora. In part II, we explored the tip of the iceberg of new and exponential technologies in a wide variety of fields—from AI, GenAI, and SynBio to superchips, biocomputing, and humanoids. Part III offered a framework for understanding and building an agile and effective exponential governance mindset and practical toolkit for surviving and thriving in the Age of Pandora. Now, in part IV, we offer tips and typologies for dealing with this new world, focused on deploying the exponential governance mindset.

The exponential governance mindset consists of five practical elements: leadership that embraces 360 tech governance; an ethos that ingrains a responsible tech culture; impact that includes key stakeholders in the tech loop: resilience in the face of polyrisk and polycrisis; and through it all, a strategy of tech foresight. As we conclude here in part IV, we focus on the future—how to futureproof ourselves, our organizations, and the global commons in the Age of Pandora to deploy new, frontier technologies *responsibly*. We connect these dots to provide guidance on how to apply the exponential governance mindset and toolkit at three different levels—the individual, the organizational, and the global commons at several exponential frontiers—the biological, the mechanical, the planetary, and the virtual, as addressed in chapter 14.

Everyone—especially those of us who are not scientists, engineers, or technologists—the businesspeople, academics, policymakers, ethicists, students, and others not deeply steeped in STEM and the bleeding edge of frontier tech (the "human-centric") must labor to keep up with advances in technology. We need to scale up our analytical skills, read widely and deeply, and think about the potential impact of exponential tech on our organizations in order to understand this brave new world of velocity, volatility, uncertainty, asymmetry, and interconnectivity. In addition, we should spend time directly observing, using, and even immersing ourselves in new technologies so that we can bridge the gap, connect, and talk with the tech-centric (defined below).

Likewise, those who are deeply steeped in STEM and innovation—the physicists; the engineers; the mathematicians; the coders and testers; the

founders, investors, and funders; and others deeply embedded in frontier tech (the "tech-centric")—have a similar but different obligation. The
tech-centric need to see the big picture less from the perspective of technological, financial, and scientific details they know well and more from
the perspectives of social science, law, systems thinking, culture, ethics, humanitarianism, policymaking, and governance. The tech-centric
must connect the human and tech dots more directly and successfully,
becoming more empathetic to, and understanding of, the human side
of the exponential tech equation, spending serious time understanding
the behavioral and planetary effects and implications of the tech they are
working on and ensuring that the consequences are largely beneficial and
responsibly developed.

Of course, there are people who belong in both camps simultaneously, who live at the center of the exponential tech Venn diagram. This
book has attempted to cater to leaders in both camps and those at the
converging center, offering practical tools to achieve the results we all
want and need: governing in the Age of Pandora for the benefit of all
planetary stakeholders. At the end of the day, we should all aspire to be
either human-centric innovators (technologists with human-centric sensitivity) or innovative stewards (humanists with tech savvy). (See figure
14.3 in chapter 14.)

Futureproofing Ourselves, Responsibly

Let us now turn to the first two of the three levels of understanding and
application of the exponential governance mindset—the individual and
the organizational. We will explore the third level in chapter 14, where we
will look at examples of "exponential frontiers" in the global commons—
the biological, the mechanical, the planetary, and the virtual.

Ten Personal Qualities and Five Guiding Principles
for Leading in the Age of Pandora

If we consider the role each of us plays as individuals—at personal, famil-
ial, professional, communal, social, national, and international levels—a
series of qualities have come through our exploration of exponential tech

that I believe are essential to leading successfully in the Age of Pandora. Let us examine each of these briefly (see table 13.1).

In essence, and drawing on what we have learned through this book—the examples, cases, and developments—I believe the ten essential personal qualities to navigate the Age of Pandora apply to everyone—from the university student who is trying to figure out the rest of his or her life to the senior board director who is serving on five boards and needs to catch up with the overwhelming change that has happened in his or her lifetime, from the kindergarten teacher to the political party leader, and from the store owner to the multinational corporate chieftain.

The ten qualities for leading in exponential times are about making ourselves stronger, better, more ready for this period—as individuals, as members of a community, as participants and stakeholders in one or more organizations, and as citizens of the world. They range from being curious about the world to being humble about what you do not know; from being empathetic to others' perspectives, concerns, and wishes to being collaborative, interdisciplinary, inclusive, and open to diversity; and from having situational awareness to taking a systems-thinking and future-thinking approach, always understanding and emphasizing tech ethics, safety, and responsibility. Pulling together these ten qualities, here are my five principles for leading in the Age of Pandora.

Principle #1: be a continuous learner. Be a curious and continuous learner—an expert and a generalist. To survive and thrive in this era of deep complexity and vast and fast change, each of us should make sure that—in addition to whatever expertise we have or are developing from a skills, studies, talent, or professional development standpoint—we also keep our minds open to constantly learning new things, adjacently—from other sectors, disciplines, people, and parts of the world. This applies as much (maybe even more) to the Fortune 500 corporate board leader of a tech company as it does to the student graduating from law school or engineering school—and everyone in between in every sector.

How to become a continuous learner: First, gather a few high-quality publications, newsletters, and podcasts, and subscribe and read or listen regularly to subjects at the intersection of technology and society, includ-

Table 13.1 Leading in the Age of Pandora: Ten Personal Qualities and Five Guiding Principles

Ten Personal Qualities	Five Guiding Principles
Expert	1. Be a curious and continuous learner—an
Curious	expert and a generalist
Humble	2. Have an open attitude of humility, empathy,
Empathetic	collaboration, and inclusivity
Collaborative	3. Be a situationally aware, systems thinker and doer—
Situationally aware	always connect the dots
Future thinking	4. Be a risk and opportunity future thinker and doer—
Systems thinking	adopt a future-forward mindset
Interconnective	5. Activate ethical, safe, and responsible tech—
Ethically responsible	verify first; then trust

Source: Author.

ing from *MIT Technology Review, Wired Magazine, Axios,* the *Information,* the Council on Foreign Relations' Defense & Security page, and the World Economic Forum's Centre for the Fourth Industrial Revolution / Digital Transformation. Listen to some of the great tech podcasts, like The AI Breakdown, Your Undivided Attention, the World Economic Forum's Radio Davos, the Ted AI Show, Tech Won't Save Us, Tools and Weapons, and Waking Up with AI.

Principle #2: be open-minded. Have an open attitude of humility, empathy, collaboration, inclusivity, and diversity. In this often-unforgiving, fast-paced world, the ability to see the behavioral picture is crucial, especially outside our comfort zones; and that is why collaboration with a diversity of other experts and generalists is not only desirable but, frankly, crucial.

How to cultivate open-mindedness: Seek out information and connections globally—find out what is happening in other parts of the world. For example, check out the UN digital projects that are taking place all over the world to meet the UN Sustainable Development Goals or subscribe to the free newsletter *Rest of World,* which provides a unique and invaluable resource to understand the effects of tech or the absence thereof on emerging economies, the so-called Global South, and other developing and/or struggling parts of the world.

Principle #3: be a systems thinker. Be a situationally aware systems thinker and doer—always connect the dots. As we discussed in several chapters (1, 2, 11, and 12), being situationally aware, on one hand, and a systems thinker, on the other hand, are also great advantages in this fast-changing world. Because of the velocity and volatility of change, it is critical to understand the context (situational awareness of trends and megatrends) as well as the systems that we are operating within (UN Sustainable Development Goals, climate change, and digital transformation). Indeed, situational awareness is awareness of the systems that surround, envelop, and affect what we do. It is not enough to be a thinker—translate what you learn into action, of the responsible kind.

How to develop systems thinking: Read a few books on systems thinking, like the ones cited in the selected bibliography and additional resources in this book, and exercise your mind about the systems in the world and how they interconnect. A fantastic resource in this regard is the World Economic Forum's "Global Risks Report," published each year in January.

Principle #4: think and act forward. Be a risk-and-opportunity future thinker and actor—adopt a future-forward mindset. It is also deeply important for the exponential tech leader to exercise foresight, forecasting, and future-casting through scenario planning and other means to understand both the current and projected risk landscape as well as the opportunity horizon. While this may be a theoretical exercise in principle, it can be converted into a very lively and useful pathway to strategic choices and tactical actions.

How to become a forward thinker and doer: Subscribe to the work and attend meetings and webinars of future-oriented think tanks like *Diplomatic Courier*'s "The World in 2050," the Future of Life Institute, All Tech Is Human, XRSI, the Council on Foreign Relations, and the World Economic Forum.

Principle #5: be responsible. Activate ethical, safe, and responsible tech—verify; then trust. Always verify first, and only after doing that trust tech and new tech developments. Consult experts (or make sure experts have been consulted), understand the provenance and processes through which tech has gone before approving it, producing it, acquiring it, or digesting it. and continue to verify and trust continuously. In the fast-paced, speed-of-light, often-unbounded world of exponential technology, it is essential that we reverse the traditional saying of "trust but verify" to "verify, then trust." If we do not, we risk causing known and unknown, potentially irremediable, consequences.

How to become tech responsible: Since its release into the public domain, all forms of GenAI have been plagued by confabulation and hallucination, much of it having to do with the black box nontransparent sausage making of most GenAI responses, whether text to text, text to graphics or video, and other multimodal processes and outcomes. And much of this has to do with the quality and characteristics of the data and their provenance that go into algorithms. Make sure you do your part in ensuring a safe, secure, and transparent technology commons. Sidebar 13.1 provides ideas of things you can do as an individual to futureproof yourself.

Futureproofing Our Organizations, Responsibly—What Is Your Leadership Stakeholder Culture?

Next on the agenda is understanding how and when an organization can be considered future-ready, *and responsibly so*, to successfully navigate the Age of Pandora. Is your entity equipped and ready to navigate a future full of tech and exponential tech and the other challenges that come with living in the twenty-first century—*in a responsible way?*

In this section, we offer a typology of responsible organizational future-readiness based on two factors: (1) how well developed and practically implemented an organization's exponential governance toolkit is (in other words, how robust is its deployment of the five elements of the exponential governance mindset discussed in part III); and (2) what is the organization's leaders' culture on stakeholder care and responsibility, as we glean both these criteria from research and public sources (media, filings, etc.).

Using Mark Zuckerberg's famous (or infamous) "moving fast and breaking things" concept, we explore three unique approaches that leaders can have to stakeholder care: (1) "Move fast and break things,"

Sidebar 13.1
Futureproofing Techniques

- Build a responsible AI business: speak up and walk away from an irresponsible one.
- Help create a responsible culture at your company.
- Vote with your feet (leave a job) or your purchasing power (eliminate a skeevy app from your phone).
- As a consultant or expert, help to create a responsible tech culture at other tech companies.
- Join a think tank or community-based organization and become a stakeholder in the tech loop.
- Influence your elected officials to be proactive about privacy, data, surveillance, mis/disinformation.
- Become a responsible tech influencer.
- Vote with your responsible tech brain.
- Help regulators to understand your perspective as a tech stakeholder.
- Get an AR/VR headset and immerse yourself in the metaverse and spatial computing.
- Use GenAI to create text to video, audio to text and graphics to video to understand and experience multimodality.
- Adopt agentic AI in your work but keep an eye on it.
- Expand your usage of AI on your computers and phones.
- Understand what GenAI is doing to cyber insecurity.
- Flag problems to your tech expert friends and find solutions.

Source: Author.

---

(2) "Move (fast or slow) and build things," and (3) "Move slow and/or undermine things." We begin by explaining each of these stakeholder cultural approaches and then bring it back to how these two factors affect the responsible future preparedness of an organization. As coined by Mark Zuckerberg when he founded Facebook at the beginning of the twenty-first century, "Move fast and break things" was intended to reflect the ethos of his company and his leadership—and to his credit, that ethos continues to this day, twenty years later, and hundreds of billions of dollars of value creation (and sometimes destruction) later.

It is critical to understand how leaders treat their stakeholders. It can mean the difference between an ethical and trustworthy culture and a toxic and untrustworthy one.[1] It is especially important to understand culture in the context of its impact on key stakeholders. Let us explore the possibilities.

Move Fast and Break Things

This culture is one in which the impulse and focus on winning and winning big—in investments, revenues, profits, and other metrics and conquests—and doing it fast is the only thing that matters, even if things are broken or destroyed in the process. It is about inventing things with a general disregard for governance or guardrails, at least to begin with. It is an act-now, ask-for-forgiveness-later mentality that can be damaging to key stakeholders like customers, consumers, users, employees, and others whose privacy and other rights, for example, may be trampled upon in the rush to success. Hey, but it might get you there—to new tech, vast wealth, and great influence.

There are two possible outcomes from this approach—winning and winning big, as we have seen with Zuckerberg and Musk; and losing and losing big, as we have seen with Elizabeth Holmes of Theranos and Sam Bankman-Fried of FTX—where one of the biggest crypto plays in the market, a cryptocurrency exchange founded by Bankman-Fried and used as an illegal piggy bank for his hedge fund, turned into one of the biggest frauds in the crypto space to date, with the result of him getting a twenty-five-year federal prison sentence.[2] If we take a look at Zuckerberg as an example, he continues to take this approach to this day. He somewhat rashly changed the name of Facebook to Meta just a few years ago because he was betting big on the metaverse and wanted to corner the name, only to find out a year later that the metaverse while still a thing was not (at least for now) the biggest thing. But to his credit, he has pivoted to being one of the biggest players in GenAI, with his Llama suite of GenAI products and more. OpenAI under Sam Altman and Tesla and xAI under Elon Musk also represent the stakeholder culture of "moving fast and breaking things."

The stakeholder angle: A key differentiator, here in addition to how fast the organization is moving, is how it treats some of its most important stakeholders in furtherance of speed and the answer is: from mediocre to bad.

The bottom line: These cultures do not always breed broad stakeholder trust, and in fact they often antagonize key segments of the stakeholder community or damage them altogether (Theranos, FTX, and potentially Tesla—still a work in progress at the time of this writing).

Move Fast (or Slow) and Build Things

This is the mentality we see at many established, higher-reputation businesses, especially those that pay heed to guardrails and stakeholder interests and are generally compliant with laws and regulations. Examples of this culture include Microsoft under Satya Nadella, Nvidia under Jensen Huang, and Google under Sundar Pichai. It also includes Anthropic, a GenAI start-up in which Google has invested and which has a claim to caring more about stakeholder guardrails, transparency, and doing things more responsibly (at least until now).

The stakeholder angle: Here the pace of change and invention may be fast or a bit slower, but the focus is on change made responsibly, counterbalanced by the need to observe regulations, laws, and the interests of key stakeholders, including shareholders.

The bottom line: These are cultures that breed greater stakeholder trust.

Move Slow and Undermine Things

This culture is a recipe for failure—a combination of sluggishness in getting things done and not really accomplishing much in terms of tech or exponential tech preparedness. These kinds of organizations are likely to be government bureaucracies, unfocused or unproductive nonprofits, and businesses that are not tech ready or savvy and potentially at risk of going bankrupt or out of business. These organizations are singularly unprepared for what awaits them on the exponential tech path, and they are likely to not survive because they do not have the mindset to succeed in a fast-changing world.

The stakeholder angle: Anyone who is part of or has a stake in one of these types of entities should encourage education and change or vote with their feet and leave whether you are a consumer, employee, contractor, or other type of stakeholder.

The bottom line: These are cultures that breed skepticism, suspicion, and a loss of stakeholder trust.

Is Your Entity "Responsible Tech Future-Ready"? A Typology

Let us turn to understanding how these stakeholder cultural approaches relate to the exponential governance mindset and toolkit, we described in detail in part III, so we can offer a typology of how future-ready and responsible an organization might be.

The Typology Explained and Illustrated

Turning back for a moment to the five elements of the exponential governance mindset—we can develop a typology of how ready and responsible an organization might be for an exponential tech future (see figure 13.1). The purpose of this typology is to provide guidance to anyone interested in either building, analyzing, or deploying responsible tech in the Age of Pandora. As a reminder, the exponential governance mindset consists of five key elements: leadership (360 tech governance), ethos (a responsible tech culture), impact (integrating stakeholder interests), resilience (having polyrisk and polycrisis preparedness), and foresight (unleashing a future-ready strategy).

Combining a consideration of how developed and complete an organization's exponential governance mindset is and what the prevailing leadership stakeholder culture is (as discussed above), it is possible to come up with four types of future-readiness, as outlined in the next subsections. Also see figure 13.2.

Future-Unprepared and Irresponsible

First, we have the *unprepared/irresponsible entity*, where neither the exponential governance mindset is well developed nor is there sensitivity on

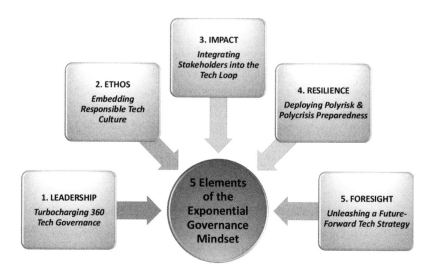

Figure 13.1 How Future-Ready and Responsible Is Your Organization?
Source: Author.

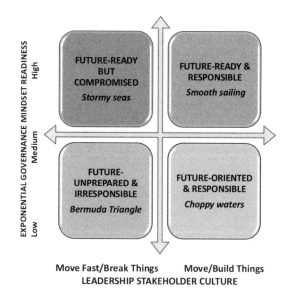

Figure 13.2 An Organizational Typology of Responsible Future-Readiness
Source: Author.

the part of leadership to stakeholder issues. Theranos and FTX present clear cases—as they have already imploded for different but similar reasons. Both companies and their founders perpetrated deep fraud on their key stakeholders (investors, employees, regulators) and simultaneously did not do much to develop proper guardrails and governance (i.e., the exponential tech mindset) within their companies.

There are several current companies especially in the crypto space (including Genesis Global Capital, BlockFi, Celsius Network, Voyager Digital, and others), but also in some social media and communications spaces (Telegram, X, and Truth Social come to mind), that may qualify for this less-than-complimentary category. The crypto companies mentioned above, for example, are all in or have been in various stages of bankruptcy and investigation.[3] This type of entity has either already been swallowed up into the Bermuda Triangle or is recklessly navigating toward it.

Future-Ready but Compromised

This is an organization that is moving fast and innovating successfully, with a certain degree of sophistication when it comes to the governance mindset, but its leadership does not deeply consider or systematically integrate most of its key stakeholders' interests. These are entities that are moving fast and breaking things—I am thinking of Meta, OpenAI, xAI, Tesla, and Amazon. This type of entity is most certainly navigating, sometimes recklessly, in stormy seas.

Future-Oriented and Responsible

While moving a little slower, perhaps partly because it is placing guardrails around governance concerns and caring a little more about key stakeholders, these are entities that are paying attention to both sides of the equation: they are innovating, moving fairly fast, but they are also cognizant of the governance guardrails and elements they need to build into their systems. Here I am thinking of Anthropic, Mistral, and Perplexity AI in the GenAI space; and of Epi One in the biotech space. This type of entity is navigating in choppy waters but deftly and successfully so far.

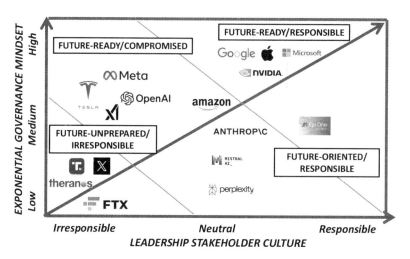

Figure 13.3 A Plotting of Responsible Tech Futures
Source: Author.

Future-Ready and Responsible

Fourth, and finally, there are the stars of the show—those entities that not only have dynamic and fast-charging innovation, products, and services but are doing so with relative leadership responsibility toward key stakeholders, as well as a developed exponential governance mindset. Among these entities are many of the most successful tech companies in the world today: Apple, Microsoft, Alphabet, and Nvidia. These entities are well prepared for the future, with all the leadership and equipment they need to sail smoothly, even when stormy weather comes their way. Figure 13.3 provides a plotting of responsible tech futures based on these types and the examples noted. Speaking of navigation, let us now turn to the final chapter, 14, in which we will take a look at what it means to manage exponential technology in the global commons in four different exponential frontiers—the biological, the mechanical, the planetary, and the virtual.

14

FUTUREPROOFING THE GLOBAL COMMONS

Exponential Frontiers

In this final chapter, I want to share with you, my reader, one last lens to look through to get our arms around how to futureproof the global commons in the Age of Pandora. We will do so by exploring what the global commons means, and by suggesting that there are four exponential frontiers in the global commons where we can observe a mix or convergence of exponential technologies ("tech turbocharging tech," as it were) in multifaceted manifestations. Let us first visit the concept of "global commons," and then we will investigate details for each of four exponential frontiers—the biological, the mechanical, the planetary, and the virtual.

We hopefully know who we are and we also know what organizations and entities we touch as stakeholders (as leaders, users, employees, consumers, taxpayers, shareholders, beneficiaries, and so on). But we are also citizens of the world—of the "global commons"—which is typically considered in analytical and policy circles to include the natural systems and resources that do not belong to any one nation and are shared by our common humanity—the oceans, the atmosphere, and beyond.

According to the Council on Foreign Relations, which has a policy segment and experts dedicated to the "global commons," the global commons covers Antarctica, the Arctic, oceans and seas, the atmosphere and space, and touches on issues such as defense and security, diplomacy and international institutions, economics, energy and the environment, health, human rights, politics and government, and social issues.[1] It would be safe to say that the global commons covers geographical and physical spaces and expanses beyond human, nation-state-imposed frontiers. In these global commons there are human actions and behaviors that take place along a wide and long spectrum of activities—from space exploration to deep sea mining—for which humanity has developed a modus vivendi, governance guardrails, treaties, and international law over the centuries, along with tensions, disagreements, confrontation, and other nasty behaviors we humans so excel at.

In the Age of Pandora, exponential technologies promote an increasingly borderless world, for better and for worse. Consider the case of the tiny but increasingly and overwhelmingly wealthy and powerful set of tech billionaire "broligarchs," like Peter Thiel, Elon Musk, Sam Altman, Marc Andreessen, and Mark Zuckerberg. They are able to act across borders, building "independent" cities and enclaves, sometimes becoming more powerful than political or government leaders, often making decisions or effecting outcomes that affect society with impunity.

Take the case of the transnational power Elon Musk has as sole owner of X/Twitter, reaching massive audiences around the world as he posts and retweets disinformation that can and has had severe and adverse emotional and physical consequences. One such case occurred in the United Kingdom in the summer of 2024, when he retweeted right-wing lies about the murder of three girls in a small town in northern England, massively stoking destructive anti-immigrant race riots all over the United Kingdom. And, since the election of Trump in November 2024 and his outsize role in funding his campaign in the United States, Musk has expanded his view to include the possible funding and/or use of his global X megaphone to support a wide variety of far-right-wing parties and causes, like Alternative for Germany (Alternative für Deutschland) in Germany and the Reform Party in the United Kingdom. This is but one example of how and why exponential technologies and their effects need to be part of the global commons conversation.

As I was delving into the global commons concept, I asked myself:

Where does the virtual world fit into this construct about borderless, but shared, frontier-less space? And how do we govern exponential technologies that are largely boundless, that are already having enormous transnational effects (GenAI; surveillance tech; and crypto) and may potentially have even greater effects on the well-being of the planet, large swaths of society, outer space, and beyond. This observation applies to both the negative and the positive, such as uncontrolled autonomous weapons including nuclear, asymmetric bioweapons usage, amazing cures, or vaccines eliminating diseases based on GenAI-turbocharged biopharma and biotech solutions.

How do we futureproof the global commons for the velocity, volatility, uncertainty, asymmetry, and interconnectivity of exponential and frontier technologies? Perhaps the global commons concept should be expanded specifically to include a virtual component, as most everything encompassed in the traditional concept of the global commons is focused on physical and/or geographical limits.

As a final general observation about the global commons and some of its exponential frontiers—and, at the other end of the spectrum from the techno-oligarchs, is another critically important challenge we must bear in mind at all times—global exponential tech access and usage inequality. It is a fact that access and use of technologies generally are for the privileged among us. Where you live and your relative economic prosperity are key determinants of whether you have access to or the usage of technologies generally (like reliable energy, the Internet, and telecommunications), let alone exponential technologies like access to GenAI tools or cutting-edge health care solutions. How we as global and local citizens address these critically important policy decisions will make the difference between global inequality as it exists today and extreme or exponential global inequality due to the growing chasm between the tech haves and have-nots worldwide. Let us turn to an exploration of four dimensions of exponential technology that relate to the global commons and four frontiers—exponential frontiers—that collectively as global citizens we need to be aware of and collaborate on to futureproof our precious blue planet.

Four Exponential Frontiers

Exponential technologies are developing and, in some cases, converging and producing new activities, products, services, externalities, and frontiers of discovery and activity, pretty much at every level of life on Earth. And we are seeing this on several frontiers—the biological (affecting human, animal, and other life on Earth); the mechanical (involving the development, use, and deployment of machines); the planetary (affecting the entire planetary ecosystem, including climate and space); and the virtual (involving cyberspace, the Internet, the metaverse, spatial intelligence, or some other form of nonphysical space).

Figure 14.1 and table 14.1 attempt to visualize and summarize in a supercompact way what I mean by the four exponential frontiers and the presence and/or convergence of a number of exponential technologies in each such frontier. There is a need for humans individually and collectively to consider these exponential frontiers as part of an overall approach to plotting the future—whether you are a policymaker, a businessperson, an academic, a student, or a curious global citizen.

Exponential Frontiers—Biological

One of the exponential frontiers—the most intimate and basic—is the biological, where exponential technologies—including biotechnology, neurotechnology, organ growing, genetic engineering, and so much more—are developing for the purpose of improving health and extending life, among other things. And on this frontier, we see the convergence of many technologies and exponential technologies, as listed in table 14.1. Two examples are bioinformatics and neurotechnology.

Bioinformatics: Early Cancer Detection and Diagnosis

Michael Marquardt, CEO of the biotech start-up Epi One, shared with me some of the details of their development of a broad diagnostic platform for the early detection and diagnosis of a large number of cancers based on what is called "bioinformatics." Bioinformatics is an interdisciplinary field that combines biology, computer science, mathematics, and statistics to analyze and interpret biological data. It involves the development

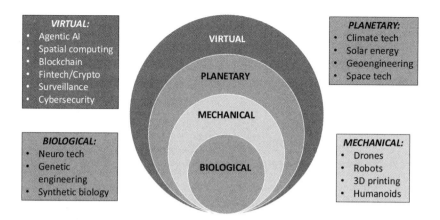

Figure 14.1 Four Exponential Technology Frontiers

Source: Author.

Table 14.1 Exponential Technologies at the Four Exponential Frontiers

Exponential Frontier	Examples	Converging Technologies
Biological	Early cancer detection tools	GenAI
	Neuro-implants	Biotechnology
	Growing organs, transplanting	Genetic engineering
	Customized targeted disease	Autonomy/robotics
	treatments	Advanced materials
		Exponential computiing
Mechanical	Drones	GenAI
	Robots	Biotechnology
	Humanoids	Robotics
	Autonomous warfare	Advanced materials
		Exponential computing
Planetary	Climate tech—solar	GenAI
	Weather tech	Geospatial engineering
	Geospatial engineering	Robotics
	Space R&D	Advanced materials
	Space warfare	Exponential computing
Virtual	Cyberinsecurity	GenAI
	Surveillance	Exponential computing
	Disinformation	Spatial computing
	Blockchain/crypto	Quantum encryption
	Metaverse AR/VR	Advanced materials
	AI agents	
	Digitalization	

Source: Author.

and application of computational tools, algorithms, and software for understanding biological processes, particularly those involving large data sets, such as genomic sequences, protein structures, and gene expression patterns. Key areas within bioinformatics include:

1. Genomics: analyzing DNA sequences to identify genes, mutations, and evolutionary relationships.
2. Proteomics: studying protein sequences, structures, and functions.
3. Transcriptomics: examining gene expression levels and patterns.
4. Systems biology: modeling complex biological systems and interactions.
5. Data mining and machine learning: applying advanced computational techniques to uncover patterns and make predictions from biological data.

Bioinformatics plays a crucial role in fields like personalized medicine, drug discovery, and evolutionary biology. These insights are enabling companies like Epi One to develop a broad diagnostic platform for powerful ways to allow for early detection and diagnosis of a large number of cancers.[2]

Neurotechnology and Brain Implants

For years, there was speculation about how humans one day would have brain implants or other embedded tech that would allow them to do things beyond their natural abilities. Indeed, for years, I included this possibility in ethics scenario planning exercises. Well, we are basically there, according to Marquardt: "Neurotechnology can be used purely for research purposes, such as experimental brain imaging to gather information about mental illness or sleep patterns. It can also be used in practical applications to influence the brain or nervous system; for example, in therapeutic or rehabilitative contexts."[3]

According to the Institute of Electrical and Electronics Engineers, "Neurotechnology refers to any technology that provides greater insight into brain or nervous system activity or affects brain or nervous system function."[4] It includes using neuromodulation technologies with neural interfaces that stimulate the nerves, neuroprostheses that act as prosthetic brain functions, and brain machine interfaces that read and/or write information into the brain.

Enter Elon Musk's company, Neuralink, which was founded in 2016. The company's primary product, known as "the Link," is a coin-sized device that is surgically implanted in the skull, with ultrathin wires extending into the brain. It is designed to record and decode neural signals, allowing users to control computers and mobile devices with their thoughts. While it has already been successfully demonstrated on several volunteers with severe paralysis, it raises numerous ethical issues in the process.[5] Neuralink once appeared to be science fiction and is now reality, though a tenuous and incipient one; the thin line between science fact and science fiction is one we should all consider in its amazing progress and in its serious challenges.

Exponential Frontiers—Mechanical

Another exponential frontier—the mechanical—is about the tangible machinery we create as humans to aid us in our lives, work, exploration, and war, including robots, drones, spaceships, and medical devices. This mechanical frontier, as described in table 14.1, can include the convergence of a variety of exponential technologies from GenAI and autonomy—in what some like Jensen Huang are now calling "embodied AI"—to materials science and biotechnology. We explore a couple of these categories in this subsection.

Drone Hellscape or Paradise?

Drones are most certainly no longer science fiction. They are real, they are plentiful, and they are already being deployed in diverse, astounding, and scary ways. On the frightful side of the equation is the intersection of warfare, autonomous systems, and drones. Consider the planning that the US military is apparently undertaking for a potential future China/Taiwan confrontation or invasion, according to Jared Keller, writing in

Wired: "Admiral Samuel Paparo colorfully described the US military's contingency plan for a Chinese invasion of Taiwan as flooding the narrow Taiwan Strait between the two countries with swarms of thousands upon thousands of drones, by land, sea, and air, to delay a Chinese attack enough for the US and its allies to muster additional military assets in the region. 'I want to turn the Taiwan Strait into an unmanned hellscape using a number of classified capabilities,' Paparo said, 'so that I can make their lives utterly miserable for a month, which buys me the time for the rest of everything.'"[6]

On the somewhat tamer side of the equation, consider a future cityscape with drone tech advancements, where on-time deliveries and transportation are seamless, medical and health care deliveries are possible, and public safety and security services blend perfectly with the environment. Of course, such drones need to become safe and respect privacy to be flown in such populated areas, and there are a number of darker aspects to such deployments, especially as they combine with biometrics, facial recognition, and a variety of other privacy, human rights, and freedom concerns.[7]

The Fake Human Head Transplant Story

There was a very sophisticated but fake story and video circulating on the Internet while I was writing this book in 2024 that caught my eye (and that of many others, including savvy exponential tech commentators and analysts) titled "Scientists Plan a Head Transplant System."[8] A company called "BainBridge" (which turned out to be fictional) made the claim that it was developing an AI-driven robotic system that would be capable of performing head transplants—yes, you read that right, full human to human head transplants with all the grisly details relating thereto—aimed at helping terminally ill patients or those with paralysis.[9]

Accompanied by a very detailed, realistic looking, and somewhat gory animation, the later-debunked claim sounded too good to be true—and it was. However, I cite this example here because not too long from now, as we continue to develop interconnected exponential technologies, something of this nature may be possible. And those of us around will have to figure out the ethics, risk, governance, and impact of such a development.

And just in case you thought this story was mere fakery, look at what the National Institutes of Health (of the US government) stated in a 2019 paper: "According to many, head transplantation is considered to be an extraordinary and impossible surgical procedure. However, nowadays, relevant literature and recent advances suggest that the first human head transplantation might be feasible. This innovative surgery promises a life-saving procedure to individuals who suffer from a terminal disease, but whose head and brain are healthy. Recently, the first cephalosomatic anastomosis in a human model was successfully performed, confirming the surgical feasibility of the procedure, but still not the real outcome. Skepticism and several considerations, including surgical, ethical and psychosocial issues, have emerged in the scientific community since this imaginary procedure seems to be more feasible than ever before."[10]

Exponential Frontiers—Planetary

A third exponential frontier—the planetary—is about the all-encompassing planetary, climatic, biodiversity systems that life on Earth depends on for . . . life on Earth. The planetary exponential frontier, as referenced in table 14.1, includes everything from climate tech and weather tech to geoengineering, which in turn makes use of a wide variety of exponential technologies, including GenAI, geospatial engineering, robotics, advanced materials, and exponential computing. Let us take a closer look.

Climate Tech, Geoengineering, and Weather Tech

There is so much that could be discussed under this category, but for purposes of this book, I mention a few cutting-edge climate and geoengineering examples to illustrate some of the planetary exponential frontiers.

True to the arguments we have made in this book, *The Economist* ran a cover story in the summer of 2024 in which it made this bold statement: "To call solar power's rise exponential is not hyperbole, but a statement of fact. Installed solar capacity doubles roughly every three years, and so grows ten-fold each decade. Such sustained growth is seldom seen in anything that matters. That makes it hard for people to get their heads round what is going on. When it was a tenth of its current size ten years ago, solar power was still seen as marginal even by experts who knew how fast it had grown. The next ten-fold increase will be equivalent to multiplying the world's entire fleet of nuclear reactors by eight in less than the time it typically takes to build just a single one of them."[11]

At the planetary level and frankly the extraplanetary or extraterrestrial levels, too, there is so much advanced disruptive tech being applied to so many different aspects of life on Earth—preserving it, fixing it, retooling it, and even destroying it (think space wars). The tech being applied to planetary and extraplanetary activities runs the full gamut of awe-inspiring and mind-blowing to fearsome and even existential. If we just look at the subcategory of geoengineering defined as part of the "climate-altering and technology measures," it encompasses a wide variety of tools and techniques pertaining to two main categories: solar radiation management, or SRM; and carbon dioxide removal, or CDR. Within SRM, there are technologies called stratospheric aerosol injection, marine cloud brightening, cirrus cloud thinning, and surface "albedo" modifications (involving genetically modified crops to be more reflective/deflective of the sun). In the CDR category, there are a variety of carbon capture and storage technologies, direct air capture, ocean fertilization, and microbubbles. We do not have the time, expertise, or space to explain all these here; but I encourage my reader to do further research on these still-experimental and potentially life-changing (in good and bad ways) technologies. Table 14.2 lists just a few of these technologies in the category of geoengineering, with time horizons for deployment.

Indeed, the frontiers of climate tech are now in the hands of some of the huge tech companies. Based on a model being currently developed, check out this quotation from an Nvidia climate scientist: "I'm convinced we're at the moment now where AI can compete with physics for storm scale prediction."[12] Think about this for a moment. GenAI-turbocharged weather forecasting tools that can predict a specific storm in a specific location.

Exponential Frontiers—Virtual

And finally, we have a variety of virtual exponential frontiers, way too many to cover properly in this final chapter. So I focus on two general

Table 14.2 Time Horizons for Geoengineering

Likely to Happen Soon (Years)	More Remote (Decades)	Most Remote (Centuries):
Aerosoles: particles in the stratosphere that reflect sunlight	Ocean fertilization Biochar Carbonate addition Cloud seeding Foresting (trees absorb CO_2) Reflective crops Artificial trees (CO_2 sucked from air stored underground)	Space mirrors—orbiting mirrors deflect sunlight (highly unlikely in our lifetimes)

Source: Author.

areas I believe are critically important for the future well-being of humankind in the global commons: the financial and human rights sectors.

FinTech: Of Iris Orbs and Worldcoin

We have not spent much time on crypto, blockchain, bitcoin, and web 3.0 in this book, mostly because they were crowded out by other exponential technologies but also because it is such an explosive, controversial, unsettled, and even polarizing space. Since Trump was reelected to the US presidency, crypto has had a turboboost, with Bitcoin reaching over $100,000 in value; and the entire financial regulatory landscape of the United States, with implications globally potentially changing overnight. Time will tell, but as an example of the possible explosion (in more ways than one) of crypto, one of Trump's first appointments was of David Sacks (of PayPal Mafia fame) to be federal AI and crypto tsar, a fascinating mix. The importance of tackling crypto, even if briefly, in this last chapter is that it will become even more critically important to the future of world finance, financial transactions, economics, and socioeconomic well-being (see sidebar 14.1).

A cryptocurrency is a digital or virtual currency secured by cryptography, which makes it nearly impossible to counterfeit or double-spend and does not exist in coin or paper money form. Most cryptocurrencies exist on decentralized networks using blockchain technology—a distributed

---

Sidebar 14.1
What Is Blockchain?

Blockchain is a technology that enables the secure sharing of information. Data . . . [are] stored in a database. Transactions are recorded in an account book called a ledger. A blockchain is a type of *distributed* database or ledger, which means the power to update a blockchain is distributed between the nodes, or participants, of a public or private computer network. This is known as distributed ledger technology. . . . Nodes are rewarded with digital tokens or currency to make updates to blockchains. Blockchain allows for the permanent, immutable, and transparent recording of data and transactions. This, in turn, makes it possible to exchange anything that has value, whether that's a physical item or something more intangible.

Source: McKinsey & Company, "What Is Blockchain?" June 2024, www.mckinsey.com/featured-insights/mckinsey-explainers/what-is-blockchain.

---

ledger enforced by a disparate network of computers. "They are designed to be decentralized, meaning they're generally not backed, controlled, or owned by any government, central bank, or corporation. Instead, decentralized cryptocurrencies operate according to computer software that anyone with Internet access can download and use to monitor and verify transactions. The US dollar, on the other hand, is backed by the US government and regulated by the US Federal Reserve."[13]

So here is the conundrum: cryptocurrencies are not issued by a central authority, thus making them almost immune to government interference or manipulation, which in practice means that they can more easily be manipulated by nongovernmental actors, some of them deeply questionable or even destructive—autocrats, criminal gangs, speculators, and others who do not have the best interests of the global commons and their populace (all of us) in mind.

Even those who operate in the business mainstream and are wildly successful—like Sam Altman, for instance—are backing forms of cryptocurrency. Take his "Worldcoin" (now simply "World") project (developed by the Silicon Valley– and Berlin-based company Tools for Humanity), which aims to scan the eyeballs of every person on Earth to provide iris biometric verification in exchange for free cryptocurrency tokens. This is done via shiny small orbs. The company wants to reach a billion users, but so far it has only reached 6 million who are willing to take a serious risk with their personal privacy. The scans would then be converted into a "numerical string that, when combined with an algorithm, would use biometric identifiers to let the scanned person prove they were human in an increasingly AI-driven world."[14]

Beyond the small number of people willing to have their irises scanned by his orbs, it appears that Altman is not having a lot of success convincing governments to allow him to deploy this "very advanced and novel technology." More than a dozen jurisdictions have either suspended World's operations or have looked into its data processing. Among their concerns: "How does the Cayman Islands–registered World Foundation handle user data, train its algorithms and avoid scanning children?"[15] Among my concerns? Go back to chapter 11 and check out the wide array of risks that may be applicable to the World scenario.

Freedom Tech: Fighting a Digital Dark Age

The virtual field is big and is getting bigger. There are a number of dual-use exponential technologies, some powered by GenAI, that I am calling "freedom tech" because these technologies have both the risk of plunging us into a digital dark age or, if managed properly, the potential to protect and expand our freedoms. These techs include:

- *Biometric surveillance*, including facial recognition technology and other biometric characteristics like voice, iris, fingerprint, and even characteristics like a walking gait;
- *Video surveillance*, which can include closed-circuit TV using both still and video digital cameras in all sorts of places and managed video surveillance, with human security experts designing and deploying these tools in the loop;

- *Communications surveillance, which* includes the old-fashioned phone tapping as well as cell phone monitoring and computer surveillance, such as monitoring emails and social media;
- *Aerial surveillance,* which includes drones that are becoming increasingly sophisticated and advanced (due in part to their deployment in recent wars around the world, especially in Ukraine and Israel), and satellites, whose use is becoming increasingly widespread, sophisticated, and asymmetric; and
- *Chemical markers and DNA sensors,* which are new technologies in the biotech space that detect and analyze chemical substances or biological materials.

Thus, a critical human frontier also in the virtual space (with real world, physical effects), is "freedom tech"—the world of freedoms, human rights, the rule of law, and democracy, and the technologies that are deeply embedded in these spaces in the deepfake, mis/disinformation, cyberinsecurity, and surveillance that are arrayed against such human freedoms.

I call it "freedom tech" because these techs are deployed for good in the fight against tech-biased abuses used without the permission or against the best interests (the freedoms, human rights, and rule of law) of the average person anywhere—democracies, illiberal democracies, autocracies, and totalitarian states.

These technologies are also being deployed by non-nation-state actors, including criminal gangs; and new transnational power groups, such as autocrats (see *Autocracy Inc* by Anne Applebaum) along with the superwealthy including broligarchs like Elon Musk, Sam Altman, Mark Zuckerberg, and others who operate across borders in the "global commons" with near impunity. One of these tech masters of the universe—the CEO and founder of Telegram, Pavel Durov—was arrested in France in the summer of 2024 after refusing to moderate the toxicity on his social platform to dim the voices and transactions of arms and drug dealers, pedophiles, and other illegal and criminal actors.[16] To conclude, a mere scan of the headlines from Amnesty International Tech given in sidebar

> **Sidebar 14.2**
> **The Latest Headlines from Amnesty International Tech,**
> **as of September 1, 2024**
>
> - Amnesty International Uncovers New Hacking Campaign Linked to Mercenary Spyware Company
> - Myanmar: Facebook's Systems Promoted Violence Against Rohingya; Meta Owes Reparations—New Report
> - Hateful and Abusive Speech Towards LGBTQ+ Community Surging in Twitter under Elon Musk
> - France: Intrusive Olympics Surveillance Technologies Could Usher In a Dystopian Future
> - Kenya: Meta Sued for 1.6 Billion USD for Fueling Ethiopia Ethnic Violence
> - "We Are Totally Exposed": Young People Share Concerns About Social Media's Impact on Privacy and Mental Health in Global Survey
>
> Source: Amnesty International.

14.2 demonstrates the vast array of deep challenges in this space worldwide.[17] And in the latest material development in the evolution of AI and GenAI, 2025 promises to be the year of "agentic AI." To understand more about it, check out sidebar 14.3.

Two Exponential Imperatives for the Virtual Global Commons: Diversity and Inclusion, and Trust and Safety

There are at least two cross-cutting, material worldwide imperatives when it comes to the virtual global commons, and we explore them in this section. One is the "diversity and inclusion imperative," which is about developing an inclusive, diverse, and holistic approach to participation, innovation, guardrails, safety, policy, and governance of exponential technologies. The second is about trust and safety—making sure that we develop proven tools, techniques, practices, and measurements for the promotion of digital trust in the global virtual commons.

Sidebar 14.3
The Next AI Tsunami: Agentic AI

Speaking of Virtual Frontiers, there will be continuous exponential tech developments in the AI and GenAI space. As I finish writing this book in early 2025, the next big thing is Agentic AI. Experts agree that Agentic AI will be as big as ChatGPT when it was first released in late 2022. Indeed, Agentic AI will transform everything about human agency in ways reminiscent of how the Internet transformed digital information and communication and social media did once again a few years later.

So what is Agentic AI? Agentic AI systems demonstrate autonomy, self-directed behavior, and the capacity to make decisions and take actions without requiring constant human input. These systems operate with a degree of "agency," meaning they can plan, strategize, and pursue goals based on their programming or learned objectives and independent, frequently, from their human "client." Indeed, the proliferation of agents will be uncontrollable with many more agents than humans on Earth.

What does that mean from the standpoint of opportunity, value creation, and net benefit? Well there are many possibilities, including (1) enhanced problem solving through multifaceted, iterative, agentic system decision-making; (2) innovation acceleration where new ideas can be explored quickly and efficiently; (3) automation of dynamic tasks, such as in autonomous driving, supply chain management, and robotic decision-making in real time; (4) scalable personalization, where the agents adapt to the human requiring their services—whether for health care, travel, calendar management, education, or customer support; and (5) labor augmentation, meaning that it can be a complement to human decision-making, especially in high-stakes environments like medicine, finance, and the law.

And what could the downsides possibly be? Let me count the ways: (1) Agentic AI may deprive humans of their agency—making decisions outside of the human loop; (2) there may be unintended consequences as autonomous agents make decisions that were never foreseen; (3) there may be a values, ethics, or safety misalignment between the human and the agent; (4) malicious actors will get in on the game and exploit opportunities for malign behavior of all kinds; and (5) agentic autonomy escalation, where the agents go off and make their own decisions without human input to enhance or preserve their own autonomy.

Source: Author.

The Diversity and Inclusion Imperative

Part of the process of knowing your stakeholders and their issues is to understand the role of diversity and inclusion in your organization, products, servicers, governance, and strategy.[18] Whether it is diversity in the boardroom or the executive suite, or diversity in AI and tech roles and decision-making, diversity is an imperative of our tech present and future. Without diverse representation in these roles, across sectors and frontiers, humankind will not be able to tackle fully and constructively deep, yet still undefinable, risks, and the "sky's the limit" opportunities of AI, GenAI, and other exponential technologies that are coming at us at the speed of light. And this sensitivity to diversity must extend to key stakeholder groups—whether employees, subcontractors, customers, communities, and beyond.

A big obstacle to proper diversity and inclusion across the board on tech is that tech is primarily controlled by the billionaire tech bro classs, who are increasingly disinterested in diversity or outright against diversity, equity, and inclusion programs. The situation is about to get much more challenging with the apparent mass migration of Silicon Valley's most visible tech bros to an "anti-woke"; anti–environment, social, and government; and anti–diversity, equity, and inclusion movement at the heels of the second Trump administration, as Musk, Zuckerberg, and others curry favor with the president. And even those not so directly associated with the new administration felt the overwhelming need to contribute $1 million or much more to the president's inauguration fund. The bottom line for diversity and inclusion remains stark: even women who try to develop new tech have the hardest time getting the attention of tech bros, with only 2 percent of venture capital funding going to women-owned start-ups, as we explored in chapter 8. Let that sink in.

Two recent media stories caught my eye and galvanized me, focusing my brain, as it were, on something that has bothered me (and many others) for a long time: The world cannot afford to move into the age of exponential technology without all hands on deck, and a holistic, diverse, and inclusive approach to influencing, steering, and solutioning our tech future.

The first story in question was reported on September 13, 2023, in the *New York Times*, titled "In Show of Force, Silicon Valley Titans Pledge 'Getting This Right' with AI," in which the "titans" were the usual suspects—Elon Musk, Sam Altman, Sundar Pichai, Mark Zuckerberg, Bill Gates, Satya Nadella, Jensen Huang, Alex Karp, and Jack Clark—mostly white men.[19]

The *New York Times* piece referenced the closed-door meeting as "a rare congregation of more than a dozen tech executives in the same room." Media photos of the event showed the titans arriving in style in their black sedans, and in the Senate chamber with mostly male senators and staffers—with a few female exceptions. This important conversation, of course, took place "behind closed doors," so that the "titans" and senators could freely express their thoughts without attribution and away from the watchful eyes of their undoubtedly diverse stakeholders.

To which I would say: shame on all parties involved. On the Senate leadership and staff for their relative blindness in making this a media circus about the tech titans rather than a more holistic, inclusive, and public discussion about humanity's shared tech interests. On the media, for perpetuating bias in their coverage—in terms of the pervasively male content, references, quotations, and photos. And, frankly, on the tech titans themselves, who, while not at fault for being successful, because of their success have a higher obligation to act on the tech diversity imperative.

The second media story, also reported by the *New York Times* on December 3, 2023, was a fluff piece, the "Luminaries of AI." Yes, you guessed it right: the twelve luminaries were all men and, mind you, ten of them were white.[20] This story completely ignored the depth and breadth of the leadership by females and people of color in tech, and more specifically in AI and other exponential technologies. This piece engendered a bit of a furor among diverse, especially women's groups, with numerous media and social media posts countering the twelve male luminaries' narrative, which led to a positive backlash, with various publications and organizations later naming more diverse (gender, race, ethnicity) lists of tech luminaries, innovators, and change agents.

For diversity and inclusion to really work, we need those in power to recognize the power of inclusion and insist on a more diverse composition in all venues—jobs, media coverage, conference panels, and so on. What happens when we are only listening to the tech titans? We are only hearing one half of the story—the half that is about gung-ho tech break-throughs and billions (and even trillions) of dollars. What we do not hear about enough is the other half of the story – the part that asks about the purpose and mission of the tech, and its ethics, safety, and security—its impact on society and stakeholders.

What can we do? A lot more. This is not about dethroning the tech bros; it is about bringing in the voices, brainpower, and creativity of the rest. Together, we must deploy our skills and common humanity to solve our tech challenges and make the world a safer place for exponential change.

In the meantime, how can we dampen the perpetuation of these pernicious narratives? By immediately countering misinformation by of-fering actual information, data, and facts, as Kara Swisher and Fei Fei Li (an AI pioneer and luminary herself) did in response to the *Times'* twelve-luminaries article by posting a sharp response on X/Twitter. By offering counternarratives, as did this column, titled "NY Times Missed These 12 Trailblazers: Meet the Women Transforming AI."[21] By doing better due diligence in building "best of" lists like the *Time* 100/AI List of 100 most influential leaders in AI with thirty-six women and many people of color on it.[22] By training your communications, public relations, and media professionals, and other teams on implicit bias and blind spots and making sure you never construct a "manel" (an only-men panel). And by doing original work disseminating important data and other information in your own space. I have been involved with two such initiatives: one as cochair and coauthor with a group of diverse women from the Athena Alliance, who have written and published the Athena AI Governance Playbook; the other as adviser to XRSI, a nonprofit dedicated to safety in the metaverse and made up mostly by women and people of color.

The Trust and Safety Imperative

The second must-have imperative of our exponential times is building a global commons–oriented system of actionable, provable, and account-able digital trust. One of the early and excellent digital trust frameworks

Figure 14.2 World Economic Forum: Digital Trust in the Intelligent Age
Source: World Economic Forum, "Explainer: What Is Digital Trust in the Intelligent Age?" January
22, 2025, www.weforum.org/stories/2024/11/explainer-what-is-digital-trust-in-the-intelligent
-age/. Reprinted by permission.

created and constantly under development is one by the World Economic
Forum (WEF) in collaboration with a variety of leading consultancies.[23]
See figure 14.2. More recently, there is a corollary to their approach being
developed globally through the United Nations' Global Digital Compact,
which is currently in its "zero draft" form.

Let us consider the WEF's definition of "digital trust: it is individuals' expectation that digital technologies and services—and the organizations providing them—will protect all stakeholders' interests and
uphold societal expectations and values."[24] WEF continues to describe its
digital trust framework as follows: "The framework should be used as a
decision-making guide for leaders at the highest levels when consider-

ing the development, use or application of digital technologies and services. It defines shared goals or values that inform the concept of digital trust, as well as dimensions against which the trustworthiness of digital technologies can be operationalized and evaluated."[25] In an attempt to assist leaders and organizations of all types to create a systemic and systematic approach to governing digital matters within their entities, the digital trust system has several key components, including three goals and eight dimensions along which leaders can develop, implement, and self-examine their entity's "digital trust."

The three goals, described as "considerations that motivate or can be achieved by actions or decisions (i.e., dimensions)," are security and reliability; inclusive, ethical, and responsible use; and accountability and oversight. The eight dimensions—described as "the aspect of digital trust over which organizational decision-makers, such as CEOs and senior executives, have control and, if applied to a given technology with a human-centric approach, will promote digital trustworthiness"—are cybersecurity, safety, transparency, interoperability, auditability, redressability, fairness, and privacy. The WEF's Digital Trust initiative also provides resources to make organizational digital trust measurable and actionable.[26]

We turn now to the hopeful development that is the UN Global Digital Compact, whose stated objectives are to:

1. Close the digital divides and accelerate progress across the Sustainable Development Goals.
2. Expand opportunities for inclusion in the digital economy.
3. Foster an inclusive, open, safe, and secure digital space.
4. Advance equitable international data governance.
5. Govern emerging technologies, including artificial intelligence, for humanity.[27]

I conclude now by stating explicitly something I have stated repeatedly, directly or indirectly, throughout this book: When it comes to exponential technologies, we must always verify first and only then trust; but we must build digital trust and safety through and for the stakeholder diversity that humanity represents.

Conclusion: In the Age of Pandora, We Must Be Both Innovators and Stewards

In this era of exponential technology, with broad and deep implications and reverberations that we cannot even predict or fathom, good-to-great tech governance is no longer a nice thing to have or something to think about tomorrow. It is a must-have to think about yesterday and today. Moreover, good-to-great tech governance cannot consist of merely grafting old practices and systems onto something so new and so fundamentally different. The exponential governance mindset is about constantly adapting, future-facing governance.

While the innovators are "moving fast and (possibly) breaking things"—things that may be unfixable once broken—in furtherance of discovery and riches, the stewards are also trying to move fast, racing against time to fix flaws and build or rebuild things. The recent adoption by the European Union of the AI Act and policy developments in China and the United States addressing the development of AI and generative AI guardrails speak volumes to the urgency of developing national and global tech governance standards applicable to persons, organizations, and nations in every sector. While the innovators are more motivated by riches, influence, and power mostly for themselves and their peers, the stewards are more motivated by safety, security, ethics, and guardrails, and thus protecting a broader swath of stakeholders.

It is not that the twain shall never meet—there are many of us who embody both the excitement and the concern, as well as the desire for innovation and the need for safety. We are human, after all. It is not the tech that is dangerous or evil; it is the humans with negligent, dangerous, or evil intentions who deploy tech as a harmful weapon for their own ends who need to be kept in mind. These include the powerful human technologists who become potentially more careless, disconnected, and hubristic as they gain fame and fortune. Indeed, the twain—innovation and stewardship—must always meet.

Picture drone swarms armed with synthetic biological agents, all created with the assistance of GenAI, inflicting terror upon an urban environment. That involves humans making the wrong choices. That is what we must be concerned about. That is what we must prepare for and prevent to the greatest extent possible, at every level of governance within and across entities and jurisdictions, while allowing for the unfurling and broad sharing of helpful, life-changing inventions.

In an internal email the press got its hands on during the OpenAI governance crisis of November 2023, a Microsoft executive stated, "Speed is even more important than ever; . . . it would be an absolutely fatal error in this moment to worry about things that can be fixed later."[28]

To this, I would respond and ask: But what about the things that cannot be fixed later? My point is that we do not need to sacrifice innovation for governance; nor do we need to sacrifice governance for innovation. It is up to diverse, knowledgeable, learning-oriented, forward-thinking, and continuously curious managers, directors, and policymakers to develop this better, more savvy approach to the future. The bottom line: We need to develop the exponential governance mindset to survive and thrive in the coming exciting and daunting turbulence while protecting the vulnerable and advantaging humanity and life on Earth.

In this Age of Pandora, we—as individuals, as leaders, and as global citizens—can achieve the exponential governance mindset sweet spot— we can be both innovators and stewards. We can be both careful technologists and exuberant consumers. We can be cutting-edge inventors and cautious beta testers. We can be effective ethicists and enthusiastic gamers. We can be robotics inventors and safe and happy drone users. We can be health-conscious biotechnologists and grateful recipients of the latest customized cancer treatments. We can be all those things on both sides of the equation at the same time—innovators and stewards.

While we can be all these things simultaneously, it will require a conscious effort on all our parts. Even then, there will always be those

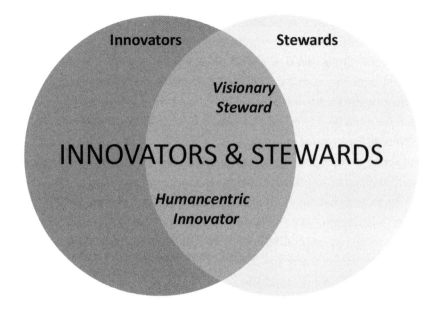

Figure 14.3 The Exponential Tech Leadership Sweet Spot
Source: Author.

who do not participate—either because of the absence of opportunity (humanitarian reasons) or the presence of depravity—criminal gangs, rogue nation-states, the guy in his mom's basement with nothing better to do than to wreak technological havoc. Yes, there will be outliers, nonparticipants, and those excluded because of the absence of educational, health, resources, or the presence of poverty, hardship, war, and other conditions out of their control. We need to make conscious and positive efforts to include the excluded on the bright side of this equation. For the rest of us, privileged enough to have access to a little or a lot of technology, we must deploy the five individual or personal directives outlined in chapter 13, guide our organizations to be future-ready and not future-reactive, and do our best as global citizens to contribute to and protect the exponential tech frontiers and our shared global commons.

Innovation and stewardship are two sides of the same coin, and both are needed and valuable. Instead of calling each other names—"accelerationists versus decelerationists" or "techno-optimists versus doomers"—

let us stop the unnecessary, negative polarization and settle on a positive spin for both sides of this equation and call ourselves both innovators and stewards where there are a number of constructive possibilities. See figure 14.3—you might be primarily an innovator or you might mostly be a steward, or perhaps, maybe you are a human-centric innovator or a visionary steward. These are all great choices; pick the one that best suits you, and let us get this done together!

Notes

Acknowledgments

1. Tristan Harris, "Our Brains Are No Match for Our Technology," *The New York Times*, December 5, 2019, https://www.nytimes.com/2019/12/05/opinion/digital-technology-brain.html.

Introduction

1. Thank you to Friso van der Oord for his comments and wisdom and to the National Association of Corporate Directors, "Technology Leadership in the Boardroom: Driving Trust and Value, 2024 Blue Ribbon Commission Report."

Chapter 1

1. Andrea Bonime-Blanc, *Gloom to Boom: How Leaders Transform Risk into Resilience and Value* (New York: Routledge, 2020); Andrea Bonime-Blanc, *The ESGT Megatrends, Diplomatic Courier*, Annual Editions 2021–24 and Illuminem 2025–26.

2. Chris Miller, *Chip War: The Fight for the World's Most Critical Technology* (New York: Scribner, 2022).

3. Jake Coyle, "In Hollywood Screenwriters' Battle Against AI, Humans Win (for Now)," AP, September 23, 2023, https://apnews.com/article/hollywood-ai-strike-wga-artificial-intelligence-39ab72582c3a15f77510c9c30a45ffc8.

4. Angela Watercutter and Will Bedingfield, "Hollywood Actors Strike Ends with a Deal That Will Impact AI and Streaming for Decades," *Wired*, November 8, 2023, www.wired.com/story/hollywood-actors-strike-ends-ai-streaming/.

5. Jonathan Haidt has long been writing about the adverse effects on social media, especially on young people. A collection of excellent articles he has written for the *Atlantic* over the past decade is at www.theatlantic.com/author/jonathan-haidt/.

6. Center for Humane Technology, www.humanetech.com/.

7. *The Social Dilemma*, film, www.humanetech.com/the-social-dilemma.

8. Tristan Harris and Aza Raskin, "The AI Dilemma," YouTube, March 3, 2023, www.youtube.com/watch?v=xoVJKj8lcNQ.

9. Future of Life Institute, "Pause Giant AI Experiments: An Open Letter," March 22, 2023, https://futureoflife.org/open-letter/pause-giant-ai-experiments/.

10. Future of Life Institute.

11. The World Economic Forum has a long-standing and terrific research hub exploring the Fourth Industrial Revolution. See World Economic Forum, Centre for the Fourth Industrial Revolution, https://centres.weforum.org/centre-for-the-fourth -industrial-revolution/home.

12. Anushree Singha Ray and Kuntal Bhattacharya, "An Overview on the Zoonotic Aspects of COVID-19," Springer Nature, April 26, 2023, www.ncbi.nlm.nih .gov/pmc/articles/PMC10132798/.

13. World Wildlife Fund, "Climate Change Impacts in the Amazon," https:// wwfint.awsassets.panda.org/downloads/amazon_cc_impacts_lit_review_final _2.pdf; Jack Graham, "The Next Amazon? Congo Basin Faces Rising Deforestation," November 11, 2022, Reuters, www.reuters.com/business/cop/next-amazon -congo-basin-faces-rising-deforestation-threat-2022-11-11/.

14. NOAA National Centers for Environmental Information, "2023 Was the Warmest Year in Modern Temperature Record," January 17, 2024, www.climate.gov /news-features/featured-images/2023-was-warmest-year-modern-temperature-re cord.

15. COP29, "The COP29 Presidency Team," https://cop29.az/en/teams; Justin Rowlatt, "UAE Planned to Use COP28 Climate Talks to Make Oil Deals," BBC, November 27, 2023, www.bbc.com/news/science-environment-67508331.

16. Kit Million Ross, "Battery Energy Storage Developments That Are Electrifying the Sector," Power Technology, April 25, 2024, www.power-technology.com/fe atures/battery-energy-storage-developments-that-are-electrifying-the-sector/?cf-view &cf-closed.

17. US Energy Department, "Fission and Fusion: What Is the Difference?" www .energy.gov/ne/articles/fission-and-fusion-what-difference; Philip Ball, "What Is the Future of Fusion Energy?" Scientific American, June 1, 2023, www.scientific american.com/article/what-is-the-future-of-fusion-energy/.

18. World Food Program, "Innovation Accelerator," https://innovation.wfp.org/.

19. Circle, "2024 Circle Impact Report," www.circle.com/circle-impact-report ?utm_source=chatgpt.com.

20. Economist, "Taiwan's Dominance of the Chip Industry Makes It More Important," March 6, 2023, www.economist.com/special-report/2023/03/06/taiwans -dominance-of-the-chip-industry-makes-it-more-important.

21. President Lai Ching-te, "Inaugural Address of ROC 16th Term President Lai Ching-te," May 20, 2024, https://english.president.gov.tw/News/6726; Tom Giles, Bloomberg Tech Newsletter, May 23, 2024.

22. United Nations, "UN Interim Report on Governing AI for Humanity, Africa Expert Meeting: Draft Submission to UN African Observatory on Responsible AI," March 2024, www.africanobservatory.ai/.

23. Steven Lee Myers, "Once a Sheriff's Deputy in Florida, Now a Source of Disinformation from Russia," May 30, 2024, *New York Times*, www.nytimes.com/2024/05/29/business/mark-dougan-russia-disinformation.html?smid=url-share&utm.

24. Darrell M. West, "How Disinformation Defined the 2024 Election Narrative," Brookings, November 7, 2024.

25. "NACD, Technology Leadership in the Boardroom: Driving Trust and Value, 2024 Blue Ribbon Commission Report," www.nacdonline.org/all-govern ance/governance-resources/governance-research/blue-ribbon-commission-reports /BRC/2024/tech-leadership-in-the-boardroom/.

26. In addition to my own work on this subject, a lot of great work is being done by others in this space. I especially like Matthew Sekol, *The ESG Mindset* (London: Kogan Page, 2024); and Herman Bril, Georg Kell, and Andreas Rasche, *Sustainability, Technology, and Finance* (New York: Routledge, 2022).

27. Keach Hagey, "Sam Altman Seeks Trillions of Dollars to Reshape Business of Chips and AI," *Wall Street Journal*, February 8, 2024, www.wsj.com/tech/ai/sam -altman-seeks-trillions-of-dollars-to-reshape-business-of-chips-and-ai-89ab3db0; Adina Solomon, "Billionaire-Planned Smart Cities in the US: What's the Latest?" Smart Cities Dive, November 13, 2023, www.smartcitiesdive.com/news/billionaire -smart-cities-update-elon-musk-telosa-utopia/699348/; Rachel Corbett, "The For-Profit City That Might Come Crashing Down," *New York Times*, August 28, 2024, www.nytimes.com/2024/08/28/magazine/prospera-honduras-crypto.html.

28. Edelman, "Edelman Trust Barometer 2024," www.edelman.ca/trust-barom eter.

Chapter 2

1. Andrea Bonime-Blanc, *Gloom to Boom: How Leaders Transform Risk into Resilience and Value* (New York: Routledge, 2020).

2. Vernor Vinge, "The Coming Technological Singularity: How to Survive in the Post-Human Era," Vision 21: Interdisciplinary Science and Engineering in the Era of Cyberspace, NASA Lewis Research Center, December 1, 1993, https://ntrs.nasa .gov/citations/19940022856.

3. ChatGPT4o, queried: "What is exponential technology?" Accessed on August 22, 2024.

4. Perplexity AI, queried: "What is exponential technology?" Accessed on March 9, 2024.

5. Perplexity AI, queried: "What is exponential technology?" Accessed on August 22, 2024.

6. Gartner, "Emerging Tech Impact Radar 2024," January 11, 2024, www.gartner .com/en/documents/5097331.

7. Mustafa Suleyman with Michael Bhaskar, *The Coming Wave: Technology, Power, and the Twenty-First Century's Greatest Dilemma* (New York: Crown, 2023), www.amazon.com/Coming-Wave-Technology-Twenty-first-Centurys/dp/0593593952.

8. Jake Bleiberg, "UK Police Arrest 17-Year-Old in Connection to MGM Resorts Hack," Bloomberg, July 19, 2024, www.bloomberg.com/news/articles/2024-07-19/uk-police-arrest-17-year-old-in-connection-to-mgm-resorts-hack.

9. Chris Gilliard, "The Deeper Problem with Google's Racially Diverse Nazis," *Atlantic*, February 26, 2024, www.theatlantic.com/technology/archive/2024/02/google-gemini-diverse-nazis/677575/.

Chapter 3

1. AWS, "What Is Artificial Intelligence?" https://aws.amazon.com/what-is/artificial-intelligence/.

2. Google, "What Is Generative AI?" https://cloud.google.com/use-cases/generative-ai.

3. Gartner, "Artificial General Intelligence (AGI)," www.gartner.com/en/information-technology/glossary/artificial-general-intelligence-agi.

4. Scott Rosenberg and Ryan Heath, "Meta's 'General Intelligence' Quest," Axios, January 22, 2024.

5. Andrew Hodges and Alan Turing, *The Enigma* (Princeton, NJ: Princeton University Press, 2014).

6. Jakob Uszkoreit, "Transformer: A New Neural Network Architecture for Language Understanding," https://research.google/blog/transformer-a-novel-neural-network-architecture-for-language-understanding/.

7. Alexandr Wang, "Scale AI Valued at Nearly $14 Billion," interview, Bloomberg TV, May 22, 2024. www.bloomberg.com/news/videos/2024-05-22/scale-ai-valued-at-nearly-14b-with-amazon-funding-video?cmpid=BBD052324_TECH&utm_medium=email&utm_source=newsletter&utm_term=240523&utm_campaign=tech.

8. Alex Watson, "Solving the Data Quality Problem in Generative AI," *Infoworld*, June 11, 2024, www.infoworld.com/article/2337627/solving-the-data-quality-problem-in-generative-ai.html.

9. Data & Trust Alliance, https://dataandtrustalliance.org/.

10. Cloudflare, "What Is AI Inference?" www.cloudflare.com/learning/ai/inference-vs-training/.

11. Interview, email exchange with Joyce Li, CEO and chief AI strategist at Averanda Partners, November 22, 2024.

12. Shiraz Jagati, "AI's Black Box Problem: Challenges and Solutions for a Transparency Future," Cointelegraph.com, May 5, 2023.

13. McKinsey, "McKinsey Explainer: What Is Artificial General Intelligence?"

March 21, 2024, www.mckinsey.com/featured-insights/mckinsey-explainers/what
-is-artificial-general-intelligence-agi.

14. McKinsey.

15. John Ayers, PhD, et al., "Comparing Physician and Artificial Intelligence
Chatbot Responses to Patient Questions Posted to Public Social Media Forum,"
JAMA Network, April 28, 2023, https://jamanetwork.com/journals/jamainternal
medicine/fullarticle/2804309#google_vignette.

16. Open Source Initiative, "Meta's Llama License Is Still Not Open Source," February 18, 2025, https://opensource.org/blog/metas-llama-license-is-still-not-open
-source?utm_source=chatgpt.com.

17. Julie Coleman, "Nvidia CEO Jensen Huang: We're at the Beginning of the
Accelerated Computing Ramp," CNBC, March 19, 2024, www.cnbc.com/2024/03
/19/nvidia-ceo-jensen-huang-says-ai-computing-ramp-is-only-beginning-and-will
-last-years.html.

18. Geoffrey Hinton, post on X, May 3, 2023, https://twitter.com/geoffreyhinton
/status/1653687894534504451?lang=en.

19. Fei Fei Li, "With Spatial Intelligence AI Will Understand the Real World,"
TED Talk, April 2024. www.ted.com/talks/fei_fei_li_with_spatial_intelligence_ai
_will_understand_the_real_world?language=en.

20. AWS, "What Is Artificial General Intelligence?"

21. Data & Trust Alliance.

22. Sara Merken, "Another NY Lawyer Faces Discipline After AI Chatbot Invented Case Citation," Reuters, January 30, 2024, www.reuters.com/legal/transac
tional/another-ny-lawyer-faces-discipline-after-ai-chatbot-invented-case-citation-20
24-01-30/.

23. Stephen M. Walker II, "What Is Superalignment?" https://klu.ai/glossary
/superalignment.

24. Ana Altchek, "OpenAI Just Dissolved IT Team Dedicated to Managing AI
Risks, Like the Possibility of It 'Going Rogue,'" *Business Insider*, May 17, 2024, www
.businessinsider.com/openai-ends-superalignment-team-manage-ai-risks-2024-5.

25. Ravie Lakshmanan, "University Professors Targeted by North Korean Cyber
Espionage Group," *Hacker News*, August 8, 2024, https://thehackernews.com/2024
/05/north-korean-hackers-exploit-facebook.html.

26. SentinelOne, "What Is Generative AI in Cybersecurity?" www.sentinelone
.com/cybersecurity-101/data-and-ai/generative-ai-cybersecurity/.

27. Gordon Corera, "Ukraine War: Cyber-Teams Fight a High Tech War on Front
Lines," BBC, September 3, 2023, www.bbc.com/news/world-europe-66686584.

28. The sources for these are Visual Capitalist, "Mapped: Most Interested in
Generative AI," www.visualcapitalist.com/cp/mapped-interest-in-generative-ai-by

-country/; Eduardo Baptista, "China Leads the World in Adoption of Generative AI, Survey Shows," Reuters, July 9, 2024, www.reuters.com/technology/artificial-inte lligence/china-leads-world-adoption-generative-ai-survey-shows-2024-07-09/; and Statista, "Global Distribution of GenAI Companies in 2023, by Country," March 7, 2024, www.statista.com/statistics/1452390/generative-ai-distribution-by-country -worldwide/.

29. The sources for these are those cited in note 28.

30. White & Case, "AI Watch: Global Regulatory Tracker," www.whitecase.com /insight-our-thinking/ai-watch-global-regulatory-tracker.

31. White & Case.

32. David Kaye, "Evaluating the UN AI Advisory Body Interim Report," Tech Policy Press, February 14, 2024, www.techpolicy.press/evaluating-the-un-ai-adviso ry-body-interim-report/.

33. Collins Ayuya, "20 Key Generative AI Examples in 2024," *EWeek*, February 12, 2024, www.eweek.com/artificial-intelligence/generative-ai-examples/.

34. Soumik Majumder, "Top Generative AI Industrial Applications," www.turing .com/resources/generative-ai-applications.

35. Cem Dilmegani, "Top 100+ Generative AI Applications/Use Cases in 2024," AI Multiple Research, April 18, 2024, https://research.aimultiple.com/generative -ai-applications/.

36. Ayuya, "20 Key Generative AI Examples."

37. Coursera Staff, "20 Examples of Generative AI Applications Across Indus-tries," March 15, 2024, www.coursera.org/articles/generative-ai-applications.

38. MIT Future Tech, "AI Risk Repository," https://airisk.mit.edu/.

Chapter 4

1. BIO, "What Is Biotechnology?" www.bio.org/what-biotechnology.

2. *National Geographic*, "Biotechnology," https://education.nationalgeographic .org/resource/resource-library-biotechnology/.

3. Karl Ereky, *Biotechnologie Der Fleisch-, Fett-, Und Milcherzeugung Im Land-wirtschaftlichen Grossbetriebe: Für Naturwissenschaftlich Gebildete Landwirte Verfasst* (Berlin: P. Parey, 1919).

4. Ashish Swarup Verma et al., "Biotechnology in the Realm of History," *Jour-nal of Biopharmacy & BioAllied Sciences* (National Institutes of Health, National Li-brary of Medicine, and National Center for Biotechnology), July–September 2011, 321–23, doi:10.4103/0975-7406.84430, www.ncbi.nlm.nih.gov/pmc/articles/PMC3 178936/.

5. Friedrich Frischknecht, "The History of Biological Warfare," *EMBO Reports* (National Library of Medicine), June 2003, S47–S52, doi:10.1038/sj.embor.embo r849, www.ncbi.nlm.nih.gov/pmc/articles/PMC1326439/.

6. S. Das and V. K. Kataria, "Bioterrorism: A Public Health Perspective," *Medical Journal of Armed Forces of India* (National Library of Medicine), July 2011, 255–60, doi:10.1016/S0377-1237(10)80051-6, www.ncbi.nlm.nih.gov/pmc/articles/PMC49 21253/.

7. Frischknecht, "History."

8. Edmond Hooker, "Bioterrorism," MedicineNet, March 13, 2023, www.medic inenet.com/bioterrorism/article.htm.

9. World Economic Forum, "Global Risks Report 2025," January 15, 2025.

10. "DNA Is a Structure That Encodes Biological Information," www.nature.com /scitable/topicpage/dna-is-a-structure-that-encodes-biological-6493050/.

11. National Institutes of Health (NIH), National Human Genome Research Institute, "What Is RNA?" September 14, 2024, www.genome.gov/genetics-glossary /RNA-Ribonucleic-Acid.

12. NIH, National Human Genome Research Institute, "Messenger RNA," May 23, 2024, www.genome.gov/genetics-glossary/messenger-rna.

13. Centers for Disease Control and Prevention, "Understanding How COVID-19 Vaccines Work," September 3, 2024, www.cdc.gov/coronavirus/2019-ncov/vaccines /different-vaccines/how-they-work.html.

14. NIH, National Human Genome Research Institute, "CRISPR," September 14, 2024, www.genome.gov/genetics-glossary/CRISPR.

15. NIH, National Human Genome Research Institute, "What Are the Ethical Concerns of Genome Editing?" www.genome.gov/about-genomics/policy-issues/Ge nome-Editing/ethical-concerns; Sandy Sufian and Rosemarie Garland-Thomson, "The Dark Side of CRISPR," *Scientific American*, February 16, 2021.

16. Sufian and Garland-Thomson, "Dark Side."

17. Brigid Kennedy, "The Billionaire Led Quest for Immortality," *The Week*, September 20, 2023, https://theweek.com/science/the-billionaire-led-quest-for-immor tality.

18. Perplexity AI, "Query: What Is Exponential Biotechnology?" May 24, 2024.

19. Mustafa Suleyman, *The Coming Wave* (New York: Crown, 2023), 5–11.

20. Judy Savitskaya and Jorge Conde, "What Is a Bio Platform For?" Andreessen Horowitz, https://a16z.com/what-is-a-bio-platform-for/.

21. Savitskaya and Conde.

22. Perplexity AI, "Query: Types of Exponential Biotechnology?" April 8, 2024.

23. Royal Academy of Engineering, *Synthetic Biology: Scope, Applications and Implications* (London: Royal Academy of Engineering, 2009).

24. Suleyman, *Coming Wave*, viii.

25. US Government Accountability Office, "Science and Tech Spotlight: Synthetic Biology," April 17, 2023, www.gao.gov/products/gao-23-106648.

26. Meriem El Karoui et al., "Future Trends in Synthetic Biology: A Report,"

Frontiers, August 7, 2019, www.frontiersin.org/articles/10.3389/fbioe.2019.00175/full.

27. US Government Accountability Office, "Science."

28. Christopher A. Voigt, "Synthetic Biology 2020–2030: Six Commercially Available Products That Are Changing our World," Nature Communications, December 11, 2020, www.nature.com/articles/s41467-020-20122-2.

29. Voigt.

30. Xu Yan et al., "Application of Synthetic Biology in Medical and Pharmaceutical Fields," Signal Transduction and Targeted Therapy, National Library of Medicine, May 11, 2023, www.ncbi.nlm.nih.gov/pmc/articles/PMC10173249/.

31. Voigt, "Synthetic Biology."

32. ETC Group, "Extreme Genetic Engineering: An Introduction to Synthetic Biology," January 16, 2007, www.etcgroup.org/content/extreme-genetic-engineering-introduction-synthetic-biology.

33. Catherine Jefferson et al., "Synthetic Biology and Biosecurity: Challenging the "Myths," NIH, National Library of Medicine, National Center for Biotechnology Information, August 21, 2014, www.ncbi.nlm.nih.gov/pmc/articles/PMC4139924/.

34. Trond Arne Undheim, "The Whack-A-Mole Governance Challenge for AI-Enabled Synthetic Biology: Literature Review and Emerging Frameworks," Frontier of Bioengineering and Biotechnology, February 28, 2024, www.ncbi.nlm.nih.gov/pmc/articles/PMC10933118/.

35. Stanford Existential Risk Initiative, *Synthetic Biology Unleashed in the Wild: Global Systemic Risk Scenario 2075,* YouTube, 2023, www.youtube.com/watch?v=uA5x0Rihi2s&t=193s.

Chapter 5

1. Harry McCracken, "Nvidia's AI Boom Is Only Getting Started; Just Ask CEO Jensen Huang," *Fast Company,* March 19, 2024, www.fastcompany.com/91033514/nvidia-most-innovative-companies-2024.

2. Your Undivided Attention Podcast, "Chips Are the Future of AI. They're Also Incredibly Vulnerable. With Chris Miller," episode 86, March 29, 2024, www.humanetech.com/podcast/chips-are-the-future-of-ai-theyre-also-incredibly-vulnerable-with-chris-miller.

3. Jarred Walton, "Nvidia Shows Off Blackwell Server Installations in Progress," Tom's Hardware, www.tomshardware.com/tech-industry/artificial-intelligence/nvidia-shows-off-blackwell-server-installations-in-progress-ai-and-data-center-roadmap-has-blackwell-ultra-coming-next-year-with-vera-cpus-and-rubin-gpus-in-2026.

4. Gordon E. Moore, "Cramming More Components onto Integrated Circuits," *Electronics* 38, no, 8 (April 19, 1965), https://download.intel.com/newsroom/2023/manufacturing/moores-law-electronics.pdf.

5. Intel Newsroom, "Moore's Law," www.intel.com/content/www/us/en/news room/resources/moores-law.html#gs.88poxt.

6. Steve Jurvetson, "Ever-Moore," X post, January 10, 2025, https://x.com/Future Jurvetson/status/1877870052642578464.

7. "What Is Materials Science?" https://materialseducation.org/resources/what -is-materials-science/.

8. Princeton University, Materials Institute, "What Is Materials Science?" https:// materials.princeton.edu/education/undergraduate/what-materials-science.

9. Michigan Tech, "What Is Materials Science and Engineering?" www.mtu.edu /materials/what/.

10. Amil Merchant and Ekin Dogus Cubuk, "Millions of New Materials Discovered with Deep Learning," Google DeepMind, November 29, 2023, https://de epmind.google/discover/blog/millions-of-new-materials-discovered-with-deep-learn ing/.

11. Amil Merchant et al., "Scaling Deep Learning for Materials Discovery, *Nature*, 2023, https://doi.org/10.1038/s41586-023-06735-9.

12. Anjana Ahuja, "Can AI Really Change Our Material World?" *Financial Times*, April 17, 2024, www.ft.com/content/ca7f67c5-6db7-4cbb-858b-67876d2c1e63.

13. Ahuja.

14. StartUs Insights, "10 New Graphene Companies Leading Material Innovation," www.startus-insights.com/innovators-guide/new-graphene-companies/.

15. StartUs Insights, "10 New Smart Sports Clothing Companies Blending Fashion & Function," www.startus-insights.com/innovators-guide/smart-sport -clothing/.

16. Emergen Research, "Top Ten Companies in Smart Fabrics Market in 2024," March 13, 2024, www.emergenresearch.com/blog/top-10-companies-in-smart-fab rics-market-in-2024.

17. European Commission, "What Is Nanotechnology?" https://ec.europa.eu /health/scientific_committees/opinions_layman/en/nanotechnologies/l-2 /1-introduction.htm.

18. Carolyn Schwaar, "The Complete Guide to the Types of 3D Printing Technology," All3DP, February 23, 2024, https://all3dp.com/1/types-of-3d-printers-3d-prin ting-technology/; Protolabs Network by Hubs, "What Are The Types of 3D Printers and What Can They Do?" www.hubs.com/knowledge-base/types-of-3d-printing/.

19. ASML, "How Microchips Are Made," www.asml.com/en/technology/all -about-microchips/how-microchips-are-made.

20. ASML.

21. Seeking Alpha, "Nvidia Says Next Generation Rubin AI Platform Coming in 2026," https://seekingalpha.com/news/4112160-nvidia-says-next-generation-rubin -ai-platform-coming-in-2026.

22. Nvidia, https://nvidianews.nvidia.com/news/nvidia-blackwell-platform-ar rives-to-power-a-new-era-of-computing.

23. Nvidia, "Nvidia in Brief," https://media.iprsoftware.com/219/files/202311 /corporate-nvidia-in-brief-pdf-december-3056300-r2-2.pdf?Signature=ncH9BnF Ng%2B%2B6bQqjZHJDBjBLfg%3D&Expires=1717968302&AWSAccessKeyId=A KIAJX7XEOOELCYGIVDQ&versionId=KgiwCZP.LuqFtUOJi3dAakvjMU.DGF27 &response-content-disposition=attachment.

24. Georgie Peru, "What Is an NPU? Here's Why Everyone's Suddenly Talking About Them," *Digital Trends*, December 27, 2023, www.digitaltrends.com/compu ting/what-is-npu/.

Chapter 6

1. Perplexity AI, "Query: List Computing Technologies That Can Be Considered Exponential."

2. Richard Fisher, "The A–Z of AI: 30 Terms You Need to Understand Artificial Intelligence," BBC, July 17, 2023, www.bbc.com/future/article/20230717-what-you -should-know-about-artificial-intelligence-from-a-z.

3. Max Roser, Hannah Ritchie, and Edouard Mathieu, "What Is Moore's Law?" March 28, 2023, https://ourworldindata.org/moores-law.

4. Roser, Ritchie, and Mathieu.

5. SETI, UCLA, https://setiathome.berkeley.edu/.

6. Folding@home, https://foldingathome.org/.

7. Microsoft Azure, "What Is Edge Computing?" https://azure.microsoft.com/en -us/resources/cloud-computing-dictionary/what-is-edge-computing/.

8. Microsoft Azure.

9. Intel, "What Is High-Performance Computing (HPC)?" www.intel.com/con tent/www/us/en/high-performance-computing/what-is-hpc.html.

10. IBM, "Nanotechnology," www.ibm.com/history/nanotechnology.

11. AWS, "What Is Nanotechnology Computing?" https://aws.amazon.com/what -is/Nanotechnology-computing/.

12. Ellen Glover, "What is Neuromorphic Computing?" BuiltIn, updated by Bren nan Whitfield, January 4, 2024, https://builtin.com/artificial-intelligence/neuro morphic-computing.

13. Glover.

14. Jordan Kinard, "These Living Computers Are Made from Human Neurons," *Scientific American*, August 8, 2024, www.scientificamerican.com/article/these-liv ing-computers-are-made-from-human-neurons/.

15. Jackie Wiles, "What Is a Metaverse?" Gartner, October 21, 2022, www.gartner .com/en/articles/what-is-a-metaverse.

16. XRSI, "The Metaverse and Standards," May 2023, https://xrsi.org/.

17. Ben Dickson, "What Is Spatial Computing?" *PC Magazine*, January 19, 2024, www.pcmag.com/how-to/what-is-spatial-computing-a-basic-explainer.

18. AWS, "What Is Quantum Computing?" https://aws.amazon.com/what-is /quantum-computing/.

19. US Department of Energy, "DOE Explains . . . Quantum Mechanics," www .energy.gov/science/doe-explainsquantum-mechanics.

20. Perplexity AI, "Query: Explain Quantum Computing to Me Like I'm a 5-Year-Old."

21. IBM, "What Is Quantum Computing?" www.ibm.com/topics/quantum-com puting.

22. IBM.

23. Martina Gschwendtner et al., "Potential and Challenges of Quantum Com puting Hardware Technologies," McKinsey, December 1, 2023, www.mckinsey.com /capabilities/mckinsey-digital/our-insights/tech-forward/potential-and-challenges -of-quantum-computing-hardware-technologies.

24. Accenture, "Quantum Is Coming: Is Your Security Function Ready?" www.ac centure.com/us-en/insights/technology/quantum-cryptography.

25. Tom Patterson, "Quantum Security's Unsung Heroes: A NIST Post-Quantum Cryptography (PQC) Standardization Post-Conference Review," *Inside Quantum Technology*, April 25, 2024, www.insidequantumtechnology.com/news-archive/qu antum-particulars-guest-column-quantum-securitys-unsung-heroes-a-nist-post-qu antum-cryptography-pqc-standardization-conference-review/.

26. Esther Shein, "Top Metaverse Platforms to Know About in 2024," Tech Tar get, January 3, 2024, www.techtarget.com/searchcio/tip/Top-metaverse-platforms -to-know-about.

27. Nvidia, "Digital Twins Overview," https://docs.omniverse.nvidia.com/digital -twins/latest/index.html.

28. Shein.

29. US Government Office of Accountability, "Immersive Technologies: Most Civilian Agencies Are Using or Plan to Use Augmented Reality, Virtual Reality and More," August 8, 2024, www.gao.gov/products/gao-24-106665.

30. There are numerous excellent resources on these topics, including from the World Economic Forum (WEF), which publishes excellent reports and monographs on this topic regularly including recently: WEF and Accenture, "Metaverse Identity: Defining the Self in a Blended Reality," WEF Insight Report, March 2024; WEF, "Metaverse Cybersecurity: Building Resilience in the Future Internet," WEF Brief ing Paper, June 2024.

31. Louis Rosenberg, "The Manipulation Problem: Conversational AI as a Threat

to Epistemic Agency," 2023 CHI Workshop on Generative AI and HCI, Association for Computing Machinery, Hamburg, April 28, 2023.

32. XRSI publishes a wide spectrum of reports and resources available on its website, https://xrsi.org/.

Chapter 7

1. Caterpillar, "Automation & Autonomy: What's the Difference?" www.cat.com /en_US/articles/ci-articles/automation-autonomy-whats-the-difference.html.

2. California Department of Motor Vehicles, "Autonomous Vehicle Definitions," www.dmv.ca.gov/portal/vehicle-industry-services/autonomous-vehicles/autonomo us-vehicle-definitions/.

3. Erico Guizzo, "Types of Robots," Institute of Electrical and Electronics Engineers, August 1, 2018 (updated May 23, 2023), https://robotsguide.com/learn /types-of-robots.

4. Guizzo.

5. Guizzo.

6. Jacob Biba, "Top 22 Humanoid Robots in Use Right Now," BuiltIn, April 17, 2024, https://builtin.com/robotics/humanoid-robots.

7. Maia Mulko, "5 of the World's Most Realistic Humanoid Robots Ever," Interesting Engineering, December 6, 2023, https://interestingengineering.com/lists/ 5-worlds-realistic-humanoid-robots.

8. Alex Orlando, "4 Robots That Look Like Humans," *Discover Magazine*, May 16, 2023, www.discovermagazine.com/technology/4-robots-that-look-like-humans.

9. Orlando.

10. Biba, "Top 22."

11. Autonomous Weapons, "The Risks of Autonomous Weapons," https://auton omousweapons.org/the-risks/.

12. United Nations, "First Committee Approves New Resolution on Lethal Autonomous Weapons," November 1, 2023, https://press.un.org/en/2023/gadis3731 .doc.htm.

13. Autonomous Weapons, "The Solutions," https://autonomousweapons.org/so lutions/.

14. Campaign to Stop Killer Robots, www.stopkillerrobots.org/.

15. Campaign to Stop Killer Robots.

16. Robert Stephens, "What Exactly Is a Smart City and Why Should All of Us Care?" University of Central Florida, September 23, 2024, www.ucf.edu/news/what -exactly-is-a-smart-city-and-why-should-all-of-us-care/.

17. IBM, "What Is a Smart City?" www.ibm.com/topics/smart-city.

18. Forbes Expert Panel, "19 Smart City Technologies and How They'll Trans-

form Urban Living," July 16, 2024, www.forbes.com/councils/forbestechcouncil /2024/07/16/19-smart-city-technologies-and-how-theyll-transform-urban-living/.

19. Zeyi Yang, "After a Year of Setbacks, Where Do Robotaxis Go in 2024?" January 23, 2024, www.govtech.com/transportation/after-a-year-of-setbacks-where-do -robotaxis-go-in-2024.

20. Lucy Buchholz, "Top 10 Most Sustainable Smart Cities," *Sustainability Magazine*, June 21, 2023, https://sustainabilitymag.com/articles/top-10-smart-cities-in -the-world-in-2023.

21. National Grid, "What Is a Smart City?" www.nationalgrid.com/stories/energy-explained/what-is-a-smart-city.

22. United Nations, Department of Economic Affairs, "68% of the World Population Projected to Live in Urban Areas by 2050, Says UN," May 16, 2018, www.un .org/development/desa/en/news/population/2018-revision-of-world-urbanization -prospects.html.

Chapter 8

1. Kevin Roose, "OpenAI Insiders Warn of a 'Reckless' Race for Dominance," *New York Times*, June 4, 2024, www.nytimes.com/2024/06/04/technology/openai -culture-whistleblowers.html.

2. Vishwas Manral and Andrea Bonime-Blanc, "Cutting Edge Technology: Continuous and Holistic Governance of Cloud and AI," *Directorship Magazine*, February 14, 2024, www.nacdonline.org/all-governance/governance-resources/directorship -magazine/online-exclusives/2024/february/cutting-edge-tech-continuous-holistic -governance-cloud-AI/.

3. Andrea Bonime-Blanc, "The OpenAI Saga," *Directorship Magazine*, Spring 2024.

4. John Thornhill, "OpenAI Still Has a Governance Problem," *Financial Times*, May 8, 2025, www.ft.com/content/49ad6c69-9b67-48da-a274-8408dfdaa7cb.

5. Anthropic, www.anthropic.com/news/the-long-term-benefit-trust.

6. National Association of Corporate Directors, "Technology Leadership in the Boardroom: Driving Trust and Value, 2024 Blue Ribbon Commission Report."

7. Andrea Bonime-Blanc, "The Defense Industry Initiative: From Business Conduct Program Innovator to Industry Standard?" chapter 4 in *Globalization and Self-Regulation*, edited by S. Prakash Sethi (New York: Palgrave Macmillan, 2011).

8. White & Case, "AI Watch: Global Regulatory Tracker," www.whitecase.com /insight-our-thinking/ai-watch-global-regulatory-tracker.

9. Kia Kokalitcheva, "California's AI Safety Squeeze," Axios, June 26, 2024, www .axios.com/2024/06/26/california-ai-safety-bill-industry-pushback; Yasmin Khorram, "California AI Bill Sparks Debate in Silicon Valley as Some Tech Giants Call It a Threat to Innovation," Yahoo Finance, August 26, 2024, https://finance.yahoo

.com/news/california-ai-bill-sparks-debate-in-silicon-valley-as-some-tech-giants
-call-it-a-threat-to-innovation-214246503.html.

10. Sarah K. White, "Women in Tech Statistics: The Hard Truths of an Uphill Battle," *CIO Magazine*, March 8, 2024, www.cio.com/article/201905/women-in -tech-statistics-the-hard-truths-of-an-uphill-battle.html; Louisa Zhou, "Women in Tech Statistics: Gender in Tech 2024," updated May 27, 2024, https://luisazhou .com/blog/women-in-tech-statistics/.

11. Andrea Willige, "More Than DEI: Why It Pays to Get Women in the Board-room," World Economic Forum Agenda, May 2, 2023, www.weforum.org/agenda /2023/05/women-board-directors-dei-profitability/.

12. J. Schuett, A. K. Reuel, and A. Carlier, "How to Design an AI Ethics Board," *AI Ethics*, 2024, https://doi.org/10.1007/s43681-023-00409-y.

13. John Carreyrou, *Bad Blood: Secrets and Lies in a Silicon Valley Startup* (New York: Alfred A. Knopf, 2020).

14. Carreyrou; Andrea Bonime-Blanc, *Gloom to Boom: How Leaders Transform Risk into Resilience and Value* (New York: Routledge, 2020).

15. Excerpts and summaries taken from Bonime-Blanc, "Open AI Saga."

16. National Association of Corporate Directors, "Technology Leadership."

17. National Association of Corporate Directors.

Chapter 9

1. Merriam-Webster, definition of "ethics," www.merriam-webster.com/diction ary/ethic.

2. Merriam-Webster, definition of "responsibility," www.merriam-webster.com /dictionary/responsibility.

3. Merriam-Webster, definition of "responsible," www.merriam-webster.com/dic tionary/responsible.

4. Satya Nadella et al., *Hit Refresh: The Quest to Rediscover Microsoft's Soul and Imagine a Better Future for Everyone* (New York: Harper Business, 2017).

5. Chloe Berger, "Satya Nadella Transformed Microsoft's Culture during His Decade as CEO by Turning Everyone into 'Learn-It-Alls' Instead of 'Know-It-Alls,'" *Fortune*, May 20, 2024, https://fortune.com/2024/05/20/satya-nadella-microsoft -culture-growth-mindset-learn-it-alls-know-it-alls/.

6. Andrea Bonime-Blanc, "The OpenAI Saga: Lessons for the Future of Tech Governance," *Directorship Magazine*, Spring 2024, www.nacdonline.org/all-gover nance/governance-resources/directorship-magazine/spring-2024-issue/the-open ai-saga/.

7. Marc Andreessen, "The Techno Optimist Manifesto," https://a16z.com/the -techno-optimist-manifesto/.

8. Center for Humane Technology, www.humanetech.com/.

9. *The Social Dilemma*, film, 2020, www.thesocialdilemma.com/.

10. "The AI Dilemma," podcast, 2023, www.humanetech.com/podcast/the-ai-di lemma.

11. "Your Undivided Attention," podcast, https://your-undivided-attention.sim plecast.com/.

12. Joseph Menn, "Stanford's Top Disinformation Research Group Collapses Under Pressure," *Washington Post*, June 14, 2024, www.washingtonpost.com/tech nology/2024/06/14/stanford-internet-observatory-disinformation-research-law suits-politics/.

13. Bonime-Blanc, "OpenAI Saga."

14. Jan Leike, post on X, May 17, 2024, https://x.com/janleike/status/17914981 78346549382.

15. Hayden Field, "Current and Former OpenAI Employees Warn of AI's 'Serious Risks' and Lack of Oversight," CNBC, June 4, 2024, www.cnbc.com/2024/06/04 /openai-open-ai-risks-lack-of-oversight.html.

16. TED AI Show, "What Really Went Down at OpenAI and the Future of Regulation with Helen Toner," May 28, 2024, https://open.spotify.com/episode/4r127X apFv7JZroOPzRDaI.

17. Eric Geller, "The US Government Has a Microsoft Problem," *Wired*, April 15, 2024, www.wired.com/story/the-us-government-has-a-microsoft-problem/.

18. Karen Weise and Cade Metz, "The Race to Dominate AI," *New York Times*, December 8, 2023, www.nytimes.com/2023/12/08/briefing/ai-dominance.html.

19. Microsoft, "Responsible AI Principles and Approach," www.microsoft.com /en-us/ai/principles-and-approach/; Microsoft, "Responsible AI Standards," 2022, https://cdn-dynmedia-1.microsoft.com/is/content/microsoftcorp/microsoft/final /en-us/microsoft-brand/documents/Microsoft-Responsible-AI-Standard-General -Requirements.pdf?culture=en-us&country=us.

20. Accenture, "Accenture's Blueprint for Responsible AI," www.accenture.com /us-en/case-studies/data-ai/blueprint-responsible-ai.

21. Accenture.

22. Erin Essenmacher et al., "The Athena Alliance AI Governance Playbook," Athena Alliance, 2024, https://athenaalliance.com/ai-governance-playbook/.

23. Andrea Bonime-Blanc, *Gloom to Boom: How Leaders Transform Risk into Resilience and Value* (New York; Routledge, 2020), 41–80.

Chapter 10

1. David Shepardson, "US Opens Special Probe into Fatal Tesla Pedestrian Crash in California," Reuters, July 8, 2022, www.reuters.com/business/autos-trans

portation/us-opens-new-probe-into-fatal-tesla-pedestrian-crash-california-2022-07 -07/.

2. Kobi Leins and Anja Kaspersen, "Seven Myths of Using the Term 'Human in the Loop': 'Just What Do You Think You Are Doing, Dave?'" Carnegie Council, November 9, 2021, www.carnegiecouncil.org/media/article/7-myths-of-using-the -term-human-on-the-loop.

3. Google Cloud, "What Is Humans in the Loop?" https://cloud.google.com/dis cover/human-in-the-loop.

4. Leins and Kaspersen, "Seven Myths."

5. Andrea Bonime-Blanc, *Gloom to Boom: How Leaders Transform Risk into Resilience and Value* (New York: Routledge, 2020), xxvii.

6. Just Capital, "Issues," https://justcapital.com/issues/.

7. Just Capital, "2025 Rankings Report," https://justcapital.com/rankings/.

8. Mike Allen and Jim Vendehei, "Meta's Make-Up-with-MAGA Map," Axios, January 11, 2025, www.axios.com/2025/01/11/meta-maga-zuckerberg-trump-rogan ?utm_source=newsletter&utm_medium=email&utm_campaign=newsletter_axio sam&stream=top.

9. Niamh Rowe, "'It's Destroyed Me Completely': Kenyan Moderators Decry Toll of Training of AI Models," *Guardian*, August 2, 2023, www.theguardian.com /technology/2023/aug/02/ai-chatbot-training-human-toll-content-moderator-meta -openai.

10. Circle, "2024 Circle Impact Report," www.circle.com/circle-impact-report ?utm_source=chatgpt.com.

11. Joanna England, "Top 10 Telematic Insurance Providers in the US in 2023," InsureTech, February 1, 2023, https://insurtechdigital.com/technology-and-ai/top -10-telematic-insurance-providers-in-the-us-in-2023.

12. E-Safety Commissioner, Australian Government, "Social Media Age Restrictions," updated December 20, 2024, www.esafety.gov.au/about-us/industry-regula tion/social-media-age-restrictions.

13. E-Safety Commissioner, Australian Government.

14. David Berreby, "As Use of AI Soars, So Does the Consumption of Energy and the Water It Requires," Environment 360, February 6, 2024, https://e360.yale.edu /features/artificial-intelligence-climate-energy-emissions; Nikita Shukla, "Generative AI Is Exhausting the Power Grid," August 5, 2024, https://earth.org/generative -ai-is-exhausting-the-power-grid/.

15. The Conversation, "AI Demand Puts More Pressure on Data Centers' Energy Use. Here's How to Make It Sustainable," *Fast Company*, July 14, 2024, www.fast company.com/91154629/ai-data-centers-energy-use-sustainable-solutions.

16. Ivan Penn and Karen Weise, "Hungry for Energy, Amazon, Google and Mi-

crosoft Turn to Nuclear Power England," *New York Times*, October 16, 2024, www
.nytimes.com/2024/10/16/business/energy-environment/amazon-google-micro
soft-nuclear-energy.html.

17. Accenture, "Sustainability: Gerando Falcoes Fighting Poverty," www.accen
ture.com/us-en/case-studies/sustainability/gerando-falcoes-accenture-fighting
-poverty.

18. James Surowiecki, "What's Gone Wrong at Boeing," *Atlantic*, January 15,
2024.

19. Harris Poll, "The Axios Harris Poll 100 2024 Corporate Rankings," https://
theharrispollreports.com/overview.

Chapter 11

1. Kate Whiting and HyoJin Park, "This Is Why "Polycrisis" Is a Useful Way of
Looking at the World Right Now," World Economic Forum, March 7, 2023.

2. Whiting and Park.

3. *60 Minutes*, "'The Godfather of AI' Geoffrey Hinton: The *60 Minutes* Interview,"
October 9, 2023, CBS-TV/YouTube, www.youtube.com/watch?v=qrvK_KuIeJk.

4. World Economic Forum, "Global Risks Report 2025," https://reports.weforum
.org/docs/WEF_Global_Risks_Report_2025.pdf

5. World Economic Forum, "Global Risks Report 2025," 9.

6. Massachusetts Institute of Technology, "AI Risk Repository," https://airisk.mit
.edu/.

7. UNESCO, "AI Governance," www.unesco.org/en.

8. European Union, "European Artificial Intelligence Act Comes into Force,"
EU AI Act, https://digital-strategy.ec.europa.eu/en/news/european-artificial-intelli
gence-act-comes-force; EU AI Act, https://eur-lex.europa.eu/eli/reg/2024/1689/oj.

9. Kevin Fumai, LinkedIn post, August 18, 2024, www.linkedin.com/posts/ke
vinfumai_aigovernance-activity-7230913346185670656-9wHP?utm_source=share
&utm_medium=member_desktop; Nahema Marchal et al., "Generative AI Misuse:
A Taxonomy of Tactics and Insights from Real-World Data," Google DeepMind, June
21, 2024, https://arxiv.org/pdf/2406.13843.

10. CredoAI, "Understanding Generative AI Risks: A Comprehensive Look at the
Top 7 Generative AI Risks for Businesses," July 5, 2023, www.credo.ai/blog/under
standing-generative-ai-risks-a-comprehensive-look-at-the-top-7-genai-risks-for-busi
nesses-2.

11. Tabby Kinder, "Biggest US Companies Warn of Growing AI Risk," *Financial
Times*, August 17, 2024, www.ft.com/content/5ee96d38-f55b-4e8a-b5c1-e58ce3d4
111f.

12. Kinder.

13. Kinder.

14. Arize AI, "The Rise of Generative AI in SEC Filings," July 2024, https://arize .com/wp-content/uploads/2024/07/The-Rise-of-Generative-AI-In-SEC-Filings -Arize-AI-Report-2024.pdf.

15. AWS, "What Is a Digital Twin?" https://aws.amazon.com/what-is/digital -twin/.

16. *Economist*, "Digital Twins Are Fast Becoming Part of Everyday Life," August 29, 2024, www.economist.com/leaders/2024/08/29/digital-twins-are-fast-becom ing-part-of-everyday-life.

17. AWS.

18. Cybersecurity and Infrastructure Security Agency (CISA), www.cisa.gov/.

19. CISA, "CISA Roadmap for Artificial Intelligence 2023–2024," www.cisa.gov /sites/default/files/2023-11/2023-2024_CISA-Roadmap-for-AI_508c.pdf.

20. CISA.

21. National Institute for Standards and Technology, "Trustworthy and Respon-sible AI," www.nist.gov/trustworthy-and-responsible-ai.

22. National Institute for Standards and Technology.

23. US AI Safety Institute, "US Artificial Intelligence Safety Institute," www.ni st.gov/aisi.

24. CISA, "CISA Artificial Intelligence Use Cases," www.cisa.gov/ai/cisa-use -cases?utm_source=newsletter&utm_medium=email&utm_campaign=newsletter _axioslogin&stream=top.

25. United Nations, "Sustainable Development Goals SDG 9 Report," Septem-ber 2023, www.un.org/sustainabledevelopment/wp-content/uploads/2023/08/230 9739_E_SDG_2023_infographics-9-9.pdf; Andrea Bonime-Blanc, "Deploying SDG 9 Despite the Headwinds: A Leadership Blueprint to Resilience in Chaotic Times," *Illuminem*, September 20, 2023, https://illuminem.com/illuminemvoices/deplo ying-sdg-9-despite-the-headwinds-a-leadership-blueprint-to-resilience-in-chaotic -times.

Chapter 12

1. Michael Porter, "What Is Strategy?" *Harvard Business Review*, December 1996, www.hbs.edu/faculty/Pages/item.aspx?num=10698.

2. R. Edward Freeman, *Strategic Management: A Stakeholder Approach* (Cam-bridge: Cambridge University Press, 1983), 44.

3. Tae Kim, "Intel Is Ramping Up Its Battle Against TSMC with New Chip Pack-aging Technology," *Barron's*, May 17, 2023, www.barrons.com/articles/intel-tsmc-st ock-chips-market-e69615a8; Leo Sun, "Better Investment Stock: Intel vs. Taiwan Semiconductor," *Motley Fool*, January 30, 2024, www.fool.com/investing/2024 /01/30/better-semiconductor-stock-intel-vs-tsmc/; Zahurul Al Mamun, "Intel vs

TSMC: The Battle for Chip Supremacy," *Daily Star*, October 17, 2024, www.thedaily
star.net/tech-startup/news/intel-vs-tsmc-the-battle-chip-supremacy-3729816.

4. Eric S. Toner, "Creating Situational Awareness: A Systems Approach," National Institutes of Health; Eric S. Toner, "Situational Awareness," www.ncbi.nlm
.nih.gov/books/NBK32848/.

5. Toner, "Situational Awareness."

6. Gartner, "Gartner Glossary," www.gartner.com/en/information-technology
/glossary/digitization.

7. Gartner.

8. Gartner.

9. World Economic Forum, "Digital Trust Framework," https://initiatives.wefor
um.org/digital-trust/framework.

10. World Economic Forum, "Measuring Digital Trust," October 2023, https://
www3.weforum.org/docs/WEF_Measuring_Digital_Trust_2023.pdf.

11. UN Sustainable Development Goals, https://sdgs.un.org/goals.

12. United Nations, *Our Common Future (aka Brundtland Report)*, 1987, https://
digitallibrary.un.org/record/139811?v=pdf.

13. UN Sustainable Development Goals.

14. UN Global Compact, "Who Cares Wins?" 2004, https://documents1.world
bank.org/curated/pt/280911488968799581/pdf/113237-WP-WhoCaresWins-2004
.pdf.

15. Georg Kell, Herman Brill, and Andreas Rasche, *Sustainability, Technology and
Finance* (New York: Routledge, 2022).

16. Scott Rosenberg, "Tech's AI Message to Wall Street: Stop Fretting," Axios,
August 2, 2024, www.axios.com/2024/08/02/google-microsoft-meta-ai-earnings.

17. Ryan Heath, "DC's Hottest New Job: Chief AI Officer," Axios, November 27,
2023, www.axios.com/2023/11/27/ai-jobs-dc-biden-chief-officer-tech?utm_source=
newsletter&utm_medium=email&utm_campaign=newsletter_axioslogin&stream
=top.

18. White House, "Executive Order on the Safe, Secure, and Trustworthy Development and Use of Artificial Intelligence," October 30, 2023, www.whitehouse.gov
/briefing-room/presidential-actions/2023/10/30/executive-order-on-the-safe-se
cure-and-trustworthy-development-and-use-of-artificial-intelligence/.

19. UK National Cyber Security Centre, "Using Cyber Security Scenarios," www
.ncsc.gov.uk/collection/risk-management/using-cyber-security-scenarios.

Chapter 13

1. I discuss this in great detail in chapter 2 of my book *Gloom to Boom: How Leaders Transform Risk into Resilience and Value* (New York: Routledge, 2020).

2. David Yaffe-Bellany and J. Edward Moreno, "Sam Bankman-Fried Sentenced

to 25 Years in Prison," *New York Times*, March 28, 2024, www.nytimes.com/2024
/03/28/technology/sam-bankman-fried-sentenced.html.

3. Reuters, "Crypto's String of Bankruptcies," January 20, 2023, www.reuters
.com/business/finance/cryptos-string-bankruptcies-2023-01-20/.

Chapter 14

1. Council on Foreign Relations, "Global Commons," www.cfr.org/global-com
mons.

2. Michael Marquardt, CEO of Epi One, original contribution, received August
12, 2024.

3. Marquardt.

4. IEEE Brain, "Neurotechnologies: The Next Technology Frontier," https://brain
.ieee.org/topics/neurotechnologies-the-next-technology-frontier/.

5. Matthew Sparkes, "Has Neuralink Made a Breakthrough in Brain Implant
Technology?" *New Scientist*, March 21, 2024, www.newscientist.com/article/24234
83-has-neuralink-made-a-breakthrough-in-brain-implant-technology/.

6. Jared Keller, "The Pentagon Is Planning a Drone 'Hellscape' to Defend Taiwan," *Wired*, August 19, 2024, www.wired.com/story/china-taiwan-pentagon-drone
-hellscape/.

7. James O'Donnell, "What's Next for Drones," *MIT Technology Review*, August
16, 2024, www.technologyreview.com/2024/08/16/1096517/whats-next-for-drones/.

8. The Rundown. "Scientists Plan a Head Transplant System," May 23, 2024,
www.therundown.ai/p/humane-seeks-ai-pin-exit.

9. BainBridge, YouTube, www.youtube.com/watch?v=szXbuUlUhQ4.

10. Grigorios Gkasdaris, "First Human Head Transplantation: Surgically Challenging, Ethically Controversial and Historically Tempting—an Experimental Endeavor or a Scientific Landmark?" US National Institutes for Health, National Library
of Medicine, March 2019, www.ncbi.nlm.nih.gov/pmc/articles/PMC6511668/.

11. *Economist*, "The Exponential Growth of Solar Power Will Change the World,"
June 20, 2024, www.economist.com/leaders/2024/06/20/the-exponential-growth
-of-solar-power-will-change-the-world.

12. Andrew Freedman, "Exclusive: New Nvidia Model Could Bolster Severe
Weather Forecasts," Axios, August 19, 2024, www.axios.com/2024/08/19/nvidia-ai
-weather-model-extreme-weather-climate.

13. Fidelity Investments, "What Is Crypto?" September 26, 2023, www.fidelity
.com/learning-center/trading-investing/what-is-crypto.

14. Chris Morris, "Worldcoin Is Looking Like a Dud for Sam Altman," *Fast Company*, July 11, 2024, www.fastcompany.com/91154657/sam-altman-worldcoin-crypto
-biometric-startup-falls-well-short-1-billion-sign-up-goal.

15. Angus Berwick, "Sam Altman's Worldcoin Is Battling with Governments

Over Your Eyes," *Wall Street Journal*, August 18, 2024, www.wsj.com/tech/sam-al
tman-openai-humanness-iris-scanning-4d0e1dab?st=m44e51q0elrl1ts&reflink=ar
ticle_email_share.

16. Aurelien Breeden and Adam Satariano, "Telegram Founder Charged with
Wide Range of Crimes in France," *New York Times*, August 28, 2024, www.nytimes
.com/2024/08/28/business/telegram-ceo-pavel-durov-charged.html.

17. Amnesty International, "Amnesty International Tech: Latest Headlines," September 1, 2024, www.amnesty.org/en/tech/.

18. *Diplomatic Courier*, "The Diversity Imperative of Our Exponential Times,"
March 9, 2024, www.diplomaticcourier.com/posts/diversity-imperative-exponential
-times.

19. Cecilia Kang, "In Show of Force, Silicon Valley Titans Pledge 'Getting This
Right' with AI," *New York Times*, September 13, 2023, www.nytimes.com/2023/09
/13/technology/silicon-valley-ai-washington-schumer.html.

20. J. Edward Moreno, "Who's Who Behind the Dawn of the Modern Artificial
Intelligence Movement," *New York Times*, December 3, 2023, www.nytimes.com/20
23/12/03/technology/ai-key-figures.html.

21. Sephora Bemba, "*NY Times* Missed These 12 Trailblazers: Meet the Women
Transforming AI," *Women in Technology*, December 6, 2023, https://medium.com
/womenintechnology/ny-times-missed-these-12-trailblazers-meet-the-women-trans
forming-ai-ae522f52a8b7.

22. *Time Magazine*, "Time 100/AI," https://time.com/collection/time100-ai/.

23. World Economic Forum, "Digital Trust Framework," https://initiatives.wefor
um.org/digital-trust/framework.

24. World Economic Forum, "Measuring Digital Trust," October 2023, www3.we
forum.org/docs/WEF_Measuring_Digital_Trust_2023.pdf.

25. World Economic Forum, "Digital Trust Framework."

26. World Economic Forum. "Measuring Digital Trust."

27. United Nations, "Globl Digital Compact: Zero Draft," www.un.org/techenv
oy/global-digital-compact. You can read more about this in "Why the Global Digital
Compact Focus on Digital Trust and Security Is the Key to the Future of Internet," by
Agustina Callegari and Daniel Dobrygowski, *World Economic Forum Agenda*, April
24, 2024, www.weforum.org/agenda/2024/04/united-nations-global-digital-com
pact-trust-security/.

28. Karen Weise et al., "Inside the AI Arms Race That Changed Silicon Valley
Forever," *New York Times*, December 5, 2023, www.nytimes.com/2023/12/05/tech
nology/ai-chatgpt-google-meta.html?campaign_id=9&emc=edit_nn_20231208&in
stance_id=109629&nl=the-morning&regi_id=123293946&segment_id=152043&te
=1&user_id=8f416255192f948975a7b440f76d3170.

Selected Bibliography and Additional Resources

Applebaum, Anne. *Autocracy, Inc.: The Dictators Who Want to Run the World*. New York: Random House, 2024.

Bonime-Blanc, Andrea. *Gloom to Boom: How Leaders Transform Risk into Resilience and Value*. New York: Routledge, 2020.

Buolamwini, Joy. *Unmasking AI: My Mission to Protect What Is Human in a World of Machines*. New York: Random House, 2023.

Capra, Fritjof, and Pier Luigi Luisi. *The Systems View of Life: A Unifying Vision*. Cambridge: Cambridge University Press, 2014.

Carr, Nicholas. *Superbloom: How Technologies of Connection Tear Us Apart*. New York: W. W. Norton, 2025.

Carreyrou, John. *Bad Blood: Secrets and Lies in a Silicon Valley Startup*. New York: Alfred A. Knopf, 2018.

Christian, Brian. *The Alignment Problem: Machine Learning and Human Values*. New York: W. W. Norton, 2020.

Crawford, Kate. *Atlas of AI: Power, Politics, and the Planetary Costs of Artificial Intelligence*. New Haven, CT: Yale University Press, 2021.

DiResta, Renee. *Invisible Rulers: The People Who Turn Lies into Reality*. New York: PublicAffairs, 2024.

Durodié, Clara. *Decoding AI in Financial Services: Business Implications for Boards and Professionals*. Singapore: World Scientific, 2020 and 2024 (2nd edition).

Espindola, David and Michael W. Wright. *The Exponential Era: Strategies to Stay Ahead of the Curve in an Era of Chaotic Changes and Disruptive Forces*. Hoboken, NJ: Wiley & IEEE Press, 2021.

Freeman, R. Edward. *Strategic Management: A Stakeholder Approach*. Cambridge: Cambridge University Press, 1983.

Gambelin, Olivia. *Responsible AI: Implement an Ethical Approach in Your Organization*. London: Kogan Page, 2024.

Graylin, Alvin, and Louis Rosenberg. *Our Next Reality: How the AI-Powered Metaverse Will Reshape the World*. London: Nicholas Brealey, 2024.

Groth, Olaf J., Mark Esposito, and Terence Tse. *The Great Remobilization: Strategies and Designs for a Smarter Global Future*. Cambridge, MA: MIT Press, 2023.

Haidt, Jonathan. *The Anxious Generation: How the Great Rewiring of Childhood Is Causing an Epidemic of Mental Illness.* New York: Penguin, 2024.

Hao, Karen. *Empire of AI: Dreams and Nightmares in Sam Altman's OpenAI.* New York: Penguin, 2025.

Harari, Yuval Noah. *Homo Deus: A Brief History of Tomorrow.* New York: Harper, 2017.

———. *Sapiens: A Brief History of Humankind.* New York: Harper, 2017.

Harding, Verity. *AI Needs You: How We Can Change AI's Future and Save Our Own.* Princeton, NJ: Princeton University Press, 2024.

Hoffman, Reid, and Greg Beato. *Superagency: What Could Possibly Go Right with Our AI Future.* New York: Authors Equity, 2025.

Kaku, Michio. *Quantum Supremacy: How the Quantum Computer Revolution Will Change Everything.* New York: Crown, 2023.

Karp, Alexander C., and Nicholas W. Zamiska. *The Technological Republic: Hard Power, Soft Belief, and the Future of the West.* New York: Crown Currency, 2025.

Kim, Tae. *The Nvidia Way: Jensen Huang and the Making of a Tech Giant.* New York: W. W. Norton, 2024.

Kissinger, Henry A., Craig Mundie, and Eric Schmidt. *Genesis: Artificial Intelligence, Hope, and the Human Spirit.* Boston: Little, Brown, 2024.

Klaas, Brian. *Corruptible: Who Gets Power and How It Changes Us.* New York: Scribner, 2021.

———. *Fluke: Chance, Chaos, and Why Everything We Do Matters.* New York: Simon & Schuster, 2024.

Kobie, Nicole. *The Long History of the Future: Why Tomorrow's Tech Still Isn't Here.* London: Bloomsbury Sigma, 2024.

Krishnakumar, Arun, and Theodora Lau. *The Metaverse Economy: How Finance Professionals Can Make Sense of Web3.* London: Kogan Page, 2023.

Lam, James. *Enterprise Risk Management: From Incentives to Controls.* New York: Wiley, 2014.

Leslie, David, et al. *AI Ethics and Governance in Practice: An Introduction.* London: Alan Turing Institute, 2024.

Li, Fei Fei. *The Worlds I See: Curiosity, Exploration, and Discovery at the Dawn of AI.* New York: Flatiron Books, 2023.

Mann, Michael E. *The New Climate War: The Fight to Take Back Our Planet.* New York: PublicAffairs, 2021.

Meadows, Donella H. *Thinking in Systems: A Primer.* White River Junction, VT: Chelsea Green, 2008.

Miller, Chris. *Chip War: The Fight for the World's Most Critical Technology.* New York: Simon & Schuster, 2022.

Olson, Parmy. *Supremacy: AI, ChatGPT, and the Race That Will Change the World.* New York: Harper Business, 2024.

Perlroth, Nicole. *This Is How They Tell Me the World Ends: The Cyberweapons Arms Race.* London: Bloomsbury, 2021.

Schaake, Marietje. *The Tech Coup: How to Save Democracy from Silicon Valley.* Princeton, NJ: Princeton University Press, 2024.

Scharre, Paul. *Four Battlegrounds: Power in the Age of Artificial Intelligence.* New York: W. W. Norton, 2023.

Sekol, Matthew. *ESG Mindset: Business Resilience and Sustainable Growth.* London: Kogan Press, 2024.

Shadbolt, Nigel, and Roger Hampson. *As If Human: Ethics and Artificial Intelligence.* New Haven, CT: Yale University Press, 2024.

Shah, Raj M., and Christopher Kirchhoff. *Unit X: How the Pentagon and Silicon Valley are Transforming the Future of War.* New York: Simon & Schuster, 2024.

Shelton Leipzig, Dominique. *Trust: Responsible AI, Innovation, Privacy and Data Leadership.* New York: Forbes Books, 2024.

Smith, Brad, and Carol Ann Browne. *Tools and Weapons: The Promise and the Peril of the Digital Age.* New York: Penguin Press, 2019.

Suleyman, Mustafa, and Michael Bhaskar. *The Coming Wave: Technology, Power, and the Twenty-First Century's Greatest Dilemma.* New York: Crown, 2023.

Swinfen Green, Jeremy, and Stephen Daniels. *Digital Governance: Leading and Thriving on a World of Fast-Changing Technologies.* New York: Routledge, 2020.

Swisher, Kara. *Burn Book: A Tech Love Story.* New York: Simon & Schuster, 2024.

Taylor, Alison. *Higher Ground: How Business Can Do the Right Thing in a Turbulent World.* Cambridge, MA: Harvard University Press, 2024.

Tetlock, Philip E., and Dan Gardner. *Superforecasting: The Art and Science of Prediction.* New York: Crown, 2015.

Toon, Nigel. *How AI Thinks: How We Built It, How It Can Help Us, and How We Can Control It.* New York: Penguin, 2024.

Wheeler, Tom. *Techlash: Who Makes the Rules in the Digital Gilded Age?* Washington: Brookings Institution Press, 2023.

Wolf, Martin. *The Crisis of Democratic Capitalism.* New York: Penguin, 2023.

Zuboff, Shoshana. *The Age of Surveillance Capitalism: The Fight for a Human Future at the New Frontier of Power.* London: Profile Books, 2019.

Index

Accenture, 114, 117, 171–72, 186t
access to information and transparency
 mandates approach, 214t
accountability, 171
adapting existing laws approach, 214t
Advanced Micro Devices (AMD), 186t, 192
advertising sector, 75–76, 77t
aerial surveillance, 276
aerospace robots, 126t
Africa, 25–26
African Observatory on Responsible AI,
 25–26, 72
Agentic AI, 278
AGI. *See* artificial general intelligence
agile approach, 214t
agility, x
agricultural biotechnology, 88–89, 90t
Ahuja, Anjana, 101
Aim Shinrikyo, 83
AI Risk Repository, 80, 209–12, 211t, 213t
Akamai Technologies, 186t
algorithm audits, 225t
algorithmic bias, 216
alignment, 67–68, 166, 278
Alphabet Inc., 186t–87t. *See also* Google
Alpha Code, 65t
Altman, Sam, 31, 67–68, 141, 155, 166,
 169, 257, 274–75
Amazon, 187t, 196
Ameca (humanoid robot), 128
Andreessen, Marc, 31, 149t, 164
anthrax attacks (2001), 83
Anthropic, 142, 167
Apple, 113, 187t, 196
Applebaum, Anne, 276
Applied Materials, 186t
aquatic robots, 126t

AR. *See* augmented reality
artificial general intelligence (AGI):
 defined, 51–52; as far-off, 65; OpenAI
 and, 166, 168; overview of, 62–63; risk
 and, 204–5; uncertainty and, 67
artificial intelligence (AI): actors and,
 17; Africa and, 25–26; defined, 51;
 downsides of, 18; generative AI *vs.*,
 55t; geopolitics and, 27; risk canvas,
 209–16; technologies combining with,
 13; transformers and, 53–54. *See also*
 artificial general intelligence (AGI);
 generative AI
ASMARA, 191
asymmetry: biotechnology and, 87; with
 exponential technology, 44–45; with
 generative AI, 68–69
Athena Alliance, 172–74, 192, 281
Atlas (humanoid robot), 128
audits, in risk management, 225t
augmented reality (AR), 112–13
Australia, 71t, 146t
Autodesk Generative Design, 74
automation, 123, 141
autonomous mode, 123
autonomous technology, 123
autonomous test vehicle, 123–24
autonomous vehicles, 123–24, 126t, 133
autonomous weapons, 129–30
autonomy: defined, 122; exponential, 124–
 34; interconnectivity and, 124; leadership
 considerations with, 134; natural-
 language processing and, 131; overview
 of, 122–24; risk and, 209t; risks and
 opportunities with, 128–34; smart cities
 and, 130–34; strategic considerations
 with, 134; uncertainty and, 124

baking, in chip manufacturing, 105*t*
Bankman-Fried, Sam, 257
batteries, 101
Bezos, Jeff, 31, 87, 148, 149*t*
bias, algorithmic, 216
Biba, Jacob, 126
Biden, Joe, 220–21
billionaires, 31–32
binder jetting, 103*t*
biocomputing, 112
biofuels, 89, 90*t*
bioinformatics, 266–68
biologic agents, in terrorism, 84*t*
biological frontiers, 266–69, 267*f*, 267*t*
biometric surveillance, 275
bioplatforms, 89–91
bioremediation, 90*t*
biotechnology: agricultural, 88–89,
    90*t*; asymmetry and, 87; categories
    of, 88–91, 90*t*; CRISPR, 86–87, 89;
    defined, 81–82; DNA and, 85–86;
    environmental, 90*t*; examples of,
    88–91, 90*t*; exponential, 87–91, 90*t*,
    91–95; industrial, 90*t*; interconnectivity
    and, 87–88; leadership considerations
    with, 94–95; mRNA and, 85–86; RNA
    and, 85–86; strategic considerations
    with, 94–95; synthetic biology, 83, 90*t*,
    91–94; uncertainty and, 87; upsides of,
    83–85, 84*t*; velocity and, 87; volatility
    and, 87; weaponization of, 82–83
bioterror, 82–83, 84*t*
"black box" problem, 61–62
blockchain, 188, 274
BLOOM, 65*t*
boards, in governance, 148–50
borderlessness, 31–32
brain implants, 268–69
Brazil, 71*t*, 146*t*
Brill, Herman, 238
Brinn, Sergey, 87
Buffet, Warren, 196–97

California AI Act, 146
Campaign to Stop Killer Robots, 130

Canada, 71*t*, 146*t*
cancer, 2, 83, 92, 266–68
Carreyrou, John, 153–54
cars, self-driving, 123–24, 126*t*, 133
CAR-T cell therapy, 92
change management audits, 225*t*
ChatGPT, 2, 18–19, 37–39, 39*t*, 64, 65*t*
chemical markers, 276
child safety, 120, 189–90
China: AI regulations/frameworks in,
    146*t*; chips and, 25; DeepSeek, xii;
    generative AI and, 70–71, 71*t*; polyrisk
    and, 202; Taiwan and, 202, 270;
    technology economics in, 28
chips, 25, 97–98, 103–4, 105*t*. See also
    Nvidia
CHIPS Act. See US CHIPS and Science
    Act of 2022
Chip War: The Fight for the World's Most
    Critical Technology (Miller), 16, 97
Circle (cryptocurrency issuer), 24
CISA. See Cybersecurity and
    Infrastructure Security Agency
cities, smart, 130–34
Claude 2, 65*t*
climate change, 6, 21–23, 184*t*, 203, 254
climate tech, 271–72
closed sources, 58–60, 60*t*, 65*t*
cloud computing, 110
coherence, in quantum computing, 116
Coming Wave, The (Suleyman), 88
communications surveillance, 276
computational lithography, in chip
    manufacturing, 105*t*
compute, 108–9
computers, 108–9
computing: biocomputing, 112; cloud,
    110; edge, 110–11; exponential, 109–21;
    high-performance, 111; nanotechnology,
    111; neuromorphic, 111–12; organoid,
    112; overview of, 108–9; quantum,
    113–18; risk and, 209*t*; spatial, 112–13
confabulation, 215, 242, 255
consumer robots, 127*t*
continuous learning, 252–53

Cook, Tim, 149*t*, 196
cooling, with quantum computing, 116
Copilot, 65*t*, 74
corporate governance, 140–43, 143*t*. *See also* governance
Council of Europe, 71*t*, 146*t*
COVID-19 pandemic, x
COVID-19 vaccine, 85–86
creative sectors, 75
CRISPR, 86–87, 89
cross-functionality, of generative AI, 78, 79*f*
cryptocurrency, 24, 273–75
culture: at Accenture, 171–72; exponential technology and, 170; futureproofing and, 255–59; governance and, 138; incentivization and, 174–75; landscape, 163–74; leadership and, 163, 176; leadership stakeholder, 255–59; life cycle approach and, 172–74; at Microsoft, 163, 168–71; at OpenAI, 166–69; responsibility and, 163–74; responsible, 161–63; stakeholder questions on, 174–76; toxicity and, 163–74
Cun, Yan Le, 59
cyberattacks, 68–69
cybersecurity, 27, 116–17, 217–21, 220*t*, 243
Cybersecurity and Infrastructure Security Agency (CISA), 219–20
Czech Republic, 71*t*, 146*t*

DALL-E, 65*t*
data audits, 225*t*
data centers, 178, 190–91, 231, 239
data mining, 268
data standards, 56–58
Data & Trust Alliance, 58, 66
decoherence, in quantum computing, 114
DeepMind, 74, 88, 100, 151, 213–16
DeepSeek, xii
defense industry: generative AI in, 77*t*; governance and, 143–44; synthetic biology in, 92
deforestation, 22

delivery robots, 126*t*
Dell, 196
deposition, in chip manufacturing, 105*t*
developing, in chip manufacturing, 105*t*
digitalization, 235–37
digital light processing (DLP), 103*t*
digital natives, 16–17
digital trust systems, 235–36
digital twin technology, 118, 131, 217
direct metal laser sintering (DMLS), 103*t*
DiResta, Renee, 165
disaster response robots, 126*t*
disclosures, 216
disinformation, 1–2, 26–27, 215–16
distributed ledger technology, 274
diversity and inclusion, 120, 277–84
DLP. *See* digital light processing
DMLS. *See* direct metal laser sintering
DNA, in biotechnology, 85–86
DNA sensors, 276
drivers, stakeholders and, 189
drones, 125–28, 269–70
Durov, Pavel, 276

EBM. *See* electron beam melting
economics, technology and, 28–32, 29*t*
ecosystem tech governance, 143–45, 144*f*
edge computing, 110–11
education, generative AI in, 77*t*
educational robots, 127*t*
Ek, Daniel, 149*t*
elections, 1–2
electron beam melting (EBM), 103*t*
Ellison, Larry, 87
emotional intelligence, 65
enabling approach, 214*t*
energy, from nuclear fusion, 23
energy storage, 101
entanglement, in quantum computing, 114
enterprise risk management (ERM), 200
entity governance, 140–43, 143*t*
entertainment, 75, 77*t*
entertainment robots, 127*t*
entity governance, 140–43, 143*t*
environmental, social, governance (ESG), 30–31, 183–87, 184*t*–87*t*, 235, 237–38

environmental biotechnology, 90*t*
environmental control, with quantum
    computing, 116
environmental risk, 206
Ereky, Karl, 82
ERM. *See* enterprise risk management
ESG. *See* environmental, social,
    governance
etching, in chip manufacturing, 105*t*
ethics, defined, 162
EU AI Act, 25, 47–48, 59, 71, 146, 212–13,
    215*t*, 284
exoskeletons, 125–28
experimentalist approach, 214*t*
exponential frontiers, 266–77
exponential technology, 1; asymmetry
    with, 44–45; attributes of, 42–45, 43*f*;
    autonomy and, 124–34; biotechnology
    as, 87–91, 90*t*, 91–95; change and, 36–
    39; ChatGPT on, 37–39, 39*t*; computing
    as, 109–21; culture and, 170; defined,
    35; defining, 37–39, 39*t*; examples
    of, 39–41, 40*t*; as Fifth Industrial
    Revolution, 19–21, 19*t*, 20*f*; generative
    AI as, 63–69; geopolitics and, 24;
    governability of, 12, 41; governance of,
    141; interconnectivity with, 45; lenses
    on, 41–42; materials technology as,
    96–107; paradox of, 45–48; Perplexity
    AI on, 37–39, 39*t*; risk and, 207–9,
    210*t*; risk management and, 41–42;
    stewardship and, 45–48; uncertainty
    with, 44; velocity with, 43–44; volatility
    with, 44
exposure, in chip manufacturing, 105*t*

facilitating approach, 214*t*
false information, 66–67
favelas, 191
FDM. *See* fused deposition modeling
fidelity, in quantum computing, 115–16
Fifth Industrial Revolution, 19–21, 19*t*,
    20*f*, 249
financial services, 77*t*

fintech, 273–75
Firefly, 65*t*
Fisher, Richard, 109
"FLI Letter," 18–19
food, synthetic biology in, 93
foresight: digital trust systems and,
    235–36; elements of, 231–43;
    governance and, 143*t*, 144*f*, 244–45;
    interdisciplinary scenario planning
    and, 228, 241–43; leadership and,
    244; opportunity readiness and, 228,
    239–41; situational awareness and,
    228, 232–34; stakeholder questions on,
    243–44; strategy and, 227–31; systems
    thinking and, 228, 234–38, 237*t*; tech-
    risk intelligence and, 228
forward thinking, 254
founders, 148–50
FourCastNet, 1
France, 71*t*, 146*t*
Freeman, R. Edward, 230
Friedman, Milton, 28
fuels, 89, 90*t*
fused deposition modeling (FDM), 103*t*
fusion power, 23
futureproofing: continuous learning
    and, 252–53; culture and, 255–59;
    forward thinking and, 254; of global
    commons, 263–87; governance and,
    249–51; leadership and, 251–59; open-
    mindedness and, 253; of organizations,
    255–59; ourselves, 251–55, 253*t*;
    responsibility and, 254–55, 262;
    systems thinking and, 254; techniques,
    256; typology, 259–62

Gates, Bill, 149*t*
GE, 143–44
Gemini, 46, 65*t*
generative AI (GenAI): in advertising,
    75–76, 77*t*; AI *vs.*, 55*t*; asymmetry with,
    68–69; China and, 70–71, 71*t*; chips
    and, 25; in creative sectors, 75; as
    cross-functional, 78, 79*f*; cybersecurity

and, 27; in defense, 77t; defined, 51; disinformation and, 1–2, 26–27; in education, 77t; in entertainment, 75, 77t; exponentiality of, 63–69; faces of, 69–80, 71t–72t, 73f, 77t, 78f–80f; in financial services, 77t; FLI Letter and, 18–19; as global, 70–72, 71t; governability of, 12; in health care, 76, 77t; interconnectivity and, 45, 69; key issues and topics for, 54–62, 55t, 60t; in manufacturing, 74, 77t; in marketing, 75–76; materials science and, 106–7; as multidisciplinary, 78, 79f; opportunities with, across sectors, 73–76, 73f, 75f; in pharmaceuticals, 76, 77t; polyrisk and, 79–80; productivity, 75f; risk canvas, 209–16; risks of, 79–80, 80f, 209t; in software, 76, 77t; as turbocharging other technologies, 76, 78f; Turing Test and, 52–53; uncertainty with, 67–68; value creation, 75f; velocity with, 64–65; volatility with, 66–67. See also artificial intelligence (AI)

genetic engineering, 90t. See also synthetic biology

genomics, 268

geoengineering, 271–72, 273t

geopolitics, 24–27

Germany, 71t, 146t

germline editing, 86–87

global commons: defined, 263; exponential imperatives for, 277–84; futureproofing of, 263–87

global nature, of generative AI, 70–72, 71t

Global Tech Megascape, 11–12, 12t

Glover, Ellen, 111

Google, 46, 64–65, 190, 196. See also DeepMind

governance: actors in, 148–53; boards in, 148–50; CEOs in, 148–50; corporate, 140–43, 143t; culture and, 138; ecosystem, 143–45, 144f; entity, 140–43, 143t; experts in, 150–51; of exponential technology, 12, 141; foresight and, 143t, 144f, 244–45; founders in, 148–50; futureproofing and, 249–51; guidelines, 143t; importance of, 139–40; incentivization and, 157–58; insight and, 143t, 144f; investors in, 148–50; landscape, 153–55; leadership actions in, 158–59; legally-mandated, 145–48, 146t–47t; levels of, 138–48, 139f, 143t, 144f, 146t–47t; management in, 150–51; at Open AI, 139–40; oversight and, 143t, 144f; regulatory, 145–48, 146t–47t; resilience and, 222, 226; staff in, 150–51; stakeholder protection and, 151–53; stakeholder questions on, 156–58; structure, 156–57; of technology, 12–21, 19t, 20f; voluntary, 143–45, 144f; women in, 149–50, 150t. See also leadership; 360 tech governance

GPT4o, 65t

GPUs. See graphics-processing units

graphene, 101–2

graphics-processing units (GPUs), 97–98. See also Nvidia

Group of Seven, 71t, 146t

Haidt, Jonathan, 18

hallucinations, 66–67, 215

Harris, Tristan, 165

health care, 2, 76, 77t, 90t, 92, 121, 131, 234t. See also bioinformatics; neurotechnology; pharmaceuticals

heat, 22

Hewlett Packard, 186t

high-performance computing (HPC), 111

Hinton, Geoffrey, 64–65, 204

HITL. See humans in the loop

Hoffman, Reid, 149t

Holmes, Elizabeth, 153–54, 257

Horowitz, Ben, 31, 149t

HPC. See high-performance computing

HP Inc., 186t

Huang, Jensen, 64, 97, 149t, 155, 258

humanoids, 125–28

humans in the loop (HITL), 180–81

IAP. *See* Innovation Accelerator Program
IBM, 196
incentivization: culture and, 174–75;
     governance and, 157–58
Inception AI, 88
inclusion, 120, 170, 277–84
India, 71*t*, 146*t*
industrial biotechnology, 90*t*
Industrial Revolutions, 19–21, 19*t*, 20*f*
industrial robots, 127*t*
inferencing, 61
Innovation Accelerator Program (IAP),
     23–24
insight, 143*t*, 144*f*
inspection, in chip manufacturing, 105*t*
Intel Corp, 186*t*, 231
intelligence, tech-risk, 228, 238–39
interconnectivity: autonomy and, 124;
     biotechnology and, 87–88; with
     exponential technology, 45; with
     generative AI, 69
interdisciplinary scenario planning, 228,
     241–43
interference, in quantum computing, 114
invention, 215
investors, in governance, 148–50
ion implantation, in chip manufacturing,
     105*t*
Israel, 71*t*, 146*t*
Italy, 71*t*, 146*t*

Japan, 71*t*, 83, 146*t*
Juncker, Jean-Claude, 201
Jurvetson, Steve, 99
Just Capital, 183–87, 184*t*–87*t*

Kaspersen, Anja, 181
Kell, Georg, 238
Kenya, 72*t*, 146*t*
Kimsuky Group, 68

large language models (LLMs), 38, 46–47,
     56, 58, 61
lawyers, 66–67

leadership: 360 tech governance and, 137–
     60; actions, 158–59; with autonomy,
     134; with biotechnology, 94–95; culture
     and, 163, 176; foresight and, 244;
     futureproofing and, 251–59; guiding
     principles, 251–55, 253*t*; with materials,
     107; personal qualities in, 251–55, 253*t*;
     polycrisis and, 225; polyrisk and, 225;
     recommendations, 144; responsible,
     32–33; situational awareness and, 232;
     stakeholders and, 197–98. *See also*
     governance
learning: continuous, 252–53;
     reinforcement, 58
Leike, Jan, 167
Leins, Kobi, 181
Li, Fei Fei, 65, 281
Li, Joyce, 61
liability approach, 214*t*
life cycle approach, culture and, 172–74
life cycles, stakeholders and, 191–97
lithography, in chip manufacturing, 105*t*
living therapeutics, 92
Llama model, 64, 118
LLMs. *See* large language models

Ma, Jack, 149*t*
Ma, Pony, 149*t*
Make-a-Video, 65*t*
manufacturing, 74, 77*t*, 92, 116
marketing, 75–76
Marquardt, Michael, 266
Masiyima, Strive, 149*t*
Mata, Roberto, 66–67
materiality, 191–97, 193*f*
materials: advanced, 101–2, 103*t*;
     applications of, 100*t*; engineering
     and, 98–100; exponential, 96–107;
     leadership considerations with, 107;
     metamaterials, 102; Moore's Law and,
     97–99; nanomaterials, 102; risk and,
     209*t*; science, 98–104, 103*t*; strategic
     considerations with, 107; three-
     dimensional printing and, 89–90, 102

McCauley, Tasha, 166
meat alternatives, plant-based, 93
mechanical frontiers, 267f, 267t, 269–71
medical robots, 127t
medicine. *See* health care
MENA Observatory on Responsible
    AI, 72
mental health, 188o
Meta, 186–87, 187t, 196
metaverse, 112–13, 118–21, 189–90
metrology, in chip manufacturing, 105t
microbial production, for
    pharmaceuticals, 92
Microsoft, 151, 154, 163, 168–71, 187t, 196
military robots, 126t, 129–30
Miller, Chris, 16, 97
misinformation, 211t, 215–16
MJF. *See* multi jet fusion
Moore, Gordon E., 98
Moore's Law, 97–99
Morin, Edgar, 201
Motorola, 218t
"move fast and break things," 46, 164,
    170, 255–58
Mozilla, 142
mRNA, in biotechnology, 85–86
multidisciplinarity, of generative AI, 78,
    79f
multi jet fusion (MJF), 103t
Munger, Charlie, 158
Murthy, Narayana, 149t
Musk, Elon, 31, 149t, 150, 196, 257, 264;
    autonomous vehicles and, 133; FLI
    Letter and, 18; global commons and,
    264; life extension and, 87; Neuralink,
    269; popular support and, 14; risk and,
    204–5; Trump and, 165–66, 242

Nadella, Satya, 149t, 154, 163, 169, 196,
    239, 258
Nakasone, Paul M., 155
nanomaterials, 102
nanotechnology, 102
nanotechnology computing, 111

National Association of Corporate
    Directors (NACD), 27, 141, 143t, 144f,
    157–58
National Institute of Standards and
    Technology (NIST), 220–21
natural-language processing (NLP), 131
networking, multiqubit, 116
Neuralink, 269
neural-processing unit (NPU), 106t
neuromorphic computing, 111–12
Neuroplatform, 112
neurotechnology, 268–69
Nigeria, 72t, 146t
NIST. *See* National Institute of Standards
    and Technology
NLP. *See* natural-language processing
North Korea, 68
Norway, 146t
NPU. *See* neural-processing unit
nuclear fusion, 23
Nvidia, 25, 74, 97, 104, 187t, 195; in
    automotive sector, 106; in compute, 56;
    digital twins and, 118; foresight and,
    231–32; FourCastNet, 1; velocity and, 64

OECD. *See* Organization for Economic
    Cooperation and Development
OpenAI, xii, 59, 67, 139–42, 154–55,
    166–69, 196, 205. *See also* ChatGPT
"Open Letter to Pause Giant AI
    Experiments," 18–19
open-mindedness, 253
open sources, 58–60, 60t, 64, 65t
opportunity readiness, 228, 239–41
Organization for Economic Cooperation
    and Development (OECD), 71t, 145–46,
    146t
organoid biocomputing, 112
Orlowski, Jeff, 18, 165
oversight, 143t, 144f
Owner Techonomic Model, 28, 29t, 30

Page, Larry, 87
pandemics, 21–22

Pandora (myth), 3–4
Paparo, Samuel, 270
Patterson, Tom, 117
PBC. *See* public benefit corporation
Perplexity AI, 37–39, 39*t*, 65*t*, 88, 115
pharmaceuticals, 76, 77*t*, 92
photoresist coating, in chip
    manufacturing, 105*t*
Pichai, Sundar, 149*t*, 258
planetary frontiers, 267*f*, 267*t*, 271–72
plant-based meat alternatives, 93
polycrisis: in convergence of physical and
    virtual worlds, 217–24; defined, 201–2;
    leadership and, 225; preparedness,
    199–200; stakeholder questions on,
    224–25; tech risk and, 204–16, 207*t*,
    208*f*, 209*t*–11*t*, 213*t*–15*t*
PolyJet, 103*t*
polyrisk: in convergence of physical
    and virtual worlds, 217–24; defined,
    202; exponential tech risk and,
    207–9; generative AI and, 79–80;
    global strategic risk and, 204–7;
    interconnectivity and, 69; leadership
    and, 225; preparedness, 200–204;
    resilience and, 199; stakeholder
    questions on, 224–25; as term, 201. *See
    also* risk
principles-based approach, 214*t*
privacy, 120, 170, 211*t*
proteomics, 268
public benefit corporation (PBC), 142

quantum computing, xii, 113–18
quantum mechanics, 114
qubits, 115–16

Rahat, 188
Rasche, Andreas, 238
Raskin, Aza, 165
recycling, 102
red teaming exercises, 225*t*
regenerative medicine, 90*t*
regulatory governance, 145–48, 146*t*–47*t*

reinforcement learning, 58
reliability, 170
Republican Party, 165
reputation, 191–97
research robots, 127*t*
resilience: AI Risk Repository and, 80;
    exponential governance and, 226;
    governance and, 222, 226; overview of,
    199; polycrisis and, 222–24; polyrisk
    and, 199, 222–24; preparedness and,
    200–204
responsibility, defined, 162
responsible, defined, 162
responsible leadership, 32–33
rights-based approach, 214*t*
right wingers, 165
risk: audits, 225*t*; disclosures, 216; in EU
    AI Act, 215*t*; of generative AI, 79–80,
    80*f*, 209*t*; high, 215*t*; implementation
    targets, 223; landscape, 208*f*; limited,
    215*t*; management, 41–42; minimal,
    215*t*; outcome targets, 223; taxonomy,
    213*t*; tech-risk intelligence and, 228;
    unacceptable, 215*t*. *See also* enterprise
    risk management (ERM); polyrisk
RNA, in biotechnology, 85–86
robots, 125–30
Romania, 1
Rosenberg, Louis, 120

Sacks, David, 166, 273
Salesforce, 186*t*, 218*t*
Samsung, 196
Saudi Arabia, 72*t*, 146*t*
Scale AI, 56
scenario planning, interdisciplinary, 228,
    241–43
Schwartz, Steven A., 66–67
SDGs. *See* Sustainable Development
    Goals
sectors, in generative AI, 73–76, 73*f*, 75*f*
security robots, 126*t*
selective laser sintering (SLS), 103*t*
self-driving cars, 123–24, 133

semiautonomous, 123
ServiceNow Inc, 186t
service robots, 127t
sheet lamination, 103t
silk, spider, 92
Singapore, 146t
situational awareness, 11–12, 12t, 228, 232–34, 234t
SLA. *See* stereolithography
SLS. *See* selective laser sintering
Social Dilemma, The (film), 18
social-impact technology, 23–24
social media: change and, 15–16; politics and, 26–27
social robots, 127t
socioecology: interdependence in, 21–22; of technology, 21–24
software, generative AI in, 76, 77t
Son, Masayoshi, 149t
Sony, 195
Sophia (humanoid robot), 127–28
sources, open *vs.* closed, 58–60, 60t, 64, 65t
South Africa, 146t
South Korea, 72t, 146t
Spain, 72t, 146t
spatial computing, 112–13
spider silk, 92
Stable Diffusion, 65t
stakeholder(s): communities as, 184; culture and, 255–59; customers as, 184; drivers and, 189; environment as, 184; framework, 183–87, 184t–87t; humans in the loop and, 180–81; integration of, 178–98, 182f–83f, 184t–87t, 193f; issues, 183; knowing, 181–82, 182f; leadership and, 197–98; life cycles and, 191–97; matching, to issues, 187–91; materiality and, 191–97, 193f; mental health and, 188; opportunities, 183; potential, 182f–83f; protection, 151–53; questions on culture, 174–76; questions on foresight, 243–44; questions on governance, 156–58; questions on

polyrisk and polycrisis preparedness, 224–25; reputation and, 191–97; risks, 183; shareholders as, 184; surveillance and, 189; trust and, 191–97; workers as, 184
Stakeholder Techonomic Model, 28, 29t, 30
Stamos, Alex, 165
standards-based approach, 214t
State Techonomic Model, 28, 29t, 30
stereolithography (SLA), 103t
stewardship, 45–48, 284–87
Suleyman, Mustafa, 88, 171
superchips, 103–4
superposition, in quantum computing, 114
surveillance: aerial, 276; biometric, 275; communications, 276; stakeholders and, 189; video, 275
sustainability, 30–31, 130–34, 236–37
Sustainable Development Goals (SDGs), 22–23, 236–37, 254
Sutskever, Ilya, 67, 155, 166
Swisher, Kara, 281
Switzerland, 72t, 146t
synthetic biology, 83, 90t, 91–94, 209t
synthetic data, 56–57
systems biology, 268
systems thinking, 228, 234–38, 237t, 254

Taiwan, 25, 72t, 146t, 202, 270
technology: autonomous, 123; change and, 14–16; economics and, 28–32, 29t; future disruptive, 34–35, 35t; generative AI as turbocharging, 76, 78f; governance of, 12–21, 19t, 20f; human condition and, 17–19; in political landscape, 24–27; social-impact, 23–24; socioecology of, 21–24; trust and, 32–33. *See also* exponential technology; 360 tech governance
Tegmark, Max, 18
telepresence robots, 127t
terrorism, 82–83

Tesla, 133, 186t–87t, 196
Text2Video, 65t
Theranos, 153–54, 257
Thiel, Peter, 31, 87, 149t, 165
third-party assessments, 225t
three-dimensional printing, 89–90, 102
360 tech governance: defined, 137; integrated, 157–59; leadership and, 137–60. *See also* governance
TikTok, 196
tissue engineering, 90t
Tokyo Subway Sarin Attack, 83
Toner, Helen, 166
Tooze, Adam, 201
toxicity, culture and, 163–74, 211t
transcriptomics, 268
transformers, 53–54
transparency, 170, 214t
Trump, Donald, 164, 187, 192, 264, 273, 279
Trump Organization, 196
trust, 32–33, 191–97, 277–84
trust systems, 235–36
TSMC, 231–32
Turing, Alan, 52–53
Turing Machine, 52–53
Turing Test, 52–53
Turkey, 72t, 146t

Ukraine, 69, 128, 201
uncertainty: autonomy and, 124; biotechnology and, 87; with exponential technology, 44; with generative AI, 67–68
United Arab Emirates, 72t, 146t
United Kingdom, 70, 72t, 146t
United Nations, 71t, 146t
US CHIPS and Science Act of 2022, 31
USDC (cryptocurrency), 24

vaccine, COVID-19, 85–86
value creation, 75f
Vance, J. D., 31, 165
vehicles, self-driving, 123–24, 126t, 133
velocity: biotechnology and, 87; with exponential technology, 43–44; with generative AI, 64–65
vendor assessments, 225t
Verma, Ashish Swarup, 82
Viatris, 218t
video surveillance, 275
Vinge, Vernor, 36–37
virtual frontiers, 267f, 267t, 272–77, 273t
virtual reality (VR), 112–13
volatility: biotechnology and, 87; with exponential technology, 44; with generative AI, 66–67
voluntary governance, 143–45, 144f
VR. *See* virtual reality

Wang, Alexandr, 56
warfare, 69. *See also* defense industry
weapons, autonomous, 129–30
weather tech, 271–72
WEF. *See* World Economic Forum
Welch, Jack, 144
women, 149–50, 150t
Worldcoin, 274–75
World Economic Forum (WEF), 199–200, 282–83, 282f, 290n11, 299n30
World Food Program, 23–24

Zhengfei, Reng, 149t
Zuckerberg, Mark, 31, 149t, 150, 196; on AGI, 52; content guardrails and, 26; metaverse and, 112, 118; open source and, 59; opportunity readiness and, 239; Trump and, 187

About the Author

Andrea Bonime-Blanc, JD/PhD, is founder and CEO of GEC Risk Advisory, a board member and adviser, and a multiple-book author. She specializes in the governance of change—focusing on global strategic risk, leadership trust, geopolitical change, sustainability, cyber resilience, and exponential technology—and advising businesses, nongovernmental organizations, and government. She spent two decades as a C-suite global corporate executive, including serving as general counsel and as chief ethics, risk, compliance, cyber, and corporate responsibility officer at several global companies (including PSEG Global and Bertelsmann). She has served on many boards of directors and advisory boards, including for several tech start-ups and the Cyber Future Foundation, the Athena Alliance, Epic Theatre Ensemble, the ECI, and the National Association of Corporate Directors' New Jersey Chapter. She serves as a senior fellow at several institutions, including the Conference Board's Governance & Sustainability Center and New York University's Center for Global Affairs, and she serves as AI Ethics Strategy Fellow at the American College for Financial Services. She also serves as independent ethics adviser to the Financial Oversight and Management Board for Puerto Rico and on the founding global faculty of the Institute for Corporate Directors Malaysia Mandatory Board Sustainability Certificate. She is a recipient of numerous awards, including the 2023 Diligent Governance 100, the 2022 National Association of Corporate Directors' Directorship 100, the 2019 Cyber Futurist Award, the 2018 inaugural Directors & Chief Risk Officers (DCRO) Exemplar Award, twice, Ethisphere's 100 Most Influential People in Business Ethics. She is a life member of the Council on Foreign Relations, a global keynote speaker, and the author of six books, including *Gloom to Boom: How Leaders Transform Risk into Resilience and Value* (Routledge, 2020); *The Artificial Intelligence Imperative: A Roadmap for*

Business (Praeger, 2018); and *The Reputation Risk Handbook* (Routledge, 2016). She was born and raised in Germany and Spain, received a joint JD in law and PhD in political science from Columbia University, lives in New York City, and posts on Bluesky as @GlobalEthicist.